Indigenous Language Politics
in the Schoolroom

INDIGENOUS LANGUAGE POLITICS IN THE SCHOOLROOM

Cultural Survival in Mexico and the United States

Mneesha Gellman

UNIVERSITY OF PENNSYLVANIA PRESS

PHILADELPHIA

Published by
University of Pennsylvania Press
Philadelphia, Pennsylvania 19104-4112
www.upenn.edu/pennpress

Printed in the United States of America on acid-free paper

10 9 8 7 6 5 4 3 2 1

Hardcover ISBN: 978-0-8122-5404-4
Paperback ISBN: 978-0-8122-2528-0
eBook ISBN: 978-0-8122-9863-5

A Cataloging-in-Publication record is available
from the Library of Congress.

For Indigenous language-keepers and learners everywhere.
Thank you for doing what you do.
Xhtiuzænyubiu' and Wok-hlew'!

And for my parents, who taught me that working for a better world,
regardless of scale, is the point.

CONTENTS

ABBREVIATIONS

ACLU NorCal	American Civil Liberties Union of Northern California
BIC	Bachillerato Integral Comunitario/Integral Community High School
BIC 29	Bachillerato Integral Comunitario Numero 29/Integral Community High School Number 29
BIPOC	Black, Indigenous, and People of Color
CEDARTMC	Centro de Educación Artística "Miguel Cabrera"/Center for Artistic Education "Miguel Cabrera"
CSEIIO	Colegio Superior para la Educación Integral Intercultural de Oaxaca/Superior College for Integral Intercultural Education of Oaxaca
DA-RT	Data Access and Research Transparency
ECS	Eureka City Schools
EHS	Eureka High School
EZLN	Ejército Zapatista de Liberación National/Zapatista Army of National Liberation
HVHS	Hoopa Valley High School
IEEPO	Instituto Estatal de Educación Pública de Oaxaca/State Institute of Public Education of Oaxaca
ILOC169	International Labor Organization's Convention 169 (on Tribal and Indigenous Peoples)
INBA	Instituto Nacional de las Bellas Artes/National Institute of Fine Arts

INBAL	Instituto Nacional de Bellas Artes y Literatura/National Institute of Fine Arts and Literature
INI	Instituto Nacional Indigenista/National Indigenist Institute
IRB	Institutional Review Board
KTJUSD	Klamath Trinity Joint Unified School District
LGBTQI+	Lesbian, Gay, Bisexual, Transgender, Queer, Intersex, Plus
NALA	Native American Languages Act
NGOs	Non-governmental organizations
PAR	Participatory Action Research
SEP	Secretaría de Educación Pública/Secretary of Public Education
SNTE	Sindicato Nacional de Trabajadores de la Educación/ National Education Workers Union
UABJO	Universidad Autónoma "Benito Juárez" de Oaxaca/ Autonomous University "Benito Juárez" of Oaxaca
UDHR	Universal Declaration of Human Rights

ACKNOWLEDGMENTS

The seed of this book began in my childhood when, as one of the few kids in my rural California elementary school classroom who spoke some Spanish, I was asked to help orient a new student, a recently arrived refugee from Central America. Over the subsequent months and years I soaked up her relationship with languages, and changed my own. I did not have a political consciousness about what it meant at the time, but I remember the way that words formed us and our ability to become friends through and within languages.

Words determined the way we participated in classroom dynamics and moved through our schoolwork, including whether or not we raised our hands in response to questions or broke into new social circles. Her story, having to rapidly immerse into an English-only setting while adjusting to a very different lifestyle in a new place, played out without comment in the community in which I grew up. I remember thinking it odd that we spent so much time trying to learn each other's languages at recess and that so few other people could talk to her in the early days of her arrival. What if we had schools that valued more languages and that better equipped us to move between worlds? It felt like a naive suggestion at age ten, but as I grew into being a scholar of democratization and human rights, I revisited her story in my head many times.

I recognize more and more with each passing year my own role in settler colonialism in far Northern California, my home region that I long to return to but ultimately do not live in full-time. As a White person who regards traditionally Native land as home, I wanted to find a way to share my acquired skills as a political scientist to address some of the implications of my own positionality. In the simultaneously ransacked and sacred spaces of Humboldt County, I looked for ways to apply the knowledge I had collected elsewhere to be of use in local efforts for Indigenous cultural survival.

The efforts of Native American language-keepers in the settler-colonial era in Northern California have been tremendous. My own minute contribution is to document their impact in one small but mighty space, the public high school classroom. This research would not have been possible without the interest and active participation of the Yurok Tribe. I thank the Yurok Tribal Council, the Yurok Language Program, and the Yurok Education Department for their permission for and engagement with this research. I also thank them for their patience with me and the process of academic publication, which does not allow for immediate results. Jim McQuillen, Victoria Carlson, and Barbara McQuillen have been instrumental in orienting me to the world of Yurok language resurgence, and James Gensaw and Carole Lewis generously opened their Yurok classrooms to me to allow this project to play out. The Yurok Tribe's Office of the Tribal Attorney worked with me on revisions so that this manuscript could officially be approved by the Yurok Tribal Council for publication, and I thank them for their time and effort. I also thank members of the Yurok Summer Language Institute for allowing me to participate in and observe their programming for several years. The work you are all doing is so important, and it has been an honor to observe and document your efforts.

I also thank the administrators, staff, and teachers at Eureka High School and Hoopa Valley High School for welcoming me and helping with the day-to-day logistics of my contact with students, and also for insight into the dynamics of their schools and surrounding communities. And for my own language skills, *Señora Quimby, Señor Rivera, y mis otras maestrxs de español, gracias por su instrucción de español, que cambió mi vida y abrió tantas puertas.*

In Mexico, the traditional community leaders of Teotitlán del Valle granted permission over multiple years for this project to take place. I thank them, as well as the school director, staff, teachers, and Parents' Committee at Bachillerato Integral Comunitario (BIC) 29 for their willingness to facilitate the research. Your dedication to the students in your care gives me hope for the future. I also thank administrators, teachers, and students at the Centro de Educación Artística "Miguel Cabrera" (CEDARTMC) and the Universidad Autónoma "Benito Juárez" de Oaxaca (UABJO). Thank you for doing what you do. The pedagogical spaces you foster are the meaning of the word *educación.*

For research support at various points in this project I thank the Sociological Initiatives Foundation, the Phillips Fund for Native American Research at the American Philosophical Society, the Alma Ostrom and Leah Hopkins Awan Civic Education Fund of the American Political Science Association, and the U.S. Fulbright García-Robles Fellowship in Mexico, which the Covid-19 pandemic sadly cut short. Within Emerson College, I am grateful to have received the Norma and Irma Mann Stearns Distinguished Faculty Award for research funding, as well as a pre-tenure leave that allowed for data collection, and a Huret Faculty Excellence Award that facilitated further research and manuscript preparation. My colleagues at Emerson are fantastic, creative, and supportive, and I appreciate their camaraderie.

Like many texts, this one had a shifting cast of support players on the technical side over many years. Thanks to Donato Cayetano Herrera García, Ana Salas, and Emily Finestead for transcription assistance, Yaling Hou for survey data visualization support, Lauren Holt for editing prowess, and Annika Falconer for editing and production assistance. Jenny Tan has been the editor I dreamed of when I thought about writing another book—thank you for talking at length about the ideas in these pages and how to make them clearer. Two anonymous reviewers also gave detailed feedback on an earlier draft that has surely made this stronger. Any remaining errors are my own.

My parents, Sherri Siegel and Steve Gellman, got me traveling, loving Mexico, and speaking Spanish at an early age, as well as developing a deep connection to far Northern California. Clearly it has been formative. Thank you for working so hard to provide a life for me. Bryan Gaynor and Lisa Miller have provided a home away from home year after year—your hospitality is an art form. Thank you for everything.

Joshua Dankoff, love of my life, thank you for following me, year in and year out, to yet another country, a different research site, more places where I need to talk to people, study, or work. Your support, from dishes to suitcases, allowed this book to get written over the din of family life. And to our children, Matolah and Chayton, thank you for your flexibility and willingness to travel. From multiple semesters in Mexico with school in Spanish, to my constant "just one more minute" when I was writing and you wanted my attention, I know this story has shaped your childhood. I hope someday you can appreciate why.

CHAPTER 1

Contemporary Culturecide: Why Language Politics Matters for Youth Participation

Introduction: Listening to Youth Voices

Oaxaca, Mexico

Sun bounces off the metal roof and cooks the concrete in the open-air classroom where I sit with a high school student, reviewing her informed consent documents before we start the interview. The young woman across from me in her school-issue blue pleated skirt and knee socks glances away from me nervously. I have invited her out of class where her friends giggled at her departure, and she tells me I am the first foreigner she has ever talked to. The mountains and cacti are silhouettes behind us, and a lone motorcycle taxi churns dust on the road up to the school, delivering a student running late.

As the audio recorder clicks on, I ask the same questions I've asked dozens of times before: "In what ways do you feel included or excluded at your school?" "How do you identify yourself culturally?" "What helps motivate you to participate in your school or community?" Eti[1] tells me she was displaced from her home community in the Sierra Mixteca mountains a few years earlier because of paramilitary violence there (Anonymous, 2018d). Her family relocated to Oaxaca de Juárez, the capital city of Oaxaca, where her parents found work, and she commutes more than ninety minutes each way, at great expense, to attend this small rural high school that centers around Indigenous cultural learning.

As we sweat in the mid-afternoon sun near the school's cactus nursery, I ask her, why not go to a better-resourced school closer to her new home in the city? She responds: "As an Indigenous person, I feel more comfortable in a school that is trying to include Indigenous values, like language, even though here they teach Zapotec and I speak Mixteca. Before we had to leave my town, I went to a similar school there too. There is more understanding, and less discrimination when I'm not the only Indigenous student" (Anonymous, 2018d). The Bachillerato Integral Comunitario (Integral Community High School, or BIC), in Oaxaca is the only high school system in the state that deliberately prioritizes Indigenous cultural continuity, including through Indigenous language instruction.

Eti's deliberate pursuit of a schooling system that includes Indigenous values and curricula in Oaxaca, even when more convenient opportunities are available, demonstrates her ability to analyze her own participation in identity negotiation and related social and political positionality as an Indigenous person. This snapshot also sheds light on the status of Indigenous peoples in Mexico today. Racism and discrimination are in no way relegated to the past and instead continue to inform the life choices of young people as they navigate the formal education sector and their own identities. This student travels to attend a school with three required years of Zapotec language study, even though her whole family speaks Mixteca, a separate Indigenous language. Yet the inclusion of indigeneity in the curriculum makes the trek worthwhile for her, despite the complicated way that students from a variety of backgrounds express socially condoned racism, sometimes against their own heritage.

The interview continues amid the rattle of cow bells as the animals move from one pasture to another. "How do students from different backgrounds get along here?" While some students are painfully shy, others talk as if they've been waiting to be asked such questions. Sometimes the chance to convey their thoughts to an adult who promises to listen, in confidence, releases a flood of intense analysis. Such was the case with Eti, who began to skittishly and quickly find her robust narrating voice:

> Indigenous students are sad to say that they speak an Indigenous
> language, because they prefer Spanish more. Regularly students use
> [Indigenous] language only to say rude things. At school students
> refer to people who do something out of the ordinary by saying
> "You are a weirdo"[2] or "You are very Indian."[3] Sometimes they say it
> as a joke, but we do not take it that way because we do not trust
> them. Usually these type of comments are said by children who

come from Oaxaca [City]. Possibly they feel inferior and that is why they make fun of the Indigenous students without knowing their emotional state. I'd say two to three times a week I hear these kind of comments. Both genders use it equally. Students also give nicknames based on skin type. Young people who mock Indigenous people are rebellious or come from families that make fun of people, so it is normal for them to mock. It is not taken as an aggression but as a joke. Sometimes people apologize for their comments if they see they went too far. (Anonymous, 2018d)

Eti's ability to navigate her social world is informed by her indigeneity, and this identity influences the kind of education she seeks out. Her identity and educational resources in turn shape the spectrum of choices available to her as a social and political actor at every level. Themes of discrimination, politics, economics, and survival surfaced across dozens of interviews with high schoolers in Oaxaca. Many young people had ideas for solutions, and all, like Eti, had acute observations of their lived experiences based on the demographics they represented.

Hoopa, California

Three thousand miles north in a newly built conference room that blocks out the thick morning fog, Jake[4] sits across from me in the glow of the digital audio recorder. A senior at Hoopa Valley High School, located on the Hoopa Valley Indian Reservation in far Northern California, he responds to a question about the importance of learning the Yurok language by saying, "Our language, it's kind of like dying out slowly, but like, us younger people are just bringing it back, reviving it. The more speakers, the better" (J. Reed, 2018). The idea that young people can help right a historical wrong of the past by revitalizing a language that the boarding school generation had beaten out of them is palpable in Yurok classrooms, and it is paired with other types of resurgence and survivance in Native communities.

The Trinity River flows just beyond the school, the lifeblood of many people who live and study near it. The Hoopa Valley Indian Reservation is a place of intense beauty, difficulty, and resilience all at once. I ask every person I interview, young people and adults alike, to let their imaginations soar, if only for a moment: What would they do with a magic wand and three wishes? "If I had a magic wand, I'd change my community. I'd build a recreation center for the kids, for the youth, so they could go there on the weekends instead of like, hanging out with friends, getting drunk, smoking weed, just make an alternative space for them," Jake says wistfully (J. Reed, 2018). His logical wish reflects a clear assessment of missing infrastructure for youth, and he links cultural loss to something bigger than language: economic investment and positive social spaces, things that highlight needs in rural Native communities and are connected to the historic and contemporary trauma of colonialism.

Language access and youth identity are joined in complex ways that form a backdrop for Indigenous cultural resurgence. This matrix is felt acutely in Hoopa, where addiction and family problems keep people locked in cycles of violence and dependency, and where socioeconomic barriers, like the lack of gas money, can prevent people from getting together. At the same time, the will to maintain cultural traditions runs strong. As an enrolled Yurok Tribal member and student in Yurok II, Jake has a stake in the cultural survival of Yurok people and others in California's Indian Country (J. Reed, 2018).

Indigenous language access alone will not solve the economic and social problems in Indigenous communities that have been marred by generations of genocidal policies from settler-colonial populations and their descendants. But culturally relevant curricula, including Indigenous language classes for young people like Eti and Jake, constitute interventions in the status quo. Settler-colonial agendas are clearly visible for minority youth in formal education curricula around the world. As policymakers continue to assimilate ethnic minorities through curricula written by and for ethnic majorities, the politics of language becomes visible as contested terrain where language access is one part of Indigenous youth resistance against their ongoing subjugation.

Research Puzzle and Central Concepts

A research puzzle is meant to identify a mystery worthy of solving. The question that drives my own puzzle is this: How do high school–level Indigenous language classes in Oaxaca and California affect the identity formation and agency of students from various backgrounds? This question is situated across literatures in Indigenous studies, human rights, and democratization. Moreover, the question is connected to concerns about the fate of pluriethnic democracy and engaged citizenship, meaning the way in which people play active roles in constructing civic and political life.

I argue that access to Indigenous language classes encourages resistance to culturecide, meaning the killing of culture, by expanding the repertoire of, and interest in, participatory practices among youth. Indicators of participation are seen through forms of civic, cultural, and political engagement by youth from Indigenous and other backgrounds. Indigenous language access foments identity-based agency for Indigenous youth that allows them to better resist culturecide, while youth from other backgrounds are able to become allies or co-conspirators in Indigenous flourishing.

Key Concepts

Resistance in social-movements scholarship is generally taken to mean some form of agentive opposition, with variation in degrees of contention and insurgency, collective versus individual actions, revolutionary intent, and idealism versus selfishness in the purpose of the action (Selbin, 2010: 10–11). There are many creative ways in which oppressed communities maintain practices of resistance as everyday repertoires of being and doing (Jasper, 1997; Scott, 1985). Such practices may include contentious conversations and stories (Tilly, 2002: 118–122), crafting public performances that discreetly subvert hierarchies (Scott, 1990: 45–69), dances and other cultural rituals (Yashar, 2005: 14–15), voter registration (McAdam, 1988), boycotts, countersummits, and other forms of transnational solidarity activism (Tarrow, 2005: 5–11). There are even "emotions of resistance" such as "pride, happiness, love, safety or confidence, and righteous anger" (Whittier, 2001: 238).

When I invoke the notion of youth resistance to culturecide, I am including their resistance within the claim-making tradition articulated by social-movements luminaries. This is because to resist is to assert the claim of agency over something, such as over one's identity or the issues facing a community. Even in "resisting arrest" the resistance is an act of claiming agency over the body and one's right to not be physically controlled. Resistance in its many forms is one way to protest something or, at its most basic, to engage in contention. Useful here is McAdam, Tarrow, and Tilly's conceptual division between "contained contention" through established actors where at least one party to the contention is the government, and "transgressive contention," where some of the actors making claims are new to such behavior and contention is innovative outside traditional scripted spaces of claim-making (McAdam et al., 2001: 7–8). Eti and Jake, the two students quoted in this chapter's opening, are engaging in contained contention by asserting a claim to Indigenous language access in public education institutions that have typically quashed Indigenous identity expression.

Resistance is a common aspect of Indigenous rights movements, including food sovereignty (Enrique, 2012: 74–76; Sowerwine et al., 2019), governance sovereignty (Fenelon, 2002; Kessler-Mata, 2017), land and water stewardship (Middleton Manning & Reed, 2019; Orcutt, 2019), governance arrangements (Indigenous Peoples of Oaxaca Forum, 2006; Kessler-Mata, 2017; Speed & Collier, 2000), and gender dynamics (Gopar, Bohórquez Martínez, et al., 2016; Nash, 2010). In linguistic rights movements, resistance can be manifested in a range of ways but frequently includes using minority languages in public spaces, or asking for or demanding more possibilities to do so. Such language rights assertions can be seen around the world, from Irish-language revival in the North of Ireland (Mac Ionnrachtaigh, 2013) to the Kaska language in Yukon Territory, Canada (Meek, 2010: 21–22). In some cases language-connected resistance includes pushing for language survival in contexts hostile to such an intent (Hassanpour et al., 2012). In others, long-time horizons are necessary to transition from language repression to language inclusion (Enrique López, 2006). In many cases, resistance as a form of claim-making to Indigenous or heritage language access from states is bound with social justice projects more broadly (Skutnabb-Kangas et al., 2009).

In the case studies included in this book, resistance comes from young people's desire for cultural continuity of Indigenous knowledge, even in the face of genocidal settler-colonial states that have sought to assimilate by force as well as through education. Indigenous education is linked to issues of identity, often as a process of assertion in resistance to dominant ethnolinguistic frameworks (Kovats Sánchez, 2018; Lara-Cooper, 2017; Olthuis et al., 2013). By seeking out and engaging in heritage language classes, minority youth send the message to schools and policymakers that they are willing to show up and work for cultural survival. Their educational choices push back against the planned destruction of Indigenous cultures that formal-sector education has long instituted.

Historically, cultural destruction was conceptually linked to physical destruction. In 1933 Raphael Lemkin, a Polish lawyer of Jewish descent, coined the term *genocide* to explain the processes of large-scale human

rights violations. His definition of genocide, put forth in an early presentation to the League of Nations, included the concept of cultural destruction
as a form of intentional annihilation, and he argued for the cultural dimen-
sion of genocide in front of many official audiences throughout the 1930s
and 1940s (Short, 2010: 834–837). The intentional destruction of a particular
group's cultural traditions, with physical elimination of its people as a by-
product, is generally referred to as cultural genocide. Lemkin argued for the
inclusion of cultural genocide in discussions about the 1948 United Nations
Convention on the Prevention and Punishment of the Crime of Genocide
(Short, 2010: 837).

The term was ultimately excised from the final Convention language due
to political pressures from the United States, Canada, and Australia (Benvenuto, 2015: 29; Mako, 2012: 175–176; Schabas, 2008: 171). Hanna Schreiber's
work shows the evolution of the 1948 Convention text as it was pared down
to achieve consensus among signatories (Schreiber, 2017). The fear that these
three powerful countries could be held accountable for the cultural genocide
of Indigenous people under the Convention, given the forced boarding school
legacies that each of them share, facilitated the potent textual edit that dis-
mayed Lemkin (Short, 2010: 834).

While the United States has slowly drifted toward recognizing settler-
colonial treatment of Native Americans as genocidal and with White suprema-
cist origins in some ways (Bonds & Inwood, 2015; Hamilton, 2019), broader
recognition of cultural destruction as genocide is still limited. (Following
the rationale of Eve Ewing [2020], I capitalize *White* throughout this book in
recognition of the shared identity of whiteness that aligns in capitalization-
as-collective-indicator practice with terms like *Indigenous* and *Black*.) Among
genocide scholars and Indigenous studies literatures, there is ongoing debate
about terminology and practices of oppression as they apply to Indigenous
experiences (Benvenuto, 2015; Gone, 2014; Norgaard, 2019; K. Reed, 2020).
I take it as fact that past treatment of Indigenous people in far Northern
California constituted genocide. My own contribution is to engage the concept of culturecide to describe what Indigenous students are resisting today
when they access Indigenous language classes.

In the academic tradition of trying to compress words to make a concept
more popularly palatable,[5] *culturecide* has been used interchangeably in some
literatures with *cultural genocide*, meaning the targeting of certain com-
munally held identities for annihilation. In this first understanding of culturecide, it has been taken to mean the intentional destruction or repression

of certain culturally bound groups of people and can be based on ethnic, political, social, or religious identities. Lakota/Dakota scholar James Fenelon's 1998 book, *Culturicide, Resistance, and Survival of the Lakota (Sioux Nation)*, offers a second understanding of culturecide through a typology in which he situates the term on a spectrum of domination ranging from genocide to acculturation, and his definition is what I employ throughout this book. Culturecide sits between cultural genocide and cultural suppression on the continuum of domination that represents state policy toward minorities (Fenelon, 1998: 41). Fenelon identifies social, political, economic, and cultural means of domination and uses culturecide as a typological tool to explain how Indigenous people have been harmed under such domination, as well as how Indigenous people have resisted it (Fenelon, 1998: 65–80).

Although Fenelon made the term *culturecide* more visible and situated it theoretically, it has not had wide resonance. This is perhaps in part because of the multiple spelling iterations that have inhibited consensus on its use. Most publications that use the term opt for the spelling *culturecide*, which I take up in this book, but Fenelon replaced the e with an i, in line with terms such as *feminicide*. Fenelon is cited by many scholars in the field of Indigenous studies, but only rarely has the term moved out of the bibliography and into the main text. *Cultural genocide* as a term continues to be more common, and "(cultural) genocide" appears in the literature as well (Bacon, 2019), but frequently there is slippage between concepts. The gap in the literature on culturecide over the last few decades needs filling because cultural genocide and culturecide claim separate conceptual terrain. I use the term *culturecide* in line with Fenelon's framework, as an expression of cultural domination that is not synonymous with cultural genocide.

Political scientist Hanna Schreiber's work also makes the case for terminological distinction. A scholar of Ralph Lemkin's work, Schreiber writes about the evolution of genocide terminology:

> In order to avoid confusion with the definition of genocide established in the Convention of 1948 (which emphasises the physical aspects of destroying a group for national, ethnic, racial, or religious reasons), in the context of the ongoing political debate I propose using the term "culturecide", which directly points to the possibility of "killing a culture", without the necessity to physically exterminate its depositaries. The principal connotation of the term "cultural genocide" suggests that members of a group are killed due

to cultural reasons. However, while such physical extermination may accompany culturecide, it does not necessarily have to be the goal. (Schreiber, 2017: 334–335)

As does Fenelon, Schreiber differentiates cultural genocide (physical genocide based on cultural grouping) from culturecide (killing culture while allowing physical persistence). Using such a definition of culturecide also sidesteps conflation between cultural genocide and ethnocide. The United Nations Commission on Human Rights' report on the 1981 Declaration of San José defined ethnocide as the denial of an ethnic group's right to cultural continuity (UNESCO, 1983). Silencing of culture may operate in tandem with physically based practices of cultural genocide, ethnocide, or *feminicide* in some places, but the terms are not synonymous.

The concept of culturecide is sufficiently narrow that it can be invoked where physical targeting for death is not the explicit agenda but killing Indigenous culture is part of daily practice. By narrowing the scope to the killing of culture, not the elimination of the body, culturecide can be conceptually applied to the type of contemporary harm that Indigenous people, discussed in the following pages, have experienced in recent history through to the present day. Culturecide is conceptually and practically important in contemporary conversations about decolonization and survivance because it reminds us of what is at stake for Indigenous communities when overt physical destruction gives way to more subtle but no less insidious practices of destruction. By naming culturecide as part of settler colonialism that perpetuates ongoing harm in the midst of democratization, I straddle the fault lines between multiple traditions that seek to document violence while also exploring potential solutions for more peaceful pluriethnic coexistence.

Having clarified the definition of culturecide, I address here the various forms of terminological expression for resistance to ongoing colonization. *Revitalization* is the term that appears most frequently in Indigenous studies literature (Baldy, 2018; Guerrettaz, 2019; Jacob, 2013; Olthuis et al., 2013); *resilience* (McCovey, 2006; Risling Baldy & Begay, 2019), *survivance* (Vizenor, 1994, 2010, 2009), *survival* (Fenelon, 1998; McCarty et al., 2014), *resurgence* (Corntassel, 2012; Simpson, 2008), and *revival* (H. Campbell, 1994; Faudree, 2013) are also used. I tend to use the term *revitalization*, as this was the most favored term among interviewees, particularly in California, but I use the other terms as synonyms when necessary. All of them refer to the effort of cultural continuity in the face of attempted culturecide.

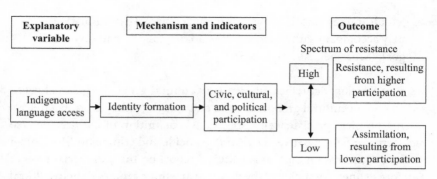

Figure 1. Causal diagram of the central argument.

Figure 1 (the causal model) shows how the explanatory variable, mechanism, indicators, and outcome fit together. Though the arrows are unidirectional in the diagram, in practice it is evident that participation feeds back into identity formation so that identity is iterative, both forming and being formed by young people's participation experiences. The arrow in the outcome box also shows an oversimplified version of a spectrum of resistance. Students may strongly resist culturecide in one aspect of their lives or at a given moment but then enact assimilation in another area of life or specific moment. Like any causal diagram, this one captures the basic dynamics of the argument but is unable to convey all the nuance of lived experience that young people qualitatively share. Nevertheless, this diagram can help readers anchor the data shared in the empirical chapters ahead.

A Note on Indigenous Terminology

This book consistently uses and references the concepts of indigeneity and Indigenousness. However, Linda Tuhiwai Smith rightly notes that "the term 'indigenous' is problematic in that it appears to collectivize many distinct populations whose experiences under imperialism have been vastly different" (2012: 6). There are numerous labels for Indigenous people in both Mexico and the United States, and most are fraught with racist origins. In my previous book (Gellman, 2017), I used the term in Spanish, *pueblos originarios* (original peoples), to refer to Indigenous people in Mexico and El Salvador, as that term has gained currency showing international solidarity across

Indigenous groups. Smith herself uses a close translation of *pueblos originarios*, "indigenous peoples," in her 2012 book, *Decolonizing Methodologies*.

In this book, I generally use the term *Indigenous* because I work across multiple Indigenous communities, state and national borders, and individual and group contexts, and there are different preferred terms across these spaces. I defer to particulars whenever possible but also need at times to refer to collectivities. Some Indigenous people prefer to reclaim the term *Indigenous*, particularly because it comes with rights, as the official term used in documents like the 1989 International Labor Organization's Convention 169 on Indigenous and Tribal Peoples, as well as in state and federal laws in many Latin American countries. In addition, there is also a current preference to capitalize the term *Indigenous*, which was not capitalized in much of the previous literature, but I follow the new convention here.

In general, I try to speak as specifically as possible about people's identities. For example, in the California chapters of this book I use the term *Yurok* when referring to Yurok people only, and *Native Americans* if speaking about more than one Native American group. I only use the term *Indian* to refer to legal frameworks, in citations, or in quotes from people who identify as such. Like the term *queer* in the LGBTQI+ community, *Indian* is frequently used self-referentially by insiders but can be seen as derogatory when used by outsiders (J. Gensaw, 2017; M. Gensaw, 2017). In the Mexico chapters I use the specific name of a person's tribe or ethnicity whenever possible but use the term *Indigenous* if speaking about more than one group, which I do frequently when referencing cases across Mexico and the United States. There is rich debate over terminology, and it is possible that the renderings I have chosen will fall out of favor in the future. I update with each new endeavor. The remainder of this chapter presents conceptual matrices and hypotheses and introduces the case studies of four public high schools in Oaxaca, Mexico, and far Northern California.

Conceptual Matrices and Hypotheses

Given existing language hierarchies, challenges abound for education policy regarding language access for ethnic minority youth. Classrooms in both Mexico and the United States are primary sites of citizen formation where youth identity is consolidated and languages are enforced (Gellman & Bellino, 2019; Hornberger & De Korne, 2018). The interrelationship among language, identity validation, and civic, cultural, and political participation is complex. I define cultural participation as running the gamut of meaning-making activities, from showing up for or taking an active role in religious, linguistic, or artistic processes, to studying family or community traditions, to possibly passing on such processes or traditions as either a learner or teacher.

Similarly broad, civic participation refers to any type of collective action that addresses concerns at the community level, for example, performing a *cargo* (required but unremunerated voluntary community service in Indigenous Mexican communities), helping pick up trash in a public area, or volunteering as a tutor. Many studies have sought to analyze the political behavior of ethnic minorities but often remain confined to the realm of formal participation indicators such as voting (Burch, 2013). In my own work, I take political participation to include the full range of institutional and contentious claim-making activities, everything from voting to protesting at the local, regional, national, or international level (Gellman, 2017: 5).

Because of this expansive notion of participation both conceptually and empirically in terms of the range of indicators documented, this book expands the notion of what is political. In doing so, I account for the numerous informal but in fact quite vital interrelationships between cultural and political realms. I address this nexus through the connection between state language regimes—meaning the way that state policies and notions of language use are embedded institutionally (Sonntag & Cardinal, 2015: 4–5)—and youth identity development in relation to civic, cultural, and political participation.

Hypotheses

In the following chapters, I present the findings from testing four related hypotheses developed in the research design phase. For each hypothesis, I offer brief examples to help convey the meaning behind the theorization.

1. For heritage-speaker students—those who have personal familial ties via ethnic group to a given language—heritage language classes facilitate greater participation in heritage communities. Indicators of the connections between language engagement and civic, cultural, or political participation are numerous, and I documented many of them in my field notes over several years. Increased language-fueled participation in Mexico sometimes looked

like a Zapotec student deciding to accompany a parent to the community assembly meetings conducted in Zapotec and paying attention to the language, or signing up to participate in cultural celebrations like a cooking competition conducted in Zapotec. In California, indicators of proof for this hypothesis looked like an ethnically Yurok student in a Yurok language class becoming more interested in Yurok politics or culture and starting to play a new role in these realms by going to a protest about the Klamath River dam[6] or joining the Yurok Tribe youth committee.

2. Indigenous language access brings with it a host of unintended yet beneficial side effects for heritage-speaker students, such as increasing student success in other high school classes, raising self-esteem, and empowering students to participate more broadly in a variety of ways. Indicators of this phenomenon include students who attend and do better in other classes at least in part because they are connecting with language teachers and students who have a shared interest, and student descriptions of how they felt at their schools or in their communities before and after their heritage language access.

   Civic participation indicators might look like students who volunteer in formal or informal ways to help others in their communities, whether through school clubs or outside organizations and regardless of type of volunteer work. Cultural participation indicators range from Mixtec[7] students going home from their Zapotec classes to quiz elders on Mixtec vocabulary, and Hmong American students asking community members to tell them folktales rooted in Hmong cosmology. Indicators of political participation include students getting involved in rights movements that pertain to their own heritage groups, and requesting that school curricula be expanded to include their heritage content too.

3. Learning a minority language such as Zapotec or Yurok helps non-heritage-speaker students develop intercultural competence skills—meaning, effective engagement with cultures other than one's own—that facilitate greater acceptance of, and interest in, Indigenous communities. Minority students, based on their own positionality, already know that multiple linguistic and cultural worlds exist, though they may or may not be versed in navigating such worlds. But ethnic-majority students often lack an awareness of multiple cultural and linguistic worlds. Some mestizo[8] and White

students are firmly rooted in majoritarian bubbles where those frameworks for speaking and being are all they know. In such cases, non-heritage-speakers from the ethnic majority may show an increase in intercultural competency due to Indigenous language access.

To address one potential criticism of the research design, it is true that some non-heritage students who sign up for Zapotec or Yurok might be the type of students who are already more interested in other cultures. But in Oaxaca, there are reasons such as cost and school location that drive non-heritage enrollment, and in California, course schedule issues sometimes determine which language students use to meet the language requirement. This is to say that while there may have been some selection bias in terms of which students signed up for Zapotec and Yurok classes, the logistical context of school and class choices meant there was significant variation in who actually took Indigenous language classes during the time of the study.

4. For non-heritage-speaker youth from other minority backgrounds, such as Mixtec students in Oaxaca or Hmong American students in California, seeing positive examples of ethnically based knowledge in minority language classes increases their interest in their own ethnic backgrounds, even though the language classes themselves have nothing to do with that particular background. This hypothesis generated the least amount of data but was included in the data collection.

Methods and Methodology

I devote all of Chapter 2 to an in-depth discussion of methods and methodology, but I briefly note here that this project is rooted in what I term *collaborative methodology*, meaning that it was designed with stakeholder partnerships and values at the forefront. This includes stakeholder participation in crafting the research questions as well as specific language in the data collection instruments. This project also fuses empirical and interpretivist research design, a rather unusual approach for a political scientist. For example, the four hypotheses listed above were assessed in ways that definitively searched for answers in a positivist sense, as well as drawing on participants' interpretations of their own realities and my interpretations of their reflections. I used a mixed-methods approach to address this ambitious self-imposed mandate, including political ethnography—meaning participant observation and participation in communities—as well as semi-structured, open-ended qualitative interviews, focus groups, and surveys. I engaged students, faculty, and administrators in the formal education sectors of public upper secondary schools known as *bachilleratos* in Mexico, or high schools in the United States.

Indicators of resistance to culturecide can be seen in the rejection of ethnic-majority norms and assimilationist behaviors more broadly. Such indicators may also include an assertion of indigeneity in a range of behaviors not limited to civic, political, and cultural arenas, including language use, traditional dress, and food-obtaining practices. In this way, Indigenous language access is but one of many factors that feed into developing a repertoire of resistance.

Navigating Education as Both Colonizing and Decolonizing

My argument presents Indigenous language access as one mechanism to work toward decolonizing education; it then shows how such access can foment resistance to culturecide among young people. In making this argument, I have no illusions about the scope of the challenge. Public education is a fundamental tool of state-building that has been used to homogenize populations and create nationally oriented citizens. Settler-colonial states like the United States and Mexico rely on public education to push Indigenous people and other minority groups to assimilate.

Using the same tool for decolonization that is used in colonization is risky. Tuck and Yang, in asserting that decolonization cannot be transposed onto settler frameworks, might argue that such an approach amounts to the metaphorical decolonization they rightly warn against (2012: 3). But the public education system is, at its base, a network for information dissemination. When Zapotec or Yurok words and epistemologies become a portion of the information disseminated, perhaps the role of the education sector in decolonization deserves another look. Surely there is the potential for Indigenous language access in schools to take place in ways that do not fundamentally change people's relationship with settler-colonial states. At the same time, students in both Zapotec and Yurok classes told me over and over again that having access to the language changed the way they defined themselves and made them prouder of and more comfortable with their Indigenous heritage. With boosted self-esteem, they were then more capable of resisting culture-cide in school and elsewhere.

In addition, the education sector is a prime space to make many societal values visible or invisible. Such an approach resonates with what Anishinaabe scholar and writer Gerald Vizenor terms "Native survivance," which is a "sense of narrative resistance to absence, literary tragedy, nihility, and victimry. Native survivance is an active sense of presence over historical absence, the dominance of cultural simulations, and . . . a continuance of stories" (Vizenor, 2010: 1). As a prime arena of narrative creation where certain stories are preserved over others, schools play a role in the politics of Indigenous presence and absence. Following these lines of argument, Indigenous language access can, through positive Indigenous youth identity formation, encourage a resistance to culturecide that constitutes a form of survivance. Insisting on visibility in spaces where invisibility is usually the rule thus becomes one part of a broader strategy of decolonization.

I acknowledge that numerous variables beyond language access are at play in Indigenous schooling experiences and identity formation processes. There are many aspects of life that inform Indigenous youth identity construction and that in turn may inform why young people choose to participate or not in aspects of political, civic, or cultural life, whether in a decolonized mode or not (Jacob, 2013: 51–59). Language access and language use each play a particular role in how identity is performed (Faingold, 2018: 37–40). Scholars have documented ways in which school (E. A. Cole, 2007), family (Crawford & Alaggia, 2008), economics (Córdova & Layton, 2015), and the social or political dynamics of surrounding communities influence young people (Kessler-Mata, 2017; Norton, 1979: 19; Tavanti, 2003). In addition, mental health or peer groups may explain certain behaviors (Duran, 2006). All of these works document truths about factors impacting Indigenous youth.

Identity construction in schools and the relationship between language and schooling are especially vital for explaining Indigenous youth identity and participation because of the history of colonialism in formal education (D. W. Adams, 1995). This is visible in the fact that Indigenous leaders continue to view education policy as a central aspect of cultural survival for their communities. In part this may be because youth resistance to colonization and domination has played out in schools, as sites of abuse, coercion, and visible state power. Because public schools serve as some of the most commonly engaged-with state institutions in ordinary people's lives, resisting within such institutions is therefore a means to push back against the colonization and domination that public education represents.

In California, for example, the Yurok Tribe's Education Department advocates for more Yurok language classes and expanded curricular integration of Native American content. Yurok leaders may not be able to change all the other factors that affect students in schools like Eureka High School and Hoopa Valley High School, but Tribal leaders can try to intervene in terms of curricular offerings. This concrete opportunity to address how young people absorb the world around them via mechanisms of formal education creates pathways to resist culturecide.

Though dynamics of globalization and migration inform the language choices people make, these forces are sometimes beyond the grasp of policymakers at the school, regional, or state level. As a researcher invested in addressing real policy changes that can promote cultural survival of Indigenous communities, I therefore focus my attention on language access as one element of resistance to culturecide. Overall, this book documents Indigenous language access in public high school education and explores how teachers, students, and community members work together to resist assimilation through the promotion of access to Indigenous language and cultural content.

Scope Conditions

I do not cover every aspect of the impact of language access with equal weight. For example, due to a range of factors, students from heritage-speaking backgrounds—those whose parents, grandparents, or ancestors spoke an Indigenous language or ethnically identified with it in some way—may struggle with school success, and sometimes fail. It is outside the scope of this book to track academic outcomes based on school records, though a future researcher may be able to tie language access to transcript-verified academic success. Instead, I document student self-reporting of academic experiences connected to Indigenous language access. By taking this approach, I am able to discuss in depth some of the many variables that play a role in Indigenous students' academic success, such as campus and community climate, mental health, motivation toward academic work, and economic barriers.

Other variables I am not able to include here for lack of space—including academic support services,[9] teen sexuality and pregnancy, and school district politics—will surely enrich other scholars' research agendas. One additional scope condition present here is a focus on state repression of culture—culturecide—rather than physical repression by the state. This scope condition allows for a deep dive into educational curricula and school climates, while recognizing that such a focus is intertwined with legacies of genocide.

Case Snapshots

Common struggles for Indigenous cultural survival cut across state boundaries. All of the schools included in this study are situated in communities that have been powerfully shaped by colonialism and continue to have a significant presence of Indigenous people. To that end, this research puts education policy debates from the central valley of Oaxaca, Mexico—where Zapotec language classes are available at some schools—in conversation with those from far Northern California,[10] where the Native American language of Yurok is now an elective in four public high schools in Humboldt, Del Norte, and Trinity Counties. Given the ethnic and racial diversity of each school, access to Indigenous and heritage languages can play a range of roles in youth identity development. I attempted to include a sample of all school community members in the study regardless of racial or ethnic background.

I invited student participation from Indigenous language classes (Zapotec in Oaxaca, Yurok in California) and control classes (French and Art History in Oaxaca, Civics and History in California), corresponding faculty for all classes, and school administrators for all schools, as well as Zapotec and Yurok community leaders from the surrounding areas. I spoke with any student who returned their signed parent/guardian permission forms and did not select respondents based on race or ethnicity. To complement the focus on Indigenous language access, I also briefly consider the role of English language learning in Mexican classrooms, as well as Spanish language learning in Californian classrooms, to understand how ideas of social and economic mobility, especially as connected to aspirations of migration and assimilation, inform educational policy and practice. However, some of the English/Spanish content would take me beyond the scope of the research puzzle at hand and has been therefore set aside for a subsequent publication.

The case-study sites are four high schools (two in Oaxaca, two in California) where language electives are offered to students from a range of ethnic-minority and ethnic-majority backgrounds. In three of the four schools,

Indigenous language courses meet the world language requirement, and English is the required language in the fourth school. Schools were selected and paired in order to capture a spectrum of schooling realities for students: rural, primarily Indigenous-serving in the primary pairing, and urban, primarily ethnic-majority-serving in the secondary pairing. Across the schools, I performed interviews, focus groups, and surveys with students in more than twenty distinct courses, with some courses serving as the classes of target interest—namely Zapotec and Yurok, and other classes such as Spanish, English, French, U.S. History, Civics, and Mexican Art History selected as controls, or additional spaces to both triangulate data and check the impact of the language classes specifically against the impact of other types of curricula. This spread of courses also allowed for insight into the way that both history and civics education directly contribute to engaged citizenship.

Each of the schools granted research access in line with Emerson College's Institutional Review Board (IRB) protocol #17-062-F-E-6/1-[R1-3]. All Yurok aspects of the research were reviewed and approved by the Yurok Tribal Council and the Yurok Education Department, while the Zapotec research was approved by the Indigenous community-elected education official (*El Regidór de Educación*) in the town of Teotitlán del Valle, as well as the Parents' Committee and school directors of the BIC and the Oaxaca de Juárez high school. Research instruments are available in the Appendices.

Transparency in Case Selection

In the spirit of full transparency in research design, I offer the following orientation to my positionality here. While some political scientists cling to claims of objectivity on par with the natural sciences (Ragin, [1987] 2014), others see centering of positionality and the interpretive capacity of the researcher as a key component of political science (Yanow & Schwartz-Shea, 2014a). For my own part, I give the following positional explanation to encourage others to be more forthright about their own case selections.

I grew up in far Northern California, and my K–12 schooling culminated in attending an urban, majority-White regional high school there that is included in this study. As I developed my scholarly career as a minority rights scholar and Latin Americanist, I began looking at the themes I studied in the Global South—violence against Indigenous peoples, distortion of historical narratives, and language rights—in my childhood backyard. Post-tenure, my work has taken a policy turn out of interest to move findings from the theoretical to the practically applicable. The chance to look at education policy in regional high schools, in partnership with the Yurok Tribe's Education Department, appeared as a way to both collaborate with stakeholders and give back to a part of the world that has not yet produced many people with PhDs. This paired well with my interest in Oaxacan Indigenous politics and violence, which had been part of the focus of my first book. I had a framework, as well as a list of contacts, to match schools across borders.

Arguably, this case selection differs from those of researchers who claim they randomly surveyed cases exhibiting certain characteristics and chose those that best met their research model. We don't yet live in a scholarly world where people can justify case selection based on where children can be cared for by grandparents while fieldwork takes place. Though I know from many informal conversations with colleagues that I am not alone in life-logistics-informed case selection, as a discipline political science has not yet reached such levels of honesty.

At stake for researchers in such an approach to case-selection transparency is the claim to objectivity and neutrality. Revealing one's positionality may invite judgment about potential bias. Yet concealing the real reasons for case selection perpetuates myths about objective research practices that reinforce social hierarchies within the academe. My hope is that this explanation of pragmatic case selection may show future researchers that it is possible to balance real-world identities and life constraints with innovative research design objectives, and that describing such aspects of design is part of research transparency, not a liability. Such transparency is a way of accounting for influences in research, all the way from question and argument design to findings. In addition, an orientation toward transparency has led me to the creation of a collaborative methodological framework for political science research discussed in depth in Chapter 2.

Mexico Sites

BIC 29 is located about an hour east of Oaxaca de Juárez in the small Zapotec village of Teotitlán del Valle and requires three years of Zapotec language study for all students, regardless of background. The BIC school system, which contains forty-nine schools throughout the state of Oaxaca, is administered by Colegio Superior para Educación Integral Intercultural de Oaxaca (Superior

College for Integral Intercultural Education of Oaxaca, CSEIIO), and follows a specific mandate to provide culturally relevant education for Indigenous students while adhering to Ministry of Education curricula.

The Centro de Educación Artística "Miguel Cabrera" (Center for Artistic Education "Miguel Cabrera," CEDARTMC) is an urban selective test-in high school run by the Instituto Nacional de las Bellas Artes (National Institute of Fine Arts, INBA) that attracts artistically minded students and has a strong legacy student presence (legacy students are those whose parents, siblings, or other family members attended CEDARTMC before them), and only offers English to fulfill the three years of language requirement at the high school level. There are eleven CEDARTMC schools in all of Mexico, with the Miguel Cabrera school situated in the southern part of central Oaxaca de Juárez.

In Oaxaca, I spoke with students from Indigenous and non-Indigenous backgrounds in this range of school experiences as they navigated their educative options in conversation with family expectations and individual desires. To foreshadow my findings, in urban Oaxaca de Juárez, like many people from minority backgrounds around the world in urban contexts, students from Indigenous families who still spoke Zapotec were sometimes the least interested in language continuity and much more eager to study English because it was seen as a vehicle for upward social mobility and a means to avoid discrimination.

At the same time, students who identified as second- or third-generation Indigenous people, meaning that their parents or grandparents were Indigenous but had not passed the language on to them, were much more inclined to study Zapotec. In rural contexts, this paradox was reversed: students who went home to Zapotec-speaking families invested in learning the language in school, while those who lacked the family reinforcement were less interested in studying Zapotec. In each scenario, studying Zapotec was treated by students as a tool of cultural survival for Indigenous people, whose languages and customs have been subverted to a dominant mestizo agenda that they still experience today.

California Sites

Hoopa Valley High School (HVHS), located on the Hoopa Valley Indian Reservation ninety minutes inland from the coastal towns of Eureka and Arcata, serves mostly Native American heritage students from Hupa, Yurok, and

Karuk backgrounds, among others, as well as a minority of White and Latinx students. HVHS's student body faces high levels of poverty, family member substance abuse, and other societal obstacles. Nonetheless, it is a bastion of culturally based knowledge in the region, with some teachers and staff members themselves of Native background and others committed to supporting Native students.

Eureka High School (EHS) is situated in a majority-White town, the largest in Humboldt County with approximately 27,000 residents. There are significant Latinx, Native American, and Asian American minority populations that have expanded over the last few decades, shifting Eureka's identity from a very high majority-White town to a White but diverse one, with communities of color spread throughout the area. As of 2022, 49.7 percent of the EHS student population does not self-identify as White (DataQuest 2022). Table 1 compares the cases demographically and on the outcome of interest.

Again foreshadowing my findings, students who identified in some way as Native American were generally enthusiastic about Yurok language access in high school. Students saw such access not only as a concrete way to deepen their own knowledge of a cultural skill set but also as a way to revalidate their community identity in a public space that has frequently trivialized or rejected their heritage. A high proportion of Native American high school students in Hoopa and Eureka deliberately seek out the Yurok language classes, as well as other Native language classes available, for personal, family, and community reasons. The overwhelming sense from students is that they feel more confident being Native in school since they have a Native teacher and Native content in the curriculum. These findings are discussed in detail in the following chapters.

Conclusion: Outline of the Book

The remainder of the book proceeds as follows. Chapter 2 contributes a theory-building framework for how to do research that is collaborative and beneficial to stakeholders, particularly Indigenous communities. Information has been extracted from historically marginalized communities by scholars and not shared back with them in ways that contribute to community needs and goals; in contrast, this chapter outlines best practices in engaging Indigenous communities as partners in research. It also describes the successes

Table 1. School case studies in comparative form across selected characteristics, 2018

School	Urban/Rural, location, dominant language	Additional languages offered	Student population total	Student demographics	Identity and participation notes	Outcome
BIC 29	Rural (Oaxaca, Spanish)	Zapotec, English	150	1/3 Zapotec, 1/3 Indigenous-descendant, 1/3 mestizo	Consolidation of Indigenous identity, local participation	Some resistance to culturecide
CEDARTMC	Urban (Oaxaca, Spanish)	English	350	Mestizo majority, some Indigenous and Indigenous-descendant students	Awareness channeled globally, artistic identity expansive	Resistance to neoliberal globalization
HVHS	Rural (California, English)	Yurok, Hupa, Spanish	300	Yurok and Hupa majority, small White population	Consolidation of Native identity, local participation	Strong resistance to culturecide
EHS	Urban (California, English)	Yurok, Spanish, German	1,000	Majority White, many Latinx, Asian American and Native students	Expansion of intercultural awareness, some increasing participation	Some resistance to culturecide

and failures of the specific methods employed in the case studies and offers summaries of key insights from the methods.

Chapter 3 documents the historical contexts for contemporary language politics in formal education settings. Drawing on discussions of how state language regimes operate in relation to linguistic minorities, this chapter argues that Mexico and the United States have crafted assimilationist agendas through Castilianization and Englishization policies, respectively, both of which undercut Indigenous language rights. These majority-dominant language regimes constitute a form of culturecide that affects contemporary Indigenous youth identities and repertoires of participation.

Chapter 4 describes how the Zapotec language requirement at BIC 29 in Teotitlán del Valle has mainstreamed conversations about and practices of Indigenous language and culture for high school students in rural Oaxaca. This chapter discusses the Zapotec renaissance proclaimed in Oaxaca in contrast to the dominant practices of racism and discrimination. Using vignettes drawn from interviews and focus groups, this chapter relays the book's themes through the eyes of students and teachers. Such an approach is utilized in each of the case-study chapters to let stakeholders speak for themselves.

Chapter 5 presents the case study of CEDARTMC, a public, arts-focused high school, noting how the English language requirement in urban CEDARTMC offers a different path for identity development than the Zapotec language requirement in BIC 29. The case shows how competing worldviews encompassed in curricular language requirements have implications for youth participation. Such worldviews inform administrative choices about socioeconomic opportunities for students, as well as prioritizations of cultural expressions in school. Identity consolidation and participation appear variegated in CEDARTMC and BIC 29, as do the challenges students face. Nevertheless, commonalities abound in what young people define as meaningful in the context of their communities.

Chapter 6 examines the role of Yurok teaching and learning at HVHS, a predominantly Native American–serving public high school located on a rural Indian reservation in far Northern California. Though factors such as unemployment and addiction affect the surrounding community, cultural resilience is an ongoing process at HVHS. Native language courses are one site of this resilience, alongside other culturally rooted activities in both the formal and informal education curriculum. While for some students Native language classes are just another class to get through, for others the classes catalyze them as the next generation of language-keepers and cultural practitioners.

Chapter 7 presents how students from a range of ethnic backgrounds relate to their Yurok language elective classes at the comparatively urban, small-town coastal school of EHS. For Yurok heritage-speakers, Yurok classes provide a self-esteem boost where they experience their heritage being valued and legitimated for curricular inclusion. In such a space, the overarching power relations between ethnic-majority and ethnic-minority students are briefly suspended or even reversed. For White students, Yurok language classes offer a space to learn about the intense and ongoing relationships between Native and settler-descendant communities, not only as history but also as contemporary reality. For students of other ethnic-minority backgrounds, discussion of Yurok language and culture validates other forms of ethnic-minority identities in a town that, though increasingly diverse, remains majority White. Yet these experiences of Indigenous language access take place in a community riddled with racist acts and institutions, and one that has not yet come to terms with its past even as young people perpetuate divisive behaviors through everyday interactions.

Chapter 8 concludes the book with an examination of how Indigenous language access is connected to decolonization. As youth form their identities and consider ways to participate in the world, they also develop repertoires of resistance to culturecide. Indigenous language access in public high schools is one part of a vast puzzle about how people learn to live together in peaceful and democratic coexistence.

CHAPTER 2

Collaborative Methodology: Research With, Not On, Indigenous Communities

Introduction: Seeking Community Access

Indigenous scholar Linda Tuhiwai Smith writes that "the word itself, 'research,' is probably one of the dirtiest words in the indigenous world's vocabulary" (2012: 1). After all, historically, "research" has been used to justify scientific racism, with both social and natural scientists lending their skills to affirm social hierarchies that justify White colonization of Black, Indigenous, and People of Color (BIPOC) communities (Kendi, 2016). In response, many scholars have advocated for ways to decolonize research with Indigenous peoples, including Tuhiwai Smith's subversion of the Western positivist approach to knowledge production (2012), Wilson's approach to research as ceremony (2008), and Stephen and Speed's fusing of feminist and activist frameworks to center Indigenous voices (2021). Much of this innovation comes from fields like anthropology, education, and cultural studies. I draw on these important interventions to discuss how more reluctant disciplines like political science can meaningfully move away from research as extraction. To do so, I share my own process of learning to work with, rather than on, Indigenous communities.

Oaxaca

The road from the municipal government office in Teotitlán del Valle, Mexico, to the local high school is lined with cacti and full of potholes. It is a road I walk many dozens of times. Following local protocol, when I arrive the very first time I present myself to the authorities in the town center, sign the book requesting an audience in the government office, and then explain my request when I am summoned for my turn. I seek permission to study youth identity and Indigenous language access at the Integral Community High School Number 29 (*Bachillerato Integral Comunitario Numero 29*, or BIC 29), which sits on community-donated land a mile from the town center. After an oral interview with the town mayor and then the local education official, or El Regidór de Educación, Joel Vincente Contreras, Mr. Contreras takes me to the school himself. My request for site access has been approved at the municipal level, but there are several more levels of permissions to be sought before I can begin research. However, as I show in this chapter, the relationship-building in a project's beginning is arguably as integral to its validity and ethics as the results that might come from later methods of data collection.

I squeeze inside the Toyota camper cab between the elderly Mr. Contreras and his ritual accompanier as we take the potholed road to the BIC,[1] where Mr. Contreras presents me to the school director, the Zapotec language teacher, and the Parents' Committee representatives. Mr. Contreras and his accompanier are both serving *cargos*, community service jobs, under Oaxaca's *usos y costumbres*, a traditional and customary system that gives official state recognition to Indigenous governance processes rather than requiring political party representation. More recently, the term *usos y costumbres* has been replaced by some organizations, including Mexico's State Electoral Institute, with the label *sistemas normativos indígenas*, or normative Indigenous systems (Gobierno de Oaxaca, 2020; Martínez de Bringas, 2013). However, since most of my interlocutors continue to use the term *usos y costumbres*, I follow their practice here. While many surrounding towns have shifted to political party elections rather than community assemblies where *usos y costumbres* play out, Teotitlán del Valle has a proud reputation as a cultural stronghold for Valley Zapotec practices, including governance, artistry, and language. Municipal leadership positions range in duration from one to three years and are taken very seriously within the community.

Señor Contreras's accompanier, in tattered T-shirt and jeans, holds the engraved and beribboned stick that shows that Contreras has come in his official capacity as a *cargo*-holder. This time-honored ritual metaphorically opens the BIC's doors for me. The school director and Zapotec teacher grant their permission for the study, as do the Parents' Committee representatives who are serving one-year cargos along with nine other parents of BIC students.

Local Zapotec researchers are not always so lucky in gaining access, as internal jealousy and gender norms have made it hard for people from within

Teotitlán del Valle to carry out cultural projects there. This is particularly true for young, unmarried, and ambitious women, as the local authorities remain firmly older men with traditional notions of gender roles (Anonymous, 2018ad: 13; Cruz, 2012). My outsider status is key to being welcome here. Zapotec community members see me as far removed from their world, and this is partly why I am granted access to it.

California

In contrast to the ease of access in Oaxaca, in 2017 I stood in front of the Yurok Tribal Council in Northern California and fielded hardball questions, seeking permission to launch my project with Yurok language students in two public high schools. Skepticism about my outsider status was evident, and rightly so, given the history of genocide and exploitation by White settlers and their descendants in the region. The fact that I grew up near the main White-majority town an hour south of the Yurok Reservation was not helpful. At first glance, my profile lumped me in with the beneficiaries of nineteenth-century militias who massacred California Indians to steal their land. To obtain the Yurok Tribal Council's permission to carry out research on anything about them, I had to overcome entrenched barriers to trust based on historical and contemporary violence of White people toward Indigenous people.

The issue of trust didn't end with just getting permission but was part of the study dynamic throughout each stage of the research. The element of trust and what it takes to earn it, as a researcher working with Indigenous people as an outsider, became so significant to the project that it led to this chapter as a stand-alone discussion of methodology. In this section I discuss how positionality operates differently across cases in comparative research.

The history of information extraction from marginalized communities by scholars who don't give back to those same communities has rightfully created an atmosphere of bitterness toward the role of scholars in general (Deloria Jr., [1969] 1988: 78–100). One element that likely enhanced my permissions request to the Yurok Tribal Council was an ongoing dialogue I had with the Yurok Education Department director over the previous year (2016). During this time, I demonstrated my commitment to making the project— through collaborative methodology—useful for the Education Department by collecting information that could be cited in tribal grant-writing projects as well as by documenting academic successes or challenges for Native students about whom the Education Department was eager to gain insight.

In the seaside town of Klamath, an hour south of the Oregon border, on the Yurok Indian Reservation at the Yurok Tribal headquarters, Education Director Jim McQuillen stood at my side in the Council meeting and essentially vouched for me and the project. Nevertheless, when the Council approved my study, it was contingent on Tribal right to review written work that had to do with Yurok people. This is an important way for Yurok people to maintain integrity over the way they are portrayed, a lesson many Indigenous peoples learned the hard way. Much scholarly exploitation and exotification of Native peoples in written studies over the last 150 years has proved that in a settler-colonial state, academics can and do publish things harmful to Native communities (Deloria Jr., [1969] 1988: 80; Hale, 2008: 11; Kroeber, 1925). Knowing this historical and contemporary dynamic of misrepresentation and self-serving academic research, I appreciate the importance of Tribal Council approval of the study itself, as well as their review of work prior to publication, as a way of addressing the power imbalance between researcher and researched.

Collaborative methodology as a framework for relationships between the researcher and the researched essentially upturns this power paradigm by opening the research design process to full participation by traditionally subjectified stakeholders. This is not easy terrain for political scientists. Yet such reframing of power relationships is vital when working with Indigenous and other historically marginalized communities in order to decolonize methodologies and halt the resource extraction status quo. As this chapter will show, collaborative research requires changing the framework of how we view the purpose of research: to what end, and for whom? It may not be easy, but collaboration is one concrete way in which research by elite outsiders interested in the experiences of historically marginalized populations can be less exploitative. Arguably, collaboration can also result in better research that is more deeply vetted by the very people it purports to affect.

The two examples above exemplify distinct approaches for gaining research access. In Oaxaca, being an outsider was helpful; in California, it was a liability. Both realities hinged on my own positionality as a White, female, middle-aged college professor asking permission to examine the experiences of Indigenous students in public school systems in relation to language curricula. Both research protocols were integral to designing collaborative research that seeks to follow and further establish best practices for doing research with, rather than on, historically marginalized communities.

Collaborative Methodology as Ethical Commitment

Education policy and the language politics landscape in which education administrators operate play a critical role in the formation of the next generation of citizens in a given demographic. So why bother with research protocol formalities? The formalities provide a legitimate method of gaining access to educational spaces, as well as collaborating with those who create them. Classrooms are sites where cultural values, norms of behavior, and aspirational goals are generated (Rojas Crotte, 2017: 264–270). The way languages are (or are not) integrated into curricula speaks volumes about the prioritization of types of identity validation or negation in public schooling.

As a result of ongoing migration combined with accelerated rates of cultural and economic globalization, language priorities for schools tend to revolve around majority languages like Spanish and English in Mexico and status languages like German or French, and increasingly Mandarin, or the practical language of Spanish in California. Given this undeniable language hierarchy, what, then, are the methodological considerations in studying political challenges for education policy as it pertains to heritage language access for youth? What methods can capture the meaning-making of young people in empirically valid ways?

This chapter explores the challenges and successes of the methodology and methods used to study language policy in public secondary schools in Oaxaca, Mexico, and far Northern California. This research was crafted as a collaboration between Indigenous communities and myself as the primary researcher, rather than as a strictly outsider-imposed framework that treated subjects as sources of data to be mined for information. This is not a small claim, as it fundamentally entails an ethical orientation toward the communities themselves as the most important aspect of the project. That is, the relationships between the researcher and the stakeholders are the ultimate priority, not just generating publications for the sake of advancing the researcher's career.

Clearly academic publication is part of the cycle of information dissemination, evidenced by the fact that you, reader, are partaking of this chapter and that I as author sought out a reputable press to publish this work. However, this step has only come to be after iterative dialogue with stakeholders about research design, project implementation, and discussion of the findings, as well as multiple tribal reviews of the manuscript, with time for stakeholder comments, prior to publication. The practicalities of collaboration are discussed below.

Collaborative Methodology Defined

Much social science research has been performed at the expense of, rather than to the benefit of, the people whose lives are being documented. Collaborative methodology attempts to change the paradigm of conventional information extraction from marginalized communities for scholarly benefit and instead engage people as actors with agency rather than as objects of research. In short, this means that stakeholders—people affected by the research puzzle itself—have been invited to participate in multiple levels of concept formation and research design rather than exclusively as data contributors.

Collaboration can mean many different things. At its most basic level, collaboration means working together, but the word itself does not define relationships in any specific way. Who works with whom, and how such working together should take place, is open for interpretation. At the most basic level, by collaboration I mean working together with stakeholders to generate each stage of the research puzzle, including formulating questions, deciding what methods of data collection to use, and making decisions about how findings should be shared. By methodology I am referring to the theoretical orientation and higher purpose of the research, which is distinct from the tool kit of methods used for data collection. Collaborative methodology entails a theoretical and practical commitment to mutually created and agreed upon knowledge frameworks, processes, and products that are available for use by various stakeholders.

What collaborative methodology looks like may vary tremendously from project to project. However, all projects that seek to operate under the umbrella term of *collaboration*, as I define it, share a commitment to addressing power relationships through research design. This includes an explicit focus on social hierarchies and how they are navigated, as well as what is at stake in the research for each actor. A strength of collaboration is thus its potential amenability to a range of methods utilized by political scientists, from political ethnography to field experiments. A risk is that the vagueness of collaboration can allow a broad range of research approaches to use the label without actually centering stakeholder voices.

Collaborative methodology as a general concept has a long history in other fields. From activist research approaches utilized in anthropology (Hale, 2008; Speed, 2006; Stephen, 2013), development studies and geography (Kindon et al., 2007), criminology (Higginbottom, 2008), feminist studies (R. Campbell & Wasco, 2000), and many others across a range of disciplines (Bradbury, 2015; Robles Lomeli & Rappaport, 2018), the notion of using the tools and resources of research to advance specific agendas that relate to empowering historically marginalized people has a long precedent. Terms like *solidarity*, *interdependence*, and *groundedness* are sometimes used to describe decolonizing work (Snelgrove et al., 2014: 19–22).

The label most commonly ascribed to a stakeholder-focused research framework is Participatory Action Research (PAR). PAR has long been used by scholars in the social sciences who seek to connect their research to direct action that will benefit communities of study. Political scientists, however, have generally avoided any type of community involvement in research because it has the potential to undermine impartiality and objectivity—prized values in the discipline. However, as the discipline looks internally to justify its existence relevant to policy, and the liberal arts in general are pushed to defend their existence in higher education, notions of collaboration to promote policy-relevant research may become more accepted.

As I have begun to publicly talk about the kind of collaborative methodology I use, colleagues most frequently assume that it is PAR, a widely recognized term across disciplines. Collaborative methodology as I practice it is similar to PAR but differs in one crucial way, discussed below. PAR is defined by three central characteristics. First, PAR is committed to action being derived from an iterative process of reflecting on information derived from research with stakeholders (Baum et al., 2006: 854–856). Second, PAR addresses power hierarchies within research relationships, working to make them more inclusive (Kemmis et al., 2014: 3). Third, PAR engages subjects as stakeholders who have a right to be involved in the process of research; researchers must not simply extract data and use it for their own benefit (Baum et al., 2006: 854–856).

These are laudable goals that have been effective in catalyzing empirically based activist agendas in many communities, and the second and third characteristics are part of what I term *collaborative methodology*. However, the discipline of political science has generally shied away from PAR research designs for a variety of reasons, in part because of the first characteristic, the notion that action must follow from research. More broadly, PAR's three aspects tend to be written off as incompatible with political science because of concerns about the objectivity and bias of researchers who are invested in communities as activists. Universities may support this work either financially or philosophically, but sometimes they don't (Simpson, 2008: 79–80).

Political scientists are increasingly addressing PAR's second (power hierarchies) and third (subjects as stakeholders) characteristics within the field. Important work on power and positionality has come from interpretivist scholars such as Timothy Pachirat (2018: 56) and Katherine Cramer (2015), and discussion specifically concerning researched communities as stakeholders was featured in the July 2018 and July 2021 issues of *PS: Political Science and Politics* (see, among others, Bleck et al., 2018: 554; Firchow & Gellman 2021: 525; Thachil & Vaishnav, 2018: 546). However, PAR's commitment to making action central is hard to mesh with empirical political science. Advocating for action is seen as activism in a field where neutral theory-testing is prized and interpretive meaning-making still contested (Yanow & Schwartz-Shea, 2014b). Headway is being made in both debates, but the discipline resists change.

As defined by the editors of *Action Research Journal* in their inaugural issue, "Action research rejects the notion of an objective, value-free approach to knowledge generation in favor of an explicitly political, socially engaged, and democratic practice" (Brydon-Miller et al., 2003: 13). PAR is therefore inherently in tension with political science. Disciplinary graduate training itself at universities across the United States is neither democratic nor socially engaged. Typically, these programs train students to engage canonical works in ways that will position them at the top of social hierarchies in the job market. Theory-making and theory-testing work is preferred by elite universities looking to hire. Because of the social reproduction process, graduate students in political science departments rarely train in PAR philosophy or techniques, and therefore the discipline reproduces itself as a non-PAR space.

Feminist methodology is also frequently invoked as a means to address power inequalities and to include stakeholders. However, collaborative methodology and feminist methodology differ with regard to PAR's third characteristic, which concerns whose voice is centered. Feminist methodology explicitly amplifies the voices of women (Bardzell & Bardzell, 2011: 3; R. Campbell & Wasco, 2000: 773–774), whereas collaborative methodology can center whichever voices in the stakeholder community are relevant to the research puzzle. In my own work, though I have a particular interest in the experiences of girls and women, it has been important to foreground the voices of Indigenous leaders, educators, and students, regardless of gender. Because of this, feminist methodology did not quite fit my own methodological framework. I needed to define a different type of methodology that shares attributes with PAR and feminist research but is distinct from both.

Though collaboration in field experiments has emerged as one way that political scientists have tried to take on some of the elements of PAR, namely through consultation with stakeholders, the notion of deeper engagement with research communities tends to be minimized or elided all together. For example, in their tome on experiments, Rebecca Morton and Kenneth Williams include a short section titled "The Promise of Collaboration," which is entirely focused on collaboration across political science subfields and makes no mention of collaboration with stakeholders (Morton & Williams, 2010: 525–529). Notably, this section follows a chapter on deception, which describes multiple ways to deceive experiment participants (Morton & Williams, 2010: 500–521). In essence, this experiment-situated approach to researcher collaboration is very clearly a privileged sphere in which treated subjects should not enter.

Early in my career, I conformed to the notion of neutrality in research while finding other avenues for activism because I wanted to succeed in academia and didn't yet know how else to do so. Finding a way to bridge the discipline and meaningful engagement of stakeholders led me to collaborative methodology. Such an approach brings researchers into closer relationship with those affected by the research. Unlike PAR, collaborative methodology as I define it has no scripted action or liberatory framework as a necessary ingredient of a study. However, it is entirely possible that communities may decide to take action based on study findings, or that researchers may advocate for democratizing practices as a recommendation based on study findings. Such actions may heterogeneously take place on a case-by-case basis. Table 2 summarizes, in simplified fashion, the attributes of collaborative methodology in relation to PAR and feminist methodology.

In this way, I offer the methodological framework of collaborative methodology as a way of doing engaged research that is compatible with the discipline of political science (Gellman, 2021a). Such an approach enables social scientists to reserve judgment about what action might flow from their findings. It also prevents a commitment to a particular type of action from shaping the research itself, a situation in which well-meaning researchers

Table 2. Simplified elements of collaborative versus other methodologies

	Critique of power relationships	Inclusion of stakeholders	Commitment to action from research	Centers women
Collaborative methodology	Yes	Yes	Only if stakeholders request it	No
Participant Action Research (PAR)	Yes	Yes	Yes	No
Feminist methodology	Yes	Yes	Varies with iterations of approaches	Yes
Traditional political science methodologies	No	No	No	No

may inadvertently take agency away from stakeholders. Letting insight flow from carefully crafted collaborative work allows a disciplinary resonance with standards of neutrality while also utilizing a decolonizing framework that critiques power and includes stakeholders, who can guide the way that the research results are used. It is possible that greater reconciliation across the methodologies discussed might be viable, and in the future consensus could be reached across disciplines about what collaboration means. The discussion above is meant to help bring political scientists to the table and encourage them to participate across disciplines in conversations about decolonizing research methodologies.

Risks of Collaboration for Stakeholder Communities and Researchers

Collaboration is not without risks, but what is at stake will vary based on the positionality of each research participant. This subsection addresses first the risks that stakeholder community members take in collaborating and then turns to address concerns for researchers. For stakeholders, including those whose communities are the subject of research, the risks of collaboration may be significant, as any partnership poses challenges in terms of time, resources, and maintaining legitimacy in one's community. Many stakeholder communities like the ones with whom I work are resource-stretched—people work for small amounts of money and have long to-do lists, and anything that requires their time means time not spent fulfilling other obligations. For those working in non-governmental organizations (NGOs) and other grassroots-level organizations, the luxury of a few hours to meet and discuss ideas with a researcher may directly threaten their ability to complete other required tasks or even their ability to clock the hours they need to collect their paycheck if they can't count interview or brainstorm time as "work."

Researchers should be sensitive to this economic dynamic and soften it whenever possible by, for example, driving to where people work rather than asking them to travel or holding a meeting over a meal that the researcher buys as a token of appreciation. While I personally have never paid people for their time, I encourage the practice of creatively figuring out how a meeting can be made most advantageous for collaborators. In my own work, this means traveling far for meetings, buying meeting meals, and saying yes to an interviewee's child or office intern who is selling raffle tickets on the sidelines of a meeting.

Beyond the imposition on time and money, another risk for researched populations in collaborating is that their participation in a project legitimates it, and people may or may not feel comfortable with the research scope or premise. By collaborating, people stake their reputations, and if a study fails in some way, or if it negatively portrays their community, it can reflect badly on them. If questions about this are raised, researchers should be prepared to have open and honest dialogue about how they would address negative results in ways that won't harm the community. Finally, the tangible benefit to collaborating may be much more ephemeral for researched communities than for researchers, and the onus is on the researcher to make the benefits of the research as concrete as possible.

For researchers, the risks of collaboration tend to center around career benchmarks, including gaining an academic position and subsequent tenure and promotion, along with the requisite publications that drive such processes. The merits of collaborative research continue to be marginalized, most notably because the majority of tenure and promotion processes do not include the impact of one's work beyond the scholarly field. In other words, tangible impact on researched communities is not rewarded, whereas the number of citations by other scholars is. Introducing collaborative methodology to graduate students and remunerating it through hiring, promotion, conference proposal acceptance, and publication processes are all changes needed to bring collaborative methodology into the mainstream.

Some may argue that asking political scientists to become collaboration-ists may never work well with disciplinary imperatives. But clearly defining collaborative methodology as an orientation that allows for analysis of power and positionality in research relationships as well as stakeholder engagement, without requiring the action that made PAR off-limits to political scientists, is arguably compatible with new ways of thinking about research transparency and reliability in the discipline.

Collaboration dovetails well with recent discussions about the role of interpretivism, positionality, and Data Access and Research Transparency (DA-RT) in political science research (APSA QMMR, 2019; Cramer, 2015; Pachirat, 2015). As the discipline struggles to find its footing on these subjects, researchers are called upon to investigate their own gatekeeping mechanisms to academia, and ultimately to question what the purpose of such mechanisms are. Bland language from grant proposals, such as intentions to share back findings with affected communities, is insufficient in the world of collaborative methodologies. How do researched people get to engage with the data once collected, or get to decide who should be in the room when such share-backs take place? These and other questions about what is at stake for researched communities signify a substantial departure from research for the sake of a researcher's career and a turn toward evaluating research as a process that affects the lives of many. Thoroughly explaining the choices researchers make about how deeply they do or do not engage with stakeholders in the research process is also a qualitative form of transparency that can help readers evaluate the research.

Collaboration does not work well in all research; there are plenty of projects that are ill-suited for collaboration. But for people who work with vulnerable and historically or contemporarily marginalized communities, collaborative methodology is imperative for ethical research. Collaborative methodology serves as an umbrella concept, with many possibilities for how to design collaborative processes based on researcher and community needs.

Impartiality and Colonialism in Research

Convenient (for scholars) extractive research has the potential to inform policy over stakeholder communities without their participation. The notion of some sort of lofty impartiality allowing for truth-selection by elites for the masses defines the facade of political science and reeks of colonialism. Jack

Norton, a scholar of Hupa and Cherokee ancestry born in 1933, went on to become the director of Ethnic Studies and Native American Studies at Humboldt State University in Arcata, California, in the 1970s. Norton was the Hoopa Tribe's first college graduate, and the Jack Norton Elementary School on the Yurok Reservation is named in his honor. In reflecting on the role of objectivity in the social sciences, Norton comments: "What I deprecate is the rarity with which the historian acknowledges either his frame of reference, or the philosophical constructs that mold and direct his interpretations of the historical record. In the past, he has assumed an attitude of splendid isolation or a so-called impartiality, as he sifts through the stuff of history and selects the 'truth'" (Norton, 1979: ix). In short, impartiality can be a form of colonization by defining some types of information as the truth. As Robin Wall Kimmerer, a Potawatomi professor of biology, reminds us, "We are all the product of our worldviews—even scientists who claim pure objectivity" (Kimmerer, 2013: 163).

Dvora Yanow has written at length about the need for a more complicated notion of what counts as subjective in order to provide an alternative to the stifling notion of impartiality described above. She writes that "the challenge is to show how that centrality of human judgement can be scientific— systematic and subject to reflective 'doubting'—without the pejorative meanings that attach to subjectivity: that 'subjectivity' needs be neither idiosyncratic, and certainly not intentionally prejudiced, nor inaccurate" (Yanow, 2014: 110). In a moment when quantitative methods and machine-based analysis continue to dominate the discipline, Yanow reminds scholars that judgment need not be outsourced for it to be reliable research.

Peregrine Schwartz-Shea has developed tables of evaluation criteria for how interpretive scholars can be guided and in turn guide readers through systematic information filtration systems that provide impartiality and transparency without the "so-called impartiality" Norton calls out above (Schwartz-Shea, 2014: 127, 129). Can interpretive logic ever be seen as sufficient by those who advocate for DA-RT? Yanow states that "a different way of engaging the 'non-rigorous' charge is on philosophical grounds. What the procedural focus misses is the philosophical context in which rigor has a particular, technical meaning: that of logic and its deliberations concerning the character of truth" (Yanow, 2014: 102). These deliberations over truth take as many forms as there are methods and methodologies, and I don't propose a universal consensus. Rather, there are potential spaces of common ethical standards that scholars working with Indigenous people can embrace.

One space of convergence across a variety of disciplinary methods to address the fallacy of impartiality is through the practice of reflexivity, where researchers understand that they are "the means, the instrument used, to produce the research study" (Schwartz-Shea, 2014: 135). The notion of reflexivity as part of a best-practices tool kit gained further visibility in the Final Report I.2 of the Qualitative Transparency Deliberations, where its authors put forth "'reflexive openness' that incorporates sustained reflection on ethical research practices" as integral to transparent research (MacLean et al., 2018: 1). The report encourages such reflexivity by scholars in relation to research participants as well, including written descriptions of ethical practices in published work, regardless of subfield or methodology (MacLean et al., 2018: 1). Such reflection goes beyond the common recipe of research puzzle explanations (Tripp, 2018: 729) and requires discussion of positionality, particularly regarding power. Reflexive openness is an alternative to DA-RT-style requirements for transparency to include, for example, full research materials such as interview transcripts, which out of context are not actually the key to understanding another scholar's logic process and can endanger respondents (MacLean et al., 2018: 7; Tripp, 2018: 730). Such an openness requires reflection not just on the positionality of the researcher but on how that positionality occurs in power relationships at play during research (Thomson, 2021).

Reflexivity allows readers to situate themselves in someone else's work to the degree needed to actually understand how the conclusions might be arrived at.[2] Yanow and Schwartz-Shea note that reflexivity has become a useful criterion for distinguishing quality interpretivist research (Yanow & Schwartz-Shea, 2014b: xxv). Using reflexivity in this way brings with it the requirement of documenting and analyzing how each step of the research process takes place, in essence allowing reflexivity to serve as an alternative criterion for objectivity (Schwartz-Shea, 2014: 133).

Some researchers have opted for tools like information feedback and member-checking to certify the accuracy of their claims. There is a potential range of depth in which such reaffirmation can occur. For example, "empirical ethics" can include the step of asking respondents to judge the research (Desposato, 2018: 740). But such processes do not necessarily change the power dynamic between researchers and stakeholders in more fundamental ways, although if used in more participatory frameworks, they could (Schwartz-Shea, 2014: 135). Also, it isn't clear what happens if researchers get it wrong, or how much research correction will be cosmetic versus substantive. Practices like member-checking might be a step toward collaborative methodology depending on how such practices are performed. However, they should not be an end point that lets scholars opt out of deeper engagement.

Even issues like field site access, a seemingly straightforward matter of appearing and getting permission to do research, carries with it "a whiff of the colonial heritage" (Yanow & Schwartz-Shea, 2014b: 148). White privilege remains firmly intact whether in field access in a Mexican Indigenous village or in political science graduate curricula. This fact pushes me to continually explore what tools exist across disciplines to address ongoing neocolonialism in scholarship, as well as how to recognize its impact.

Eduardo Duran, a psychologist who spent time in his youth as a migrant farmworker and went on to develop the idea of the "soul wound" as part of historical trauma in Indigenous communities, notes that "when the research is of a purely Western form, we have a neocolonial activity being imposed on a community that is already suffering from historical trauma brought on by colonial processes" (Duran, 2006: 114). Such neocolonialism might look like scholars claiming certain knowledge as new, in particular ideas that have long been known within Indigenous communities (Heugh & Stroud, 2019: 8). Michelle Jacob, in her work with the Yakama community in Oregon of which she is a part, talks about the necessity of "using Indigenous communities' own ideas as central to an analysis that seeks to contribute to Indigenous self-determination" (Jacob, 2013: 13). Such collaboration demonstrates respect for Indigenous knowledge and a willingness to elevate it with the tools available to scholars in privileged academic positions.

While there are many logistical constraints that inform fieldwork decisions, when working with marginalized communities, including Indigenous ones, the potential to do extractive research is all the greater with short time frames for research, which may preclude deeper relationships and understandings from informing the research. Helicopter research, named as such because the researcher lands, extracts, and then disappears without a trace, leaves scarce benefits for people deemed research subjects (Duran, 2006: 113). In my graduate school days, this approach was also called the surgical strike approach to fieldwork and was actively promoted at conferences and methods symposia.

Interestingly, although much time and energy have been spent debating DA-RT, the notion of ethical obligations to give back to researched communities still receives far less attention than how accessible someone's raw data is. In my work, access to sites of resistance to culturecide across all study sites requires a kind of trust-building not possible through helicopter research. The trust is built not just in being visible in a community for an extended period of time but in actively working with stakeholders to explore ways in which they may want to be involved in the research or make use of it at various stages. What such collaboration can actually look like is the subject of the sections that follow.

Collaborative Methodology Challenges and Strengths in Oaxaca and California

There is an inequality built into this particular comparative project right up front. Because I carried out research that is meant to be comparable across two distinct regions, I was able to be highly collaborative in the field site in California, where I began working on this project first, but less so in Oaxaca. In the Oaxaca communities I was implementing research instruments that were translated from English to Spanish and, for comparability's sake, needed to be the same, barring minor adjustments for comprehensibility across languages. The utilization of identical survey and interview questions is a limitation of comparative research in relation to collaborative methodology.

In addition, it is also important for full transparency in positionality as part of research design to say that because I am from Northern California and still deeply connected to family and community there, I prioritized returning there for meetings quite frequently. Because staying with family, borrowing a car, and having built-in grandparent childcare made trips economically viable, I was able to regularly meet with stakeholders in a way that was quite distinct from my ability to do so in Oaxaca. Though in Oaxaca I spent many more concentrated months "on the ground"—five months during a pre-tenure leave in 2018 and three months during a Fulbright Fellowship in 2020—the research instruments did not go through the same collaborative input process in Oaxaca that I was able to do in California. In large part such comparative challenges are related to basic logistics of fieldwork in addition to the access dynamics described in the chapter's opening.

My hope is that future collaborative scholars will continue to try new processes to optimize fieldwork logistics and communicate with multiple groups of stakeholders. At the same time, the unpredictability of when a key interlocutor will have a death in the family or some other incident that makes them unavailable is impossible to pre-schedule. Understanding those limitations gracefully might be just as important to collaborating successfully through relationship-building as getting the perfect meeting.

In California, building trust with the Yurok Tribe's Education Department to be able to conduct the study at all required finding ways for the research to serve their needs as well as mine. In this way, the parameters of community stakeholders helped determine what the collaboration would look like. In Oaxaca, no such restriction was placed on my work. This contrast was deterministic in the sense that California became the research puzzle–shaping site and Oaxaca the comparative site. This is not because I did less work in Mexico but because I was allowed to bring my outside-created research project and implement it in Oaxaca, whereas in California there was the iterative necessity of showing up in person to talk through research ideas before I could move to implementation. Thus, in California the project was more fully collaborative and ultimately may be more practically useful to stakeholders in the longer term.

The project in Oaxaca was collaborative in a smaller sense. Because of the comparative framework requirements, some elements of the research design were already fixed by the time the study began there. I was able to repeatedly meet with teachers and administrators for input regarding issues they wanted more information on, and I built that feedback into the data-gathering process in the form of extra questions that I added in interviews and focus groups. In fact, input from teachers and administrators yielded an entirely new angle of inquiry on the impact of Covid-19 and migration experiences on youth identity and school success, which I published elsewhere (Gellman, 2020a). Though it might seem mundane, the logistics of fieldwork frequently inform the research process more than many social scientists may want to admit. I write now what I wish I had been able to read as a graduate student and junior scholar.

Multilayered Collaboration

What did collaboration actually look like at each stage of the project? In terms of study design, before I arrived at the final research question for the project, I met several times with members of the Yurok Tribe's Education Department to discuss some of the issues they faced and were interested in gaining more insight and data on. This included school attendance and participation in relation to school success, racism and discrimination against Native students, and the impact of Yurok classes in the public high schools, which the Yurok Tribe partially funds.

It was relatively straightforward to expand both my initial qualitative interview questions and survey questions to include these issues. Our interests were thematically connected but on slightly varied tangents. Both led to questions about curricula, identity, and the long-term healthy development of young people as active participants in their worlds.

It was advantageous that administrators in both school districts in California echoed interest in the questions the Yurok Tribe's Education Department raised. This overlap in interest meant that with minor adjustments, I was able to capture multiple themes that could serve different stakeholders. This was perhaps luck in my case, or possibly the result of a plausible study design conceptualized while thinking about applicability and relevancy for stakeholders. Regardless, I recognize that engaging collaborative methodology in other projects might not be so viable and even lead researchers along tangents that clash with or push back against their original designs. I encourage colleagues to find the usefulness in such scenarios rather than give up on collaboration as a problem. Collaborative methodology is an orientation that can help evaluate the strengths and weaknesses of stakeholder-relevant research.

After finalizing the core research questions with iterative consultation, I began developing the instruments for qualitative interviews, focus groups, and surveys. In doing so I met with a variety of staff from the Yurok Tribe and school administrators at multiple districts. While the school administrators concentrated their feedback on the permission forms necessary for student participation (with instructions such as "cut down the text" and "make it less jargon-filled!"), teachers helped modify the language of the survey questions to make them more comprehensible to young people.

In summer 2017 at a Yurok language workshop with several language-keepers from the Yurok Tribe, I read through the survey questions and made copious notes on the text in response to confusion about what I was trying to capture based on question wording. Collaborative methodology in this scenario was compatible with member-checking the research instrument or, specifically, pre-testing a survey. Being a researcher and college professor didn't prepare me to formulate questions that address the lived experiences of Indigenous high school students, and my interlocutors took it upon themselves to improve the language, for which I am grateful.

However, the language-keepers did more than just provide feedback on the wording and concepts of the survey questions. They also urged me to include questions that captured some of their own interests, which I agreed to, and talked about how they might want to use the data after the survey was complete. Without their input, my questions would not have been calibrated appropriately to capture the information I was seeking from the particular respondent group. And without larger engagement with the project by language-keepers, it wouldn't have meant as much to carry the research out. By contrast, it was clear in Oaxaca, from the confusion exhibited over a few of the survey questions, that engaging in translation rather than member-checking and deeper collaboration diminished the relatability of the survey. This is a clear weakness in the fusion of comparative and collaborative design and one that can be improved through iteration.

Another form of collaboration that occurred was through sharing preliminary results and analyses of the data collection and soliciting feedback on the analyses. In practice this looked like, within a few months of completing the majority of the data collection at each school, my compilation of school-specific preliminary analysis reports. Reports included a data snapshot showing the number of each type of data collected, meaning quite a few interviews with teachers, students, administrators, survey respondents, and focus groups, as well as summarized data on obstacles to student success, sources of student support, school climate, community climate, impact of migration, and specific issues for Indigenous students. Each analysis also included brief recommendations to address the challenges documented.

The preliminary analyses were emailed to school directors or principals, teachers whose classes had participated in the study, and upper-level administrators at district or system-wide offices. Preliminary analyses were complete for BIC 29, CEDARTMC, and EHS in spring and summer 2018, and for HVHS in winter 2018–2019, with the documents for Oaxaca schools written in Spanish and the California schools in English. I also did numerous research presentations specifically for stakeholder communities in each school area; my general rule is always say yes to invitations to present to stakeholders, regardless of scheduling inconveniences. Zoom ubiquity in the Covid-19 pandemic made such presentations easier in California than in Oaxaca, where my hasty departure owing to Fulbright shutting down in spring 2020 interrupted numerous scheduled presentations.

Navigating Stakeholder Timelines and Communication Patterns

Collaborative methodology requires slowing the research timeline to accommodate stakeholder communication patterns and time frames. In both California and Oaxaca, administrator stakeholders from Indigenous communities did not always respond to my requests for their input, or sometimes deferred to me to make a decision about a project choice. For example, some schools reached out for more information after receiving the preliminary reports while others did not. The intent behind sharing the preliminary analysis was to explore the potential for the research to be formulated into policy interventions. The success of this approach could have easily been missed if I had been rushing to complete a project in a dissertation-length time frame or making a mad dash for tenure. With the luxury of a longer time horizon, I was able to let the preliminary analyses percolate in the hands of stakeholders for a year or more, with periodic check-ins as we found ways to follow up on any recommendations.

Despite long silences, I continued to send my questions and to provide analyses at each step of the project, thinking that even if people didn't have time to respond or have input to offer at a given moment, it was my responsibility to continually invite stakeholders in and provide information, but not to significantly slow the project in the absence of a response. I did spend more time waiting and hoping for returned messages and calls than I would have if I wasn't in a collaborative mode, and future researchers should factor that waiting time into research timelines. It is worth noting that nearly all stakeholders much preferred face-to-face meetings rather than phone or email check-ins, and the cultural importance of trust-building in person should not be underestimated. For projects like mine that are multisited and far from where I live and teach, this adds an extra layer of complexity to research logistics.

Positionality in Qualitative Fieldwork

I am a fortyish, White, English-as-first-language speaker, and professor, a cisgender woman married to a man, and mother to two young children I bring with me on research trips. I recognize that as a non-Indigenous scholar working on Indigenous studies, I perpetually run the risk of further colonizing, of advancing culturecide in my very work and way of being. Reflexive openness about positionality is critical to avoid such pitfalls, and I embrace the challenge of my colleagues to deeply reflect on who I am and how my identity influences my research (MacLean et al., 2018).

Reflexive openness is especially useful in thinking about how respondents perceived me and how that might influence how we engaged. Because I was introduced to student participants by their teachers, which included a discussion of my credentials in front of classes, participants in Oaxaca showed significant deference to me in ways that aligned with cultural norms. In each research site, my warm relations with teachers and administrators were evident to students and thus lumped me into the same category as teachers as far as students were concerned. This meant that I was perceived as an official authority that should be treated with respect. This generally worked to my advantage in garnering participation, but it was also clear that students were careful about what they said to me, and it took more digging to get below the surface of their answers.

I tried to soften this dynamic with small talk and by encouraging participants to simply have a conversation, but it was mostly eyes on me, with stakeholders trying to answer what I asked for and no more. For example, in Oaxaca, any time I made a gesture to speak, participants in focus groups and interviews would fall silent and wait to listen to what I had to say, which meant I had to be more aware of my facial expressions and body language than in other contexts. In California my status also granted me deference, but more modestly than in Oaxaca, and with more casual socializing between myself and the students—this was also in line with local cultural norms.

While in some participant-observation situations my positionality felt glaring, it was also clear that in other moments students did not appear to care much about my skin color, age, or other demographic features. I was simply another adult observing them in the classroom that they could joke about, or in the case of ordering breakfast from the food stalls during the BIC recess in Oaxaca, another person to cut in front of in line. While my positionality was central to accessing each school and to the way students generally related to me in interviews and focus groups, during numerous participant-observation hours I noticed that I was able to blend into the scenery of the school in such a way that student behavior did not seem different toward me than that toward other adults in the same space. Ultimately, more attention must be paid to the reality of positionality in social science work, with fewer pretenses about the ability to be objective simply by testing ideas in the field.

Who is testing and with what ideas are part and parcel of the research design (Cramer, 2015; Tuhiwai Smith, 2012).

An Honest Evaluation of the Mixed-Methods Tool Kit

In this section I take the reader under the hood of the project, so to speak, to share the successes and challenges of each method I employed, in the spirit of increasing research transparency. Research presented in this book is rooted in collaborative methodology and uses a mixed-methods comparative politics research design. I engage positivist tenets of theory-testing and causal analysis, as well as a mode of political ethnography that elicits meaning from people themselves as to how they form and operationalize the concepts that shape their everyday sociopolitical realities. In this way the project is both empirical and interpretive, which are strange methodological bedfellows indeed.

Political science methods and methodology remain contentious and fractured over multiple camps, with contestation between "truth-seekers" and "sense-makers" (Blatter, 2017). This project walks the line, incorporating elements of causal analysis with interpretivist approaches in a research design that allows me to both isolate variables and identify mechanisms, while also qualitatively documenting people's experiences and generating analysis of how people describe their own perceived realities. This mixed approach allows for multiple orientations to coexist, even if there is perpetual disciplinary tension in breaking down silos.

This tension is worthwhile for two reasons. First, the Yurok Tribe, like many under-resourced groups, need hard data to demonstrate program benefits to funders. They asked for research that tested and proved something. A solely interpretive project on the same topic might have satisfied colleagues in my field, but some members of the Tribe rightfully wanted a different kind of data, given that Native people are too often pigeonholed with soft stereotypes that rely on impressions rather than facts. My willingness to include a survey and frame the project around causal mechanisms resonated with the objectives of the Yurok Tribe's Education Department.

Second, themes of identity formation and participation as central phenomena of interest work well with interpretive methods. Internal reflections on the self, shared through individual and group conversations, coupled with observations of biopolitics gauged through ethnographic work, are suited to the project themes. Taken together, these two points drive my empirical-interpretive continuum, as well as the mixed-methods approach. My unconventional fusing of two ends of the political science research spectrum allows for layers of information to be handled in different modes (Blatter, 2017) across time, space, and method. In short, it makes for rich data that stands up to both theory-testing and agentive, people-centered research paradigms.

Comparative Method

The comparative method is rooted in the proposition that by comparing and contrasting information drawn from the same unit of analysis, we can gain unique insights into cases that we wouldn't be able to by drawing upon only one case study (Collier, 1993: 105; Mahoney, 2001: xi; Skocpol, 1979: 41). This method trades depth for breadth. For example, if I had taken all the time I spent in each of the four schools and communities I researched and channeled that time and energy into just one case, I would know the one case more deeply. However, the comparative gaze allows a nuanced ordering of information from any one case in relation to similar or different information in other cases.

This ability to compare increases the likelihood of situating a given case within a larger universe of information that may reveal applicability to other cases. In this way, the comparative method may facilitate an ability to generalize from small-n results that is missing from single case studies. Drawing on comparative analysis of ethnography, interviews, focus groups, and surveys in the four high schools, I highlight case similarities and differences in the coming chapters.

Data Snapshot

Using mixed methods and multiple methodological orientations, I address how youth identity is formed in curricular spaces of public high schools and how this identity translates into civic, cultural, and political participation. In doing so, I document how affirmation of minority identity, particularly for Indigenous youth, serves as a tool of resistance to culturecide and highlight the importance of culturally relevant curricula to promote multiethnic coexistence. Building on eight months in Oaxaca over two trips and six two-to-four-week trips to Northern California for this project, the majority of this book's data is from 2017 to 2020. My intensive fieldwork in the school sites is complemented by two decades of involvement in documenting Oaxacan politics as a student and scholar, as well as a lifetime of growing up in the far Northern California region.

I engaged both qualitatively and quantitatively with students from the target Indigenous language classes and control classes who returned their completed permission forms, regardless of ethnicity, race, or any other demographic factor. Some participants are heritage-speakers with varying levels of identification with specific ethnic communities; others are part of different minority groups that may be adding a given language as a third or more language. Finally, some students may primarily identify as mestizo from monolingual Spanish backgrounds or White from monolingual English backgrounds, among other possible demographics.

Political ethnographic work allows for the documentation and assessment of how concepts such as identity and participation operate within and across microcommunities as well as across regions and states. Interviews allowed for elicitation of one-on-one personal reflections with both privacy and anonymity for interviewees. The majority of interviewees were students, but teachers, administrators, and Tribal and Indigenous leaders were also included. Focus groups were only with students and meant to gauge themes based on interaction.

Surveys provided baseline quantitative data from a wider number of student respondents than purely qualitative methods could reach; they also allowed for theory-testing in a way that was separate from the interpersonal interactions of the interviews and focus groups. There are two versions of the survey: V1 for students participating in the research via their language classes (Zapotec or English in Oaxaca, Yurok or Spanish in California) and V2, a control version. V2 simply replaces language about taking the survey in a "target language class" with taking it in "your class" to account for the fact that students may have been in civics, history, or art classes in the control versions.

I administered the survey to high school students across the four high schools who were enrolled in classes ranging from Yurok, Spanish, United States History, and Civics in California to Zapotec, English, Mexican History through Art, and Local History in Oaxaca. The English language V1 version for language class students is included in full in Appendix 5.

The survey attempts to capture student self-assessments across several themes, namely interest in languages and cultures outside their primary

Table 3. Total data pool across all schools

School	Survey responses	Interviews with students	Interviews with teachers and administrators	Focus groups	Class observations
BIC 29	21	22	9	2	30
CEDARTMC	25	18	4	2	40
HVHS	23	24	10	3	40
EHS	87	56	14	2	70
Totals	156	120	37	9	180

identities, types of participation or non-participation, and sense of inclusion at the school and community levels. Each of these themes was discussed in depth in interviews and focus groups, as well as observed ethnographically during my time at the schools. The survey captures students' self-response when alone with their thoughts and a written question, rather than as part of the interactive dialogue that interviews, focus groups, or hallway conversations entail. The themes are discussed in the four case-study chapters.

Roughly half the time, surveys were completed by students who also participated in interviews or focus groups, but the other half of survey-takers were those who did not have parent or guardian permission to participate in any other aspect of the study beyond the survey or did not give permission themselves if eighteen or older. Every student who participated in an interview or focus group also completed the survey. Therefore, the survey demographics present a fairly broad lens of whom I spoke to at each school. However, teachers, administrators, and community members whom I interviewed did not take the survey, so the survey captures the high school–aged youth demographics rather than the entire study population. Table 3 presents the data totals, minus the intangible hours spent in informal ethnographic interactions with students, teachers, administrators, and community members in each location.

Informed Consent Challenges

The permissions process for this study was rigorous and difficult in multiple ways. All students under the age of eighteen had to obtain parent or guardian signatures on a consent form that included options to participate in each of the study activities. For interviews, students, as well as invited faculty and administrators, could choose to participate using their name or anonymously and with or without audio recording. Focus groups were always anonymous and audio recorded. Permission forms were approved by Emerson College's Institutional Review Board (IRB) and the Yurok Tribe's Education Department. The number of detailed options on the permission form, which required active consent by opting into an activity through checking corresponding boxes, and the IRB-required legalese language in the informational letter were disadvantages in terms of participation rates but required by IRB. (See Appendices 1 and 2, respectively, for English versions of the informational letter and permission form.)

While readily recognizable and digestible by the handful of formally educated administrators and academics whom I interviewed at each research site, the format and language of the IRB forms were not accessible for young people and their parents who came from communities of high economic marginalization and generally low levels of formal education. This issue, which was compounded by justifiable suspicion of White outsiders in Indigenous communities in both Oaxaca and California, and among immigrant parents and their children in California, resulted in overall low youth response rates. While response rates were sometimes over 50 percent in Eureka High School, at Hoopa Valley High School on the Hoopa Valley Indian Reservation response rates were as low as 10 percent in some classes. In Oaxaca, both schools had similar response rates of roughly 50 percent, with many reminders and a significant time lag in delivery of completed permission forms.

To illustrate the challenges with permissions forms, in an average class of twenty-five students, roughly five would turn in their forms on time, and another ten would then follow suit after my repeated reminders, which required me to show up at the schools day after day. Given the driving distances in California and the public transport time it took to get to and from schools in Oaxaca, these repeat reminder visits ate up many days that I might have otherwise spent working on the project in other ways (writing, reading) but were nevertheless a vital part of the study, and also got me into the classroom as a simple observer more than I had planned. The remaining ten forms would never materialize, despite the option on the form to indicate that the student would not participate in any aspect of the study.

Of the fifteen students who turned in their forms, generally three to seven would decline participation of some type, including a few in each school who declined any aspect of participation. This suggests that despite barriers to readability based on IRB requirements, families did understand the forms enough to make decisions about participating in particular ways. In addition, my description of each type of participation to the student classes may have influenced how students themselves filled out the forms or instructed their parents to do so, as I let them know that interviews and focus groups would mean a conversation with me, while surveys only required time on a tablet, phone, or paper form, without researcher contact. Surveys were the most frequently accepted form of participation, with focus groups the least likely form of accepted participation.

In California I distributed permissions documents in both English and Spanish, and in Mexico only in Spanish. An administrator for Eureka City Schools suggested I also translate the documents into Hmong, as Eureka has a significant Hmong immigrant population, but this translation proved cost-prohibitive at the time. It is worth noting that students who identified as Asian or Asian American actually had the highest response rates overall in Eureka, so while the ethical issue of full informational access for parents and guardians remains, the lack of Hmong translation did not appear to be a barrier to the data collection itself. It does, however, put a burden on students to translate for their parents or guardians. This burden is something numerous Latinx and Asian American students at Eureka High School mentioned is a regular part of their lives, as many school and community documents are provided only in English.

In Oaxaca, particularly at the school located in a rural Indigenous community, in retrospect, translating the permission forms into Zapotec would have been beneficial, even though it was generally not necessary for familial comprehension. Given community language shift, today only a small percentage of Teotitlán del Valle residents are monolingual Zapotec-speakers, and they are all elderly. Also, while spoken Zapotec is still the dominant community language, most reading and writing is in Spanish since formal education in practice takes place only in Spanish. Nevertheless, for future research I recommend translating the forms into the Indigenous language of interest. Not only would it validate the language's role in official use and provide work to a translator, but such translation could increase response rates for permission forms if families are more willing to have their children participate in activities that show that level of respect for their heritage language.

Political Ethnography

Much of the ethnographic work I carried out was on the school campuses and centered on classroom observations as well as observations between classes and interactions before and after school. I took copious field notes by hand in all locations, as opening a laptop or other digital device would have been incongruous in all the schools, where students only occasionally used Chromebooks or their phones for classroom activities. I chatted with teachers before and after class, but during class I tried to sit in the back and out of the way. The first time I observed a given class, the teacher would introduce me, and then I would present myself and the research project, but I mostly tried to stay quiet. I would often have lunch with teachers in their classroom or the faculty lounges but sometimes would sit near groups of students and casually observe as we all ate.

Among my observations, I particularly focused on making notes about identity-related indicators (language and speech patterns, clothing and accessory choices, eye contact and physical interactions), school climate (language and behavior that was exclusive or inclusive, representation through school or classroom decorations, posters, and textbooks), and civic, cultural, and political participation (conversations about what people did over the weekend, before or after school, and over holidays, announcements about activities at school or in the community). I also observed and documented these elements in each community surrounding the school, frequently by walking or sitting in public spaces and documenting what I saw or speaking to people with whom I shared those spaces. I mostly achieved the disciplined practice of typing up my field notes each night after returning to where I was staying, but sometimes, due to other time constraints such as parenting my own children, I fell behind and had to take extra time to get back in the mindset of a given day to fully type up my own handwritten notes.

Interviews

Semi-structured qualitative interviews make up a large contribution to the project data, with 186 interviews, all conducted by me, across all schools and surrounding communities in Oaxaca and California. In all four schools I was faced with the issue of lack of physical privacy for interviewing because all are strapped for space, or, in the case of the BIC, lack interior spaces that are soundproof. I did not have an office with a door that closed at the field sites except when generous colleagues allowed me to use theirs, and this posed a real problem in terms of guaranteeing confidentiality of conversations.

I interviewed students in supply closets, spare classrooms, teacher's lounges, borrowed offices, the cafeteria, and an open-air shed. I was constantly searching for private space and frequently had to move to another location (sometimes in mid-conversation with an interviewee) if someone else needed the space I was in. This situation made some interviewees anxious, many of whom were already nervous to begin with. But for other students, it provided a comedic break that humanized me and made students relax as they saw their interviewer dropping papers and scrambling to clutch folders and the audio recorder as we traversed construction sites, ditches, and study groups in hallways in search of another quiet corner.

When interviewees, predominantly students, were shy, nervous, or close-lipped, I used rhetorical strategies to gently draw them into participating in ways that allowed them to have control over the conversational direction and content. Yet other students would pour out their issues without filter. The profiles of the quiet and the talkers were very heterogeneous and not linked to gender or racial and ethnic categories. It was interesting to note that at times students veered toward over-confessionalism. I understood this tendency in light of the lack of mental health services and high student-to-administrator ratios in many of the schools.

For many students, the interview was one of the first times they'd had to sit down alone with an out-of-network adult who asked them about their lives. Thus, interviews were often characterized by initial reluctance or uncertainty about what to say followed by an outpouring of words unleashed by students with much to say and few adult confidants with whom they could share. As one forthright student from the rural Oaxacan BIC put it, "In my town, if you walk down the street with a boy, the next day the whole town knows" (Mata Moreles, 2018). In this context, my guarantee of confidentiality gave students a chance to share about their lives in ways that they ordinarily could not.

Occasionally, the written promise of confidentiality led to very intense sharing episodes; one student whose family had recently fled a civil war in another Indigenous Oaxacan town had not told anyone but the school director about her situation. In other encounters, students either relished the chance to hear their own voices or tried to make the awkwardness end quickly by dutifully answering my questions as fast as possible. In all scenarios, students provided details about their own identities, types of participation, and understandings of the political world that would not have been obtainable any other way. The guarantee of confidentiality for those who chose to speak anonymously—however compromised in terms of privacy—created a space to access perspectives that are seldom solicited, let alone systematically gathered, among Indigenous youth.

Most students agreed to be audio recorded for interviews; the highest number of students who declined to be recorded attended the BIC in Teotitlán del Valle. In either case, my process for both interviews and focus groups, as well as ethnographic observations, was to type up my handwritten notes and then send audio files to a research assistant for full transcription. I analyzed the interviews based on my original interview notes as well as the transcriptions, to which I added my ethnographic notes in relation to each interviewee.

Focus Groups

Focus groups were conducted to observe student conversations on challenging topics like discrimination at school and obstacles to education. Focus group expert Jennifer Cyr identifies three units of analysis that can yield information in focus groups: the individual level, the group level, and the interaction level (Cyr, 2016: 232). Given that focus groups in Oaxaca and California were completed in addition to, rather than instead of, a large number of semi-structured interviews, the individual unit of analysis was not invoked in the "marketing approach" in order to gather perspectives from numerous people quickly (Cyr, 2016: 234). Rather, individual perspectives were recorded as a way of triangulating information collected in interviews and participant observation. The group level of analysis, referring primarily to the degree of consensus reached by participants about a given topic (Cyr, 2016: 235), was similarly used to triangulate information from interviews.

The main impetus for my using focus groups as a research method was to document the interactional level of analysis by including the social aspect of identity formation in the study through collective conversations (Cyr, 2016: 248). The interactive elements of the focus groups were captured, for example, in how conversation processes between youths contributed to their concept formation processes, for example, regarding what I meant by "political participation." Students would often say things like "but I'm not old enough to vote" or "voting doesn't matter," and I, as the facilitator, would say, "but what does it mean to participate more broadly?" Focus group participants would then discuss different ways that they participate, redefining what participation means for them and ascribing political intentions to things that were not previously understood through a political lens, such as supporting parents who participated in community assemblies or making art that invoked themes of corruption (Focus Group 3.1 BIC, 2018).

The interactive element of focus groups also helped me as the facilitator form iterative questions that translated more clearly across languages and cultural contexts. This was particularly important in Oaxaca where the research instruments had not gone through the same collaborative process, nor member-checking, as they had in California. It became clear that the concept of *political participation* was more readily understood in California, whereas in Oaxaca the term *community participation* tended to better capture the same range of behaviors. In an ideal research setting, I would have run preliminary focus groups first in each location to allow this insight to inform eventual interview questions. However, the reality of research logistics meant that this was not always possible. In the BIC, focus groups took place later than most interviews, as it was harder to get teacher permission to exempt multiple students from class than to excuse just one at the high school level.

The interactive unit of analysis in focus groups revealed spaces of tension or convergence across gender, place of origin, or ethnic identity factors. The majority of the thirteen focus groups included three participants, with one made up of four participants and one with two participants, and two that had five to seven participants, based on who showed up at the allotted time or who had turned in their permission form on time. While I strove for mixed-gendered groups, I did not have access to demographic information that would have allowed me to intentionally craft diverse groups. However, each group ended up having significant and varied ethnic and place of origin diversity, as well as academic field of interest variation.

One drawback of conducting focus groups at high schools is that the participants know each other. The potential breach of confidentiality by a participant in a way that could be embarrassing to another was much higher than it would have been using a larger disassociated population to sample from. I discussed this very frankly in each of the classes where I distributed permissions forms, and subsequently I saw a much lower rate of permission granted for focus groups as opposed to permission granted for surveys or interviews. While my highlighting the warning about loss of privacy in focus groups may have inadvertently intervened in determining the sample population, it also felt ethically important, as most of the students, ranging in age from four-teen to eighteen, had little context for what it actually meant to participate in a focus group.

Issues of positionality and power dynamics between participants them-selves, not just between myself as facilitator and the participants, also pre-sented challenges and produced insights. Although it is perpetually a struggle to get nervous teenagers to open up with a stranger about sensitive issues, this is even more the case when their peers are present. In each of the four schools across both Mexico and the United States, there were some students in both focus groups and interviews who were at ease with themselves, be-mused at being asked their opinions, and willing to fearlessly explore their own ideas with me. However, the majority of focus group participants were nervous and close-lipped, ceding the floor to others to speak, looking down to indicate passivity, and answering questions concisely and without offer-ing much dialogue. This was mostly the case at the BIC, and somewhat less evident at CEDARTMC, HVHS, and EHS.

In general, at the high school level female students ceded the floor to male students. Students who, in the course of the focus group, gave indicators that they came from more economically well-off backgrounds—assessed by asking what neighborhood or town they lived in, and sometimes their par-ents' occupations—would regularly speak more, and students from lower economic status groups would defer to them. This economic hierarchy was true across all research sites. In addition, Indigenous students were gener-ally the quietest except when discussing Indigenous-related topics such as family language history, at which point non-Indigenous students would lis-ten respectfully and not interrupt. In short, power hierarchies between stu-dents were operating constantly and determined the amount and sequence of speaking, and therefore whose voice was heard on which topic.

Surveys

While I am primarily a qualitative researcher, in consultation with the Yurok Tribe's Education Department we decided that a survey would be helpful to establish baseline quantitative data from a wider number of student respon-dents. I included the survey as part of the permissions form for schools in both Oaxaca and California, and in both places at least a quarter of invited students chose to participate only in the survey, which was perhaps viewed by

students and guardians as less intrusive because it was automatically anonymous and was completed during class time. This meant that students were not
pulled from class to participate, as was the case for interviews and focus groups.

Except for the initial demographic questions, all other survey questions
asked students to select from a five-point scale, from strongly disagree to
strongly agree, and most left space for write-in answers. The survey allowed
for evaluation of the hypotheses through questions such as "I know how to
change my language and behavior when spending time with people from different backgrounds." I proctored all surveys myself. Regardless of survey
interface, students took between ten and fifteen minutes to complete the survey, with a few extra minutes to troubleshoot accessing the Google form for
online survey-takers.

Technical obstacles were also an issue in survey implementation in two
of the four schools. Only at EHS and CEDARTMC was there reliable internet where all students were able to take the survey online. At the BIC, in the
absence of a dependable internet connection, I initially had students take
the survey on my phone to avoid the step of inputting data from paper, but
this created a backlog of students waiting to take the survey, so I switched to
a paper survey. In Oaxaca, roughly half of the surveys were taken on paper
and then manually entered into Google Forms by a research assistant at Emerson College, whereas in California, all surveys were taken online. This
variation was based entirely on internet availability at each school.

A significant amount of time was wasted in pursuit of taking the survey
online instead of simply using paper surveys in all locations. Students were
visibly more stressed in the online testing environment because they had to
enter a URL exactly, and they frequently made mistakes that required my intervention. In contrast, the paper surveys were handed out, completed, and
turned in in roughly fifteen minutes, during which time students displayed
more curiosity about the research and also appeared more relaxed in the process. Surely these contrasting environments influenced the attention paid to
the actual questions on the surveys, although this is not systematically studied
in the project itself and data analysis does not show any significant divergence
in results based on the survey interface.

Finally, the "anti-robot" question I included on the survey, meant to ensure students responding to the surveys were real live humans who were paying attention, was a surprising failure across all research sites. The question
asked, "The sun rises from which direction?" and then listed "East, West,
South, North, Other" as the available options. I naively assumed that kids,

regardless of background and whether they lived in an urban or rural environment, had been exposed to this basic knowledge and would merely find the question an oddity, answer it, and move on.

In fact, the anti-robot question generated giggling and whispering for help in every research site, where students would prod their neighbors and occasionally ask me directly for help. The lack of knowledge about this question in the rural Mexican school, where many students help their families in outdoor kitchens or work side by side with fathers and uncles in the fields on the weekends, was particularly interesting. Was this a case of culturally based knowledge not translating into survey question format, or are Generation Z[3] youth just tuned out to ecology? I didn't pursue this further but note it here as a reflection on the surprises research can deliver. Numerous students in each school answered this question incorrectly. However, the question served its purpose in ensuring students were not filling in bubbles by rote and provided a way for them to break the tension of survey-taking as they nudged each other in amusement.

Survey Data Demographics

To maximize the utility of the survey to understand the themes of interest in relation to student demographics, my research assistants and I cross-tabulated the questions across a range of demographic fields including gender and race/ethnicity. Table 4 shows that more female students than male students participated in the survey at each school. EHS also stands out as having a much larger survey population compared to the other three schools, but this is simply in proportion to its student body, as I was able to distribute the permission forms to many more students there. While the survey text includes both a transgender and write-in option, no students at the four high schools selected those options.

Table 5 shows the racial and ethnic demographics of each school broken down by year in school. While BIC 29 and CEDARTMC are both three-year programs and EHS and HVHS are both four-year programs, the only school years shown are those that include respondents, meaning that, for example, no third-year students at BIC 29 nor second-year students at HVHS returned their signed permission forms and therefore were not included in the data pool.

As Table 5 shows, a significant portion of the students who participated in the survey self-identify as Indigenous, in both Oaxaca (25 students out of 46)

Table 4. Survey demographics by gender across all schools

School	Total survey responses	Female	Male	Total student body during fieldwork in 2018
BIC 29	21	12	9	180
CEDARTMC	25	14	11	350
HVHS	23	17	6	267
EHS	87	48	39	1,170
Total	156	91	65	1,967

and California (35 students out of 109). All other racial and ethnic categories show significant divergence across the schools, with Latinx/Hispanic and White the two next most populous categories, and EHS's diversity distinct from the other three schools in the number of students who identify as Asian/Asian American, Black/African American, or multiracial.

Given the research focus on the way that three distinct categories of students experience the impact of language access (Indigenous, ethnic majority of community, and minorities from other backgrounds) at the broadest level, the data snapshot in Table 5 shows that respondents reflect these three groups. The data pool at each school is sufficiently representative across demographic background and year in school, as well as constituting 5 to 10 percent of the population at each school, to be considered sufficiently representative to generalize to other students.

However, the above data does not capture local levels of diversity such as the number of Indigenous students from non-Zapotec backgrounds at BIC 29, which is much better captured in the interviews and focus groups. The significance of different levels of analysis in a project like this clearly points to the importance of a mixed-methods design. While the survey data addresses a wider number of respondents than available from qualitative methods, vital details would be lost without the qualitative component.

Critiquing the Survey

The survey results do a reasonable job of assisting in the assessment of key aspects of the study hypotheses about the impact of Indigenous language access in high school curricula across a range of students. However, the survey

Table 5. Survey demographics by race and ethnicity across all schools at each year

		Native American/ Indigenous	White	Latinx/ Hispanic	Asian	Mixed race	Black/ African American
BIC 29	First year of high school	4					
	Second year of high school	16		1			
	BIC 29 Total	**20**		**1**			
CEDARTMC	First year of high school	2		7			
	Second year of high school	1		4			
	Third year of high school	2		9			
	CEDARTMC Total	**5**		**20**			
HVHS	First year of high school	5					
	Third year of high school	3	1				
	Fourth year of high school	11		2		1	
	HVHS Total	**19**	**1**	**2**		**1**	
EHS	First year of high school	1	3				
	Second year of high school	5	10	2	6	3	
	Third year of high school	6	13	2	2		1
	Fourth year of high school	4	15	5	5	1	2
	EHS Total	**16**	**41**	**9**	**13**	**4**	**3**
Total		**60**	**42**	**32**	**13**	**5**	**3**

does not include questions about obstacles to student educational success, something of concern to stakeholders in each study community. This is because the specific details of obstacles emerged in interviews with students, teachers, and administrators after the survey had been finalized, but I did not have enough context for the obstacles at the survey design stage. In this way, one drawback of the comparative mixed-methods design is the inability to revise a fixed instrument over time. Interview questions can evolve based on previous comments made, but surveys are static in a way that qualitative methods are not. One potential solution to this situation for future researchers could be to wait to finalize survey questions until deeper preliminary research has taken place or to delimit a narrower scope for the survey that can be fleshed out prior to fieldwork.

Conclusion: Decolonizing Research with Indigenous Peoples

Regardless of the specific methods tool kit used, collaborative methodology as a philosophical and practical orientation to research design and process is a vital ethical imperative for researchers who work with historically and contemporarily marginalized peoples. What methodological decolonization actually looks like may be as varied as the projects undertaken, but the guiding principles hinge on building meaningful relationships of trust that frame researchers interacting with people not as "subjects" but as collaborators in projects of mutual interest. Collaborating with Indigenous community leaders is a way to help integrate knowledge outcomes into the communities themselves rather than extract the knowledge solely for the privilege of the academy.

Instead of conducting a study *on* Indigenous people involved in cultural survival, this book attempts to model best practices for collaborative methodology by presenting work done *with* stakeholders in each community. The Yurok Tribe's Education Department leaders and language-keepers were valuable partners every step of the way in developing the research design, including which methods to employ and which questions to ask. Zapotec community partners were also engaged in shaping the process of the research. In the face of disciplinary methodological tensions, it is clear that collaboration is not just a fruitful approach for quality research but an ethical necessity when working with communities that have been marginalized and continue to be exploited in the present day.

Collaborative research may be slower and less independent than some researchers are able to handle for a variety of reasons. There can be failures along the way—no researcher wants to deal with unreturned phone calls or emails when deadlines loom or publication pressures swell. My honesty regarding the real challenges of carrying out comparative mixed-methods fieldwork collaboratively serves as a form of research transparency. In unveiling the parts of the project that were hard rather than hiding them behind cleaned data, I hope to inspire other researchers to do the same. When more of us begin to articulate reflections on methodology and methods in less conventional and radically honest ways, we can grant greater perspective on the reality of the conditions in which data is collected and sometimes co-created.

The importance of decolonizing research with Indigenous peoples makes the range of methodological challenges worth it. The methodological premise to make political science less extractive and more willing to serve the interests of stakeholders also aligns with an increased call for policy relevancy in the discipline (V. Herrera & Post, 2019). Drawing on the insights of decolonizing scholarly practices through methodological commitment to collaboration can help us strengthen the ethics of political science. It also has the potential to produce research that is more meaningful to the communities with which we work.

Reflexivity about positionality is key. In particular, White outsider scholars have a responsibility to find ways to work together with communities that are open to such collaboration. This means not just arriving at a preselected research site and getting to work but asking to be invited in and being prepared to have your request denied. Engaged scholarship shows that culturecide is not just a problem for those whose culture is being repressed but a problem for everyone, including those of us who may unintentionally perpetrate it through our mode of research.

CHAPTER 3

Language Regimes, Education, and Culturecide in Mexico and the United States

Introduction: "Hay que parar tapar la boca" (We have to stop silencing ourselves)

Both Zapotec-speaking communities in Oaxaca and Yurok-speaking communities in California have been subjected to culturecide, the intentional killing of a specific group's culture, in part through language regimes of federal and state institutions. This chapter addresses the connections between culturecide, Indigenous languages, and education. I begin with a vignette showing the way Zapotec adults talk about language loss in southern Mexico.

Two parents from different families who volunteer to help maintain the BIC 29 school in Teotitlán del Valle, Oaxaca, where their children attend high school, sat across from me in folding chairs in the Parents' Committee office at the school. We talked about Mexico's language regime, meaning how Spanish has been enforced over Zapotec, the Indigenous language traditionally spoken in the town. I asked them about how language transmission has happened or been interrupted in their families, and they offered their own perspectives.

Mr. Mendoza, in a loose button-down shirt and sneakers, glanced back and forth between me and the computer screen as we talked, checking the closed-circuit cameras used to make sure students don't sneak off campus or that anyone suspicious does not sneak in. He responded, "I speak Zapotec, and we speak it at home with my wife and kids. The kids understand and can speak some, but they don't really want to, and with their friends they speak Spanish. Their movies, TV, and games on their phones are all in Spanish, along with all their schooling" (Mendoza Jiménez, 2020).

Ms. Ortiz, in her forties, clad in sweatpants and constantly getting up to tend to the students who stopped to make photocopies or to use the office's tire pump to inflate soccer balls for physical education, responded shyly. "I don't speak Zapotec—I grew up in another village that had already lost the language by the time I was growing up. My husband is from here and speaks it, and my children understand it, from spending time with his family, but they don't speak it. We speak Spanish at home" (Ortiz Mendoza, 2020). Both Mr. Mendoza and Ms. Ortiz speak of the cultural forces at work both historically and contemporarily that have led to their children mostly not speaking Zapotec. Even though Mr. Mendoza's children understand much of what is said in Zapotec in the home, they respond mostly in Spanish, and their media, social interactions, and educational landscapes are dominated by Spanish. This is true for Ms. Ortiz as well, although in her case Spanish dominance had already taken root in her community by the time she was growing up.

The informal aspects of language regimes, represented by media and social pressures to assimilate, are directly informed by the formal aspects, most directly seen in Mexico through the public education system. Until the 2010s, Zapotec was still not allowed to be spoken in primary and secondary schools in Teotitlán del Valle, a community that identifies almost ubiquitously as Zapotec. Language discrimination has changed significantly in both Mexico and the United States, from immediate and severe physical punishment for speaking Indigenous languages in the nineteenth and much of the twentieth century, to ignoring the existence of Indigenous languages while promoting the state language in the later twentieth century, and finally to a new renaissance of Indigenous language appreciation since the 2010s. Mexico and the United States must grapple with how language regimes of Spanish and English, respectively, have operated as culturecide mechanisms in each country. In both Oaxaca and California, Indigenous parents and heritage-speaking students whom I interviewed talked about reasserting Indigenous presence, with many saying iterations of "we are still here" and "we have to stop silencing ourselves" (Anonymous, 2018j; J. Gensaw, 2017; Mendoza Jiménez, 2020; Wonnacott, 2018).

Culturecide is not something new; it gives a name to the destruction of cultural aspects of particular social groups deemed dangerous or unworthy of existence by another group. In the 2007 United Nations Declaration on the Rights of Indigenous Peoples, Article 8 addresses the right of Indigenous peoples not to be forced to assimilate or have their cultures destroyed. Like many human rights provisions, it is not enforceable but relies on individual countries to embrace it (Pruim, 2014: 302–307), making it an aspirational rather than protective mechanism.

Culturecide's impact can be seen in the erosion of identity generation after generation. This leads to compounded historical trauma, which is a heavy burden for young heritage-speakers as they navigate the already perilous waters of identity formation. Though many non-Indigenous people see the destruction of Indigenous peoples as something that is part of the past, it is in fact part of the present. Culturecide continues to shape public school curricula as part of state assimilationist agendas.

Multilingualism has been the target of culturecide by numerous states during homogenization projects. By multilingualism I refer to a multiplicity of languages and manners of "communicative exchanges of information" (Heugh & Stroud, 2019: 4). In some communities, multilingualism occurs in homes or other non-institutional spaces as the result of mixed marriages or because of trade and transportation patterns. While these familial and private spaces are vital in language repertoires, my interest is in how institutions contribute to or inhibit Indigenous language access as a signifier of democratic commitment to pluralism.

One of my theoretical contributions in this book is to show how Indigenous language classes, for both students and teachers, operate as arenas of resistance to culturecide. My argument that Indigenous language learning constitutes an act of resistance against culturecide is rooted in findings from working with students, teachers, and community members who used phrases like "we are still here" to define the importance of their resistance (Anonymous, 2018o). This chapter presents historical context for how language regimes inform education policy in Mexico and the United States. In the following sections, I investigate the institutions and practices at play in restricting or expanding Indigenous language access in the formal education sector. I then look at the language regimes in Oaxaca and California to frame the institutional context that young people navigate in specific language communities. The chapter concludes with a discussion of the potential for language survival and its challenges.

To briefly note, I do not weigh in on the vocabulary that should be used to talk about language survival efforts. Many language activists I have spoken with talk about language *restoration* or *revival* rather than survival because the former terms are more positive (B. McQuillen, 2017). But the reality is that with languages like Zapotec and Yurok, people are fighting for their very survival. My use of the term *survival* is not meant to dramatize the situation but rather to be clear about what is at stake for Indigenous communities as they resist culturecide.

Comparative Language Regimes at the State Level

Schooling takes place under the regulation of education policies. By policy, I refer to both the official and unofficial texts, discourses, and practices that inform the regulatory framework for a given issue (McCarty et al., 2014: 32). As Teresa McCarty astutely notes regarding language policy, "Policy is not a disembodied thing, but rather a situated sociocultural process—the complex of practices, ideologies, attitudes, and formal and informal mechanisms that influence people's language choices in profound and pervasive everyday ways" (McCarty, 2014: xii). The many forms of language policy in a given state— including the rules regarding what language can be used in what context, the standardization of language, and who can learn what language at a given time (McCarty, 2014: 8)—form the backbone of the language regime. This regime is visible in education policy, where administrators determine which languages will be available in a given school, to whom, and for what purpose.

Language regimes do not necessarily enforce culturecide, but they often accelerate the demise of some languages in pursuit of state homogenization efforts. Linda Cardinal and Selma Sonntag (2015) brought the concept of language regimes to the forefront of the discussion on language rights in relation to institutional and ad hoc practices that capture state agendas for citizen formation. In their edited volume, numerous authors show how formal education is the foremost manifestation of language regimes in case studies from around the world (2015: 4–5). In Sonntag and Cardinal's words, a language regime is composed of "language practices as well as conceptions of language and language use as projected through state policies and as acted upon by language users" (Sonntag & Cardinal, 2015: 6). My contribution to the language regime field centers around the relationships between historic language regimes in public schools and identity formation processes that young people experience in language-learning spaces as these processes inform their larger civic, cultural, and political sense of self.

Education policies are part of language regimes. Studies show that learning in one's mother tongue can increase student success and contribute to overall well-being (Baker, 2011; Fishman, 2006; García et al., 2006; UNESCO,

1953). But whether or not schools are sufficient or even appropriate sites of language revitalization, and how to improve their impact, are ongoing issues (Hornberger, 2008, 2009). Promoters of monolingualism continue to advocate for language planning in education, most notably through the Englishization movement both in the United States and globally, which has strongly opposed linguistic diversity (Dor, 2004; Modiano, 1984; U.S. English, 2021). Similarly in Mexico, Spanish-only teaching was instrumental in the process of creating a Mexican national identity (Crystal, 2013; Jiménez Naranjo, 2017: 98; Ogulnick, 2006; Valdés et al., 2006). In both countries, notions of who citizens should be and what language they should speak were important elements of the state's agenda for citizen formation, as seen through school language policies and practices.

As federal states, both Mexico and the United States balance federal law and policies with those of individual states, meaning that there is a certain degree of local character permitted through decentralization. States such as Oaxaca and California have significant autonomy at the subnational level to run institutions like schools to meet the needs of their particular communities. While I take the subnational state, community, and school units as the central foci of analysis, the larger federal framework of each country remains relevant for potential generalizability from the case studies; it also allows for analysis of institutional design itself.

In each country, Indigenous affairs are served by massive federal bureaucracies with varying degrees of devolution to states, where Indigenous citizens are a small minority of citizens served. In Mexico, Indigenous communities have the right to be self-governing and are economically and politically integrated into state and national institutions to various degrees. The Mexican Secretary of Public Education, for example, governs bilingual and intercultural education, but that is not at all what occupies most of the agency's time.

In the United States, throughout the nineteenth century, Indigenous people lost their lands to a variety of state-level reservation schemes designed to concentrate them in small parcels of land while making the majority of land available for White settlers. The Dawes General Allotment Act of 1887 allowed the federal government to parcel out land to individuals rather than tribes, essentially a forced acculturation policy that is a manifestation of culturecide. Today, some tribes have federal recognition and reservations while others do not, with grave political and economic consequences. Indian affairs are mostly addressed by the executive branch through the Department of the Interior, the Department of Health and Human Services, and the Department of Education (Kessler-Mata, 2017: 25).

In both Mexico and the United States, official attempts to eliminate Indigenous peoples first through direct genocide and later through culturecide, especially through language repression, were significant. The intergenerational trauma from boarding schools and forced Castilianization and Englishization contributed to low self-esteem and less advocacy for cultural rights in some Indigenous communities (Jacob, 2013: 11–12). In such circumstances, Indigenous people took paths of assimilation into dominant language frameworks as the safest way to guarantee their physical survival and that of their descendants. Because of this, much Indigenous language knowledge has been lost across Zapotec and Yurok communities in varying degrees.

In both states, Indigenous peoples are demanding increased inclusion in formal governance mechanisms to facilitate their ability to be separated from them through decentralization. For example, in Mexico the Zapatista Army of National Liberation (Ejército Zapatista de Liberación National, EZLN), a predominantly Indigenous social movement demanding autonomy from the state, made a compelling example of symbolic and practical rights-claiming for international audiences. The EZLN's goals include autonomous governance (Marcos & Ponce de Leon, 2001; Mora, 2015; Nash, 2001; Rus et al., 2003), human rights (Speed & Collier, 2000), citizenship rights (Moksnes, 2012), collaboration across social divisions (Leyva Solano et al., 2015), and gender rights and justice (Eber & Kovic, 2003; Speed et al., 2006). The EZLN uprising in Chiapas pushed governments in Indigenous-populated states like Oaxaca to create institutionalized ways for Indigenous governance within state-recognized channels. Therefore, in addition to language regimes, cultural regimes blend with political regimes in traditional Indigenous governance in Oaxaca. Such governance ideally serves as a mechanism for people to demand community-level autonomy without relinquishing rights to participate in federal politics through political parties.

During colonization, Indigenous people in the United States were forced to learn English for their physical survival (Gómez de García et al., 2010: 105), and now many minorities do so for economic survival. Language regimes operate as one aspect of colonization processes that shape how people are allowed to exist in relation to the people and environments around them. Political scientist Kouslaa Kessler-Mata (Yak Tityu Tityu Northern Chumash and Yokut) has argued that "tribes will be able to exercise more self-governance rights and have expanded opportunities for self-determination" through greater participation in non-tribal political systems (2017: 91–95). True Indigenous sovereignty may include settler-descendant land return and environmental contamination cleanup as part of decolonization agendas (K. Reed, 2020), alongside language revitalization. Decentralized and autonomous governance might facilitate these agendas.

Mexico's Language Regime

State-based definitions of culture, ethnicity, and race shape social under-standings and self-perceptions that feed directly into experiences of citizen-ship. Although Mexico gained independence from Spain in 1810, the region never regained the linguistic autonomy and diversity that existed prior to colonization. Post-independence, the goal was to consolidate the country into a governable entity. In Mexico's case, utilizing language as the key marker of indigeneity paved the way for a Castilianization-based nation-building proj-ect, "with one language, one general law, one unified school system, one civic morale that would make all resident citizens dignified and responsible" (Gellman, 2017: 32–35). The Mexican language regime, in other words, was intricately bound up in notions of nation-making and modernity. By 1883, Justo Sierra, a Mexican intellectual and education champion who occupied numerous government posts including undersecretary of instruction from 1901 to 1911, stated that "our idea is absolutely opposed to the conservation of these [Indigenous] languages for any other reason than as simply archaeo-logical documents" (Ramírez Castañeda, 2014: 65, my translation).

After the Mexican Revolution of 1910, the issue of how to assimilate In-digenous citizens became the primary focus of the Mexican (mostly mestizo) intelligentsia, culminating in the creation of the National Indigenist Insti-tute (Instituto Nacional Indigenista, INI), a government institution dedicated to addressing the role of Indigenous people in Mexico's national development. INI operated as a mechanism of paternalistic assimilation known as *indigen-ismo*, or indigenism, where Indigenous Mexicans could gain economic or social benefits if they renounced their Indigenous practices, including lan-guage, and agreed to participate in social and economic projects as *campesi-nos*, or peasant farmers. This "father knows best" attitude of the government was justified not only through overt racism but more discreetly through increased access to electricity, water, agricultural technology, roads, and medical services, in exchange for assimilation into mestizo culture (cited in Ramírez Castañeda, 2014: 88, 244).

Schools operate as a state-society interface in many countries around the world. In Mexico, for much of the twentieth century under the mandate of assimilation, public school teachers physically punished and economically taxed Indigenous students for speaking their languages on school grounds (Jiménez Naranjo, 2017: 100). This set a clear precedent that schools were Spanish-only spaces where deviation from this state agenda was not permitted. While bilingual schools were implemented as pilot projects in the second half of the twentieth century in select locations, the use of Indigenous language was seen as a transitional measure with full Castilianization of the student population as the ultimate goal, rather than with real bilingualism in mind (Aguirre Beltrán, 1957; Jiménez Naranjo, 2017: 102–103). In policy, the Mexican state communicated its language regime to citizens by mandating the use of Spanish in school, with the exception of instrumental use of an Indigenous language as a means to Castilianization. In practice, punishment for Indigenous language use in schools from teachers, combined with discrimination by mestizo students toward Indigenous students, reinforced the primacy of Spanish as the language of national belonging.

Mexico's congress ratified the International Labor Organization's Convention 169 on Tribal and Indigenous Peoples (ILOC169) in 1990, making it the second country to sign on, following Norway. Numerous Latin American countries have followed suit, but at the time, Mexico's signature demonstrated a turning point in *indigenismo* toward the recognition of Indigenous peoples' rights in Mexico, after most of the twentieth century had been dedicated to assimilation. ILOC169 requires consultation with Indigenous people, mostly notably for development projects that might affect them or their traditional resources, and solidifies a commitment to allowing *usos y costumbres*, understood as customary Indigenous law, for traditional governance (Aguirre Beltrán, 1957; Jiménez Naranjo, 2017: 102–103).

Notably, ILOC169 does not contain enforcement mechanisms. Mexico's signature might have been nothing more than a way to show Indigenous communities that their concerns were being taken seriously without actually being bound to anything. In addition, ILOC169 alludes to but does not mention culturecide in any of its variations, although it does denounce assimilation as something that needs to be replaced by practices that support self-determination (Benvenuto, 2015: 31).

To bring the country more in line with the provisions of ILOC169, in 1992 Mexico's 1917 Constitution was updated to include, in Article 2, recognition of the state's multicultural composition, rooted in Indigenous identities, as well as the right of Indigenous communities to "preserve and enrich their languages" (Gellman, 2017: 36). While these achievements are significant, they have not held the state sufficiently accountable for previous assimilation programs. However, they do have symbolic importance in terms of Mexico's self-perception and international reputation as a democratizing state.

Even with Article 2 in place, schools that purport to offer bilingual education do not serve Indigenous communities well. The creation of the General Directorate for Indigenous Education (Dirección General de Educación Indígena, DGEI) in the late 1970s, followed by the General Coordination of Intercultural, Bilingual Education (Coordinación General de Educación Intercultural y Bilingüe, CGEIB) around the turn of the twenty-first century, have tried, with various degrees of success and failure, to implement language programming that respects the cultural rights of Indigenous communities while also bringing them into line with the state vision of who modern citizens should be and what they should speak (Government of Mexico, 2011 [1917]). In short, international best practices of language rights challenged the Mexican state's language regime, but in the absence of enforcement mechanisms to ensure implementation, this has led to weak and wavering bilingual education projects that have been pro-rights on paper but pro-assimilation in practice.

Language regimes have long legacies. In more than eighty interviews with Indigenous students across three different schools and one community organization in Oaxaca in 2018 and 2020, fewer than one-quarter reported speaking the Indigenous language of their parents or grandparents. Out of close to fifty interviews with Indigenous students, more than three-quarters said, nearly verbatim, "my grandparents didn't teach my parents their language because they didn't want their children to suffer like they had" (Anonymous, 2018h). Other comments included: "my parents didn't want me to be disadvantaged like they were, so they didn't teach me" (Anonymous, 2018k) and "people in my community feel shame about speaking their language" (Mata Moreles, 2018).

In some cases, students' parents were passive speakers—defined as those who absorb enough of a target language to understand but cannot respond back in the language—and in other cases the students themselves were passive speakers. But in all cases, there was a clear pattern of deliberate disconnection in intergenerational language transmission to avoid discrimination. This occurred despite the fact that the Mexican federal constitution recognizes sixty-eight Indigenous languages as national languages and provides legal backing for Indigenous language rights in the formal education sector. In practice, Spanish is prioritized at the expense of Indigenous languages in schools.

Mexican governmental institutions do not hold all the responsibility for the discord between the policy of multilingualism and the practice of Spanish language dominance. Several other factors influence school language practices. First, the National Education Workers Union (Sindicato Nacional de Trabajadores de la Educación, SNTE), which is Mexico's enormous and powerful teachers' union, has for decades undermined the practice of genuine bilingual education through their seniority system, which is blind to language matching between teacher and community. In other words, though an Indigenous community has the legal right to request a teacher who is certified as a bilingual teacher, there is no mechanism to ensure that the teacher speaks the same Indigenous language as that of the community where they are sent to teach. I and others have documented this phenomenon (Gellman, 2017: 49; Hamel, 2008: 304–305). When I asked teachers and administrators in Oaxaca about this challenge, they responded that it continued to be an issue. However, SNTE leadership has not acknowledged teacher-community mismatch as a problem, let alone fixed it.

A second factor that influences language practices in Mexican education is out-migration to the United States, which makes English language acquisition a pragmatic goal. This goal is connected to a third factor: familial interest in upward economic and social mobility. Among upwardly mobile Mexicans today, bilingual education is assumed to mean Spanish and English, rather than Spanish and Indigenous language. This is a result of mobility patterns from migration as well as domestic contact with the international economy through the tourism and business sectors.

In Oaxaca de Juárez, most private elementary schools include English as a daily class, and in 2017 a federal educational reform project called "Mexico in English" required that English classes be taught at all public primary and secondary public schools, although there has not been a clear timetable for implementation or for defining what type and level of language skills teachers need to assume such a post.[1] The demand for English, and its practical link to economic mobility, makes it more of a tangible good than Indigenous language instruction. This new reform furthers Mexico's Spanish language regime, as it will most likely further deprioritize Indigenous language teaching even in communities where there are still active speakers of Indigenous languages—indeed, Indigenous communities in Oaxaca have some of the highest rates of migration to the United States (Gellman, 2017: 49).

The United States' Language Regime

The United States has been defined as a melting pot, meaning that in theory everyone, regardless of their background, is supposed to melt into a national culture and assimilate into a shared social contract. This proposition is problematic for numerous reasons, not least of which is that the notion of "national culture" is vague and raises issues concerning whose culture gets to dominate as the national norm. While the United States has never had an official language policy, English, as the language of the U.S. government, acts as a de facto official language, enforced by the melting pot myth, which brings with it linguistic assumptions that immigrants should "melt" into the majority language of English.

This has played out historically with the expansion of U.S. territory as a result of the Louisiana Purchase of 1803, when French-speakers became citizens, and the conclusion of the Mexican-American War in 1848, when the current states of California, Arizona, New Mexico, Nevada, and a portion of Texas were added to the Union, increasing the population by roughly 75,000 Spanish-speakers who previously were considered Mexican citizens (P. H. Smith, 2013: 22–23; Stephen, 2007: 66). In addition, waves of immigration from Europe and then China and Japan in the nineteenth century created further linguistic diversity in the population. The second half of the nineteenth and early twentieth centuries saw a series of language-related legislation to enforce English-only policies in public schools in states such as Nebraska, Wisconsin, and Illinois, as well as in the U.S.-controlled territories of Hawaii, Puerto Rico, and the Philippines. However, such laws were sometimes challenged successfully: in Nebraska, an elementary school teacher was charged with violating the state language law by teaching a student to read a Bible passage in German, and the Supreme Court ruled the state law unconstitutional (*Meyer v. State of Nebraska*, 1923).

English-only boarding schools for Native American children were legally constituted in the 1870s and banned the use of Native languages, mandating that only English be used. U.S. Commissioner for Indian Affairs J. D. Atkins stated in 1887 that in the mandatory mission schools "barbarous dialects should be blotted out and the English language substituted. . . . The object of great solicitude should be to break down the prejudices of tribe . . . and fuse them into one homogenous mass. Uniformity of language will do this" (U.S. Congress 1868 in Field & Kroskrity, 2010: 11). Using Native American languages became illegal in mission schools (Field & Kroskrity, 2010: 11).

Teaching English was never just about the language but rather the idea that language by proxy represented a White Protestant worldview that students were expected to assume (D. W. Adams, 1995: 139; Field & Kroskrity, 2010: 16; Moorehead Jr., 2019: 68). Physical abuse was a socially and institutionally accepted way to reinforce lessons within boarding schools (D. W. Adams, 1995: 140–141). In 1895, Captain Richard Henry Pratt of Indian Industrial School at Carlisle, Pennsylvania, declared the school objective to be to "'kill the Indian, save the man'" (D. W. Adams, 1995: 52). This statement has long been used by scholars and activists as proof of the White genocidal agenda against Indian people (Baldy, 2018: 69). It is also an indicator of culturcide.

Indigenous rights activists have been raising awareness about the insulting portrayal of Indigenous peoples in California textbooks for decades. Beginning in 1965 the American Indian Historical Society, a national all-Indian organization based in California, began a campaign to correct the misrepresentation in public school textbooks (Norton, 1979: 19). Rubert Costo, a Cahuilla Indian educator, testified in a 1968 California Senate subcommittee hearing[2] on Indian Education that the United States' public education system and its textbooks in particular were demeaning to Native Americans. He proclaimed: "There is not one Indian in the whole of this country who does not cringe in anguish and frustration because of these textbooks. . . . There is not one Indian child who has not come home in shame and tears after one of those sessions in which he is taught that his people were dirty, animal-like, something less than a human being" (Norton, 1979: 19; War Soldier, 2019: 99–100). Costo and his fellow activists continued to speak out and bring their concerns to California's congressional committees throughout the twentieth and twenty-first centuries, arguing for re-centering Native people as contemporary people, rather than solely as relics of the past (War Soldier, 2019: 104). One victory, California Assembly Bill 738, was signed into law in 2017 and requires California's Instructional Quality Commission to "develop, and the state board to adopt, modify, or revise, a model curriculum in Native

American studies," although the process for such curricular development is unclear, and the timeline means changes may not be visible until at least 2022 (A. Herrera, 2019).

In terms of Indigenous rights, change has been slow to come. The Indian Child Welfare Act of 1978 was passed to grant Native communities autonomy over their children, but it was not until 1990 that Congress passed the Native American Languages Act (NALA). NALA recognizes that "the status of the cultures and languages of Native Americans is unique and the United States has the responsibility to act together with Native Americans to ensure the[ir] survival" (U.S. Congress, 1990: 104 STAT. 1153). A century of deliberate culturecide of Native American children, with forced Englishization as one aspect of culturecide, occurred in the boarding schools. As in Mexico, the legacy of denying Indigenous language use in U.S. schools has meant language loss and a culture of shame around indigeneity among Native people, many of whom cite the forced internment and Englishization of grandparents and other relatives as part of their own identity stories (J. Gensaw, 2017; Jacob, 2013: 51, 59).

The ongoing genocide of Native American people remains a contemporary atrocity (Jacob, 2013; Lara-Cooper & Lara Sr., 2019). Yet the United States has avoided any sort of label for culturecidal school policies, leaving it instead to therapists to develop terms such as "soul wound" to refer to intergeneration trauma (Duran, 2006: 7). The extension of culturecide policies to contemporary immigrant groups in the United States shows how Englishization policies continue to shape the United States' language regime in both formal and informal (Ballotpedia, 2016; California Department of Education, 2000) practices.

The implicit requirement of English competency in order to enjoy the full benefits of the social contract has been made explicit over the years through ongoing legislative battles over language policies in public schools. The 1968 and 1974 Bilingual Education Acts enabled students to receive mother tongue instruction as they were learning English, with English fluency rather than genuine bilingualism as the ultimate goal. In the 1980s, White perception of the cultural threat of Mexicans and other immigrants spawned the English First movement, which pushed California and twelve other states to declare English as the official language and sent a clear message about language assimilation as a state value (Ai Camp & Mattiace, 2020: 298). Around the world, many youths and adults see English as both utilitarian and universal, as well as something that can further economic survival (Gellman, 2020b; McCarty et al., 2014: 40). Accompanying the acquisition of English is a host of episte-mological beliefs and ontological practices designed to maintain and grow Eurocentric worldviews (Johnson, 2019: 14).

In California, Proposition 227 passed as a ballot initiative in 1998, elimi-nating bilingual education in schools and replacing it with an English-only immersion policy, and similar propositions in Colorado and Arizona quickly followed suit. These states intended to promote English immersion as the approach for schools working with immigrant students, which has not ac-tually improved student success rates (California Department of Educa-tion, 2000) because the Proposition 227 provisions essentially amount to dropping students into English-language classrooms without the linguistic tools to navigate the required content.

In short, the late twentieth-century public school classroom in Califor-nia discontinued bilingual education in a student's first language in favor of English-only curricula. This transpired even as the percentage of public school students in California whose first language was not English grew (Jackson, 2019). This policy has its roots in White fear, exemplified by the U.S. English movement, which has promoted, without success at the federal level, the adoption of English as the official language of the United States. In fact, the United States has no official language, and arguably therefore no official language regime (Faingold, 2018). However, the U.S. federal system, which provides tremendous autonomy to states, has proven fertile ground for states to devise soft language regimes which, while not officially declaring English-only policies at the state level, have done much to create institutional hostility to linguistic diversity.

In recent years California voters have pushed back against English-only schooling laws, most notably with the overwhelming passage of Proposition 58 in 2016, which readmitted non-English languages into public school edu-cation. A 2017 project by the California Department of Education has led to the creation of some resources for working with English Language Learners in non-English immersion classrooms (California Department of Educa-tion, 2017). And yet, states only have so much leeway with language rights. The English language requirement, a test of language competency, remains a component of the U.S. naturalization application process at the federal level; the only exceptions are for people who are over the age of fifty at the time of their test and have lived in the United States for at least twenty years as permanent residents. The role of federalism as a governance model in the United States thus continues to inform state language regimes. While the devolution of power to the state level has many benefits in terms of local contextualization and responsiveness in Mexico and the United States, it still does not fix the problem of language hegemony.

Barbara McQuillen, a Yurok language teacher at Del Norte High School[3] and staff member in the Yurok Education Department's language project, recounted how students have told her, "I can't take Yurok next semester because my mom or my dad said, 'how is that going to help you get a job?' You know, if you learn Spanish or another language you can always put that on your application. But you can't put Yurok, you know" (B. McQuillen, 2017). However, McQuillen said she hears Native students using what they know in Yurok, "giggling and saying stuff, words and phrases but not fluent speech really, but they can talk to each other" (B. McQuillen, 2017). There is intergenerational transmission resulting from these high school classes as well. McQuillen recounted that family members of some of her students express curiosity about what they are learning in Yurok class, and students will tell her, referring to a Yurok word or phrase, "'oh I taught my little sister that'" (B. McQuillen, 2017).

McQuillen identifies English as the biggest obstacle to revitalizing Yurok, because that is what most Yurok people use to communicate now and people don't like to be judged or make mistakes while they are learning something new (B. McQuillen, 2017). She also noted that the lack of people to talk to in Yurok makes it harder to practice because the language-keeper population is so small (B. McQuillen, 2017). Some young people themselves resist or express hostility to heritage language learning. They may question, in an English-speaking world, the necessity of preserving something seen as part of the past (McCarty et al., 2014: 42). In fact, it is not always so straightforward. A person may have multiple language perspectives, thinking, for example, that "speaking an Indigenous language is crucial to one's identity as a member of that group but that one prefers one's children to be monolingual speakers of English because one perceives the dominant language as more useful for economic success" (Field & Kroskrity, 2010: 22).

One manifestation of culturecide is the "epistemic violence" inflicted on Indigenous communities through teasing, physical punishment, and exclusion in schools (McCarty et al., 2014: 35). The hegemony of English in California, like the hegemony of Spanish in Mexico, is partially a result of coercive language regimes in schooling. Rendering Indigenous cultures, including language, as "dead," "unimportant," or "vanished" is a tactic of validation for genocide and culturecide, and alleviates White guilt for things like land appropriation (Jacob, 2013: 89). It allows settler colonialism to persist.

Summarizing Access to Minority Languages

For centuries, in both Mexico and California, Indigenous languages have been categorized as backward and something to be overcome in pursuit of modernity. This state tradition, enacted by ruling non-Indigenous elites who staffed educational institutions, was encoded in the hiring of schoolteachers, in norms for school curricula, and in approaches to discipline for Indigenous students. The goal of "civilizing" Indigenous citizens overruled other considerations and fostered acceptance of the practices of discrimination, physical punishment, and economic penalties for Indigenous language use in schools (Reyes de la Cruz, 2015: 24–29).

Instead of being considered fringe ideas of a few outliers, state agendas of genocide and culturecide in both Mexico and the United States were in fact a bedrock of mainstream ethnic majority culture. In California there have been many attempts to occlude the widespread support for various forms of Indigenous annihilation, but whether by direct participation or apathetic passivity, White people widely participated in these abuses against Indigenous people for generations (Lindsay, 2015: 4–9). In fact, the ideology of Manifest Destiny, meaning the God-given right of Euro-Americans to expand their territory, essentially permitted genocide as a divinely sanctioned aspect of this growth (Lindsay, 2015: 38; Wilshire, 2006: 26, 86). When events such as the 1860 Duluwat Island massacre[4] occurred in California, the slaughter of up to 250 members of the Wiyot Tribe, mostly women and children, by a White militia was heralded in the local press as an accomplishment for White settlers, and the eventual removal of Native children to boarding schools only furthered the genocidal mission through physical and cultural oppression (Greenson, 2019; Lindsay, 2015: 328–346).

Throughout the twentieth century in both Mexico and the United States, schools operated on the assumption that immersion in the dominant language (Spanish and English, respectively) was a necessary component of making Indigenous and immigrant people members of the national polity by rendering them less Indigenous (D. W. Adams, 1995; Gopar, Bohórquez Martínez, et al., 2016: 127; Gopar, López, et al., 2016: 39; Gopar, Vásquez Miranda, et al., 2016: 84; Jiménez Naranjo, 2017: 102–103). In addition, in Mexico, schools in Indigenous communities were and remain plagued by a lack of resources and infrastructure, as well as overworked and undertrained teachers who are not capable of addressing all the community's problems, including a history of forced Castilianization, in the classroom (Gopar, 2016: 12–13; Jiménez Naranjo, 2017: 99). This was mirrored in the under-resourced schools located on Native American reservations in the United States that continued the project of culturecide that had begun through forced boarding schools the century before.

In Mexico, education was specifically defined as a right in Article 3 of the Mexican Constitution in 1993, and subsequent reforms in 2013 emphasized the equitable, free, and obligatory (primary school through high school) nature of Mexican schools (Ruiz López, 2017: 68–69). While myriad challenges abound to make aspirational constitutional language reality, Mexico is ahead of the United States in at least clearly articulating a commitment to free and fair education. The United States, unlike all other peer countries, has no constitutional or statutory language guaranteeing equitable educational access, although all states provide compulsory free education for children ages six to sixteen.

Instead, in United States education policy discourses, the Tenth Amendment to the Constitution is invoked to clarify that education is a states' rights issue, given that the Tenth Amendment affirms state autonomy in the federal system and the Fourteenth Amendment provides for equal protection under the law. The U.S. Supreme Court in 1954 unanimously held in *Brown v. Board of Education* that racially segregated public schooling violated the Equal Protection Clause of the Fourteenth Amendment. However, in *San Antonio v. Rodriguez* (1972) the Court held that there is no fundamental right to education guaranteed in the Constitution. The Fourteenth Amendment acts as an indirect means to ensure the right to education and does not articulate education as a right with the same force as numerous other constitutions, including that of Mexico.

Linking Education Policy and Human Rights

All people have a right to obtain an education, as articulated in the United Nations' 1948 Universal Declaration of Human Rights (UDHR). As defined in Article 26: "Education shall be directed to the full development of the human personality and to the strengthening of respect for human rights and fundamental freedoms. It shall promote understanding, tolerance and friendship among all nations, racial or religious groups, and shall further the activities of the United Nations for the maintenance of peace" (UN, 1948). The aspirational goal of having education promote the "full development of the human personality" has repeatedly been undermined by racist and nationalistic agendas for worthwhile citizenship. Yet it is important for the collective human consciousness that such rights exist, albeit as aspiration. The Mexican Constitution has embraced the right to education for all in Article 3 and the right to Indigenous autonomy and cultural expression in Article 2. By contrast, the U.S. Constitution contains no right to education or cultural diversity beyond religion.

While some schools in both Oaxaca and California implement policies to allow Indigenous language learning, this is done solely at the discretion of administrators because there has been no systematic policy regarding minority-language classes. This means that if and when federal level education administration changes or curricular reforms are mandated, as in 2001 with No Child Left Behind[5] and in 2009 with Race to the Top in the United States, or with Inglés Para Todos (English for All) in Mexico, language landscapes could change dramatically. The larger education policy community is not yet convinced that robust language curricula can serve a wider purpose in citizen formation. Language electives are often treated as burdens by administrators, students, and their families—boxes to be checked off on the path through high school rather than a vital space for cross-cultural learning that can have a major impact on one's civic experience and contribution to democracy, as well as on economic and cultural opportunities.

Language Learning as Resistance to Culturecide

Social and curricular exclusion has a major impact on Indigenous children's self-esteem (Lara-Cooper, 2019: 31). While the particular reach of state institutions varies considerably from country to country, examples from around the globe reveal state language regimes at work with the goal of producing specific kinds of citizens. From overt twenty-first century quashing of minority languages in places like Turkey and China to ostensibly accommodating policies that mask homogenization projects in Mexico and the United States, there is little doubt that, as Joseph Stalin once said, "teachers are the engineers of the human soul" (Qin, 2019: 11). But ascribing such power to teachers alone is not wholly accurate. Teachers respond to the directives of their administrators, who make a range of practical and political decisions for a given school, district, or system. Such decisions, taken together at top administrative levels, form educational policies and enforce language regimes that shape students' schooling experiences.

While language regimes can be enforced locally, they are derived from state and national policies, and therefore changing educational policy to better include minority languages is something that needs to come from both the top and the bottom. Eduardo Faingold, in his volume on language politics in the United States and its territories, argues that because "neither the U.S. Constitution nor the Civil Rights Act of 1964 defines de jure obligations of the United States toward members of language minorities . . . the United States should consider granting certain language rights to minority groups by drafting new legislation" (2018: 35). Specifically, Faingold recommends that lawmakers redefine the term *national origin* by amending the Civil Rights Act of 1964 in order to add "language" to the protected categories already included: "race, color, religion, sex, or national origin" (2018: 62–63). Such an amendment would help clarify the vague status minority languages face in the United States. However, Mexico's passage of the Ley General de Derechos Lingüísticos de los Pueblos Indígenas (General Law on Linguistic Rights of Indigenous Peoples) in 2003 has made minority languages protected merely on paper, not necessarily in practice.

Laws alone will not eliminate the culturecide that is fostered through language regimes. Indigenous language courses in formal education are the result of openings in education policy that challenge long-standing language regulation. Ongoing discrimination against Indigenous people in both states continues to this day in both institutional and non-institutional ways, for example, through land appropriation and normalized everyday practices of racism, respectively. Such discrimination has real effects on school success.

In California, for example, Native American youth drop out of high school at double the national average and are 50 percent more likely to drop out of high school than any other ethnic group in the state (Lara-Cooper, 2019: 16). In light of this, Indigenous language inclusion in required public school curricula therefore represents a challenge to state policies of nation-making through homogenization. While state language regimes remain firmly entrenched, the revitalization of languages through schools radiates out into expanded community language use in everything from community theater to grocery store interactions. Indigenous visibility through the normalization of Indigenous language use thus constitutes a challenge to states that have defined their futures as decidedly monolingual.

The language regimes in Mexico and the United States are of course quite distinct. Mexico gives national language status to Indigenous languages and has numerous government-funded agencies that are meant to support language preservation. In contrast, the United States has no official language policy and no coordinated approach to Indigenous languages. Instead, Indigenous language access is carried out piecemeal by individual tribes. Yet there are similarities in how language learning and teaching constitute forms of resistance to state agendas, creating cracks in the facade of systems that have striven for, but not achieved, a melting pot, or *mestizaje*, in Mexico[6] that renders everyone homogeneously whiter. While teachers and students in each site frequently articulate feelings that they labor in isolation against majority-dominated language ideals, in fact, their very operation as multilingual actors challenges certain assumptions about what it means to be Mexican or U.S.-American.

Resistance

Political resistance takes many forms. Repertoires of resistance develop based on people's positionalities, which is to say that someone's power framework, meaning their class status and social standing, feeds into the kinds of resistance strategies they perform. Indigenous language teachers are important actors in language-based resistance. Similarly, students who are enthusiastic Indigenous language-learners send a message to their schools, peers, and communities that their notion of self includes more than being proficient in Spanish or English. They are demonstrating resistance to culturecide through their educational choices.

In Mexico, resistance to state agendas by the working and peasant classes has historically been militarized, as exemplified by Emiliano Zapata and his disciples, the contemporary EZLN, or by unions. In Oaxaca especially, but in other parts of Mexico as well, iconic syndicates of everyone from teachers to transportation workers shut down basic services for days or weeks at a time when their demands are not met. Such unions embody resistance in its overt form, as roadblocks or strikes. In more covert forms, resistance might be much more subtle. For example, in one of James Scott's canonical works, he dedicates a chapter to different vocal modes, such as gossip, rumors, and euphemisms, that enable oppressed people to resist against their dominators (Scott, 1990: 136–182).

In the United States, Indigenous students enacted resistance to boarding school policies by running away from schools, setting them on fire, or passively undermining school objectives through work slowdowns or general withdrawal from school life (D. W. Adams, 1995: 223–225). Contemporary subterfuge as resistance to culturecide can include parents insisting that their children respond to them in Zapotec even though people around them might enforce Spanish dominance. Resistance to culturecide can be as simple as answering the phone in Yurok, with an "Aiy-ye-kwee" instead of "Hello" momentarily reminding callers that another language is just as valid as the dominant one. Indigenous language social media posts by young people can be a type of resistance to language regimes even as they make use of mainstream corporate forums. The refusal to die out, disappear, or assimilate is itself a form of resistance to culturecide. When languagekeepers teach Indigenous languages within the confines of public education systems to heritage-speakers and non-heritage-speakers alike, they are resisting culturecide and asserting their right to exist within formal education systems.

The "Renacimiento de Orgullo" (The Rebirth of Pride): Steps Toward Language Revitalization

The history of culturecide in Mexico and the United States reveals parallels between colonial identity construction and economic exploitation as part of nation-making. In Mexico, never is this tension more evident than in the story of La Malinche, the Nahua woman who became Hernán Cortés's concubine and translator. The story of Mexico's formation as a modern mestizo state through the Indigenous Malinche's conception of a child with a *chingón*[7] White father sits in Mexico City's Plaza de las Tres Culturas as a permanent reminder of how deceit and violation were key state-building ingredients (Saldaña-Portillo, 2016: 13–14). In the United States, the myth of the nicknamed Pocahontas, who is inaccurately portrayed similarly as serving as translator for and lover to colonist John Smith, has also played a potent role in misinforming many schoolchildren and adults about how culturecide actually took place. In both countries, the potency of culturecide and its accompanying gendered myths of colonial White male superiority have made language revitalization efforts a powerful part of the decolonization movement.

There is a wealth of research on language revitalization (Crystal, 2014; May, 2012; McCarty, 2014; Olthuis et al., 2013). Christopher Loether, for example, outlines five actions that communities can take to bolster the preservation and revitalization of endangered languages: (1) increase arenas of language use; (2) promote language literacy with written materials on different interests at a range of levels; (3) create a language governance body to oversee orthography, certification of speakers, and maintenance of a reference grammar and dictionary; (4) create jobs in the language, including teachers, translators, and curricular creators; and (5) devise incentives for speaking the language through contests or other language-centric events (Loether, 2010: 253).

In Oaxaca, many of these steps have been put in motion, though they work against the mainstream language regime within the state. The market in Teotitlán del Valle remains a Zapotec language arena, and students attending BIC 29 are able to witness the value in gaining increased fluency in the language. For example, in 2018, a cooking competition all in Zapotec took place in the town as a way to encourage young people to both speak the language and learn the recipes of their elders, and events like this have taken place in Indigenous communities throughout the state.

In many respects, there is a language renaissance happening in Oaxaca, in the form of poetry readings, book publications, and songs in many Indigenous languages performed throughout the city and regions with growing frequency, drawing audiences who support the local economy through buying food and handicrafts near the events. While this cultural shift still mostly takes place among intellectual elites and the institutions they dominate, such cultural legitimation has the potential to continue to grow in both formal and informal educational spaces. For example, the International Mother Language Day celebration in 2020 brought dozens of family members of the 150 participating BIC 29 students, alongside hundreds of students from the other 48 BICs and their family members, into the capital city's central plaza. There, they watched BIC students perform Indigenous language, music, poetry, and dance in front of large, supportive crowds of mostly Mexicans and some tourists. Zapotec is far more visible in public life in Oaxaca than Yurok is in public life in California.

In the United States, many Native American tribes have been trying a range of approaches to heritage language maintenance and revival for decades

(Field & Kroskrity, 2010: 3). But in California, outside formal classrooms, Yurok-focused community events still do not contain much Yurok language, something that language-keepers would like to see change (B. McQuillen, 2017). Part of the mandate for the Yurok Tribe's Education Department is to increase Yurok language learning and use. Director Jim McQuillen states:

> Well, of course, we want to see the language continue on for the next generation and continue to thrive on the face of the Earth, you know. I think that's the main purpose, to remove it from an endangered language into a thriving language. There's a lot of information and knowledge within the language that can be retained for the next generation. And then, of course, we owe it to our elders . . . who are here, the elders who have passed, to learn the language and retain the language. They've sacrificed a lot, Yuroks who have passed, for us to have what we have in terms of information and traditions and the language itself, so we owe it to them to continue to try to pass it on to people. (J. McQuillen, 2017)

While fluency and communicative ability are prized in any language-learning context, Indigenous language use, as something that symbolically challenges the status quo of mestizo (Mexico) or White (United States) dominance, has power even in small doses. Melanie Gensaw, who works in social services in Humboldt County, summarizes: "I don't speak a lot of Yurok language, but what I feel about language is that every Native word is like an act of rebellion. . . . It was a literal act of rebellion at one point to be able to speak it. . . . And every time we speak it, we remind people around us that there is a different worldview and a different frame of reference that some people use to live their lives" (M. Gensaw, 2017). The notion of language as a central frame of reference is echoed by Jule Gómez de García and colleagues: "one's sense of oneself as an individual and as a member of a community is shaped by one's language" (Gómez de García et al., 2010: 120).

In her research with her own Yakama people, scholar Michelle Jacob describes how one of her respondents connects language survival to tribal survival because the knowledge systems inside language address natural resources, nutrition, and spiritual matters (Jacob, 2013: 58). Sometimes, respondents couldn't quite describe what the correlation was exactly, but they knew that when knowledge of language and culture was strong, Indigenous sense of self was too (Jacob, 2013: 86).[8] This anecdotal evidence was in abundance across all my research sites as well, and was borne out by the study data, with numerous personal testimonies from heritage-speakers as to the language-identity connection. The inverse of this connection is also true, however: "When language use and practice are diminished, the spiritual power and abilities of our people are likewise diminished" (Jacob, 2013: 58).

In addition to having the baseline ability to both strengthen and remind others of the existence of Indigenous peoples and worldviews, Indigenous language access has also been shown to have a tangible effect on healthy ethnic identity, which translates into broader school success (McCarty et al., 2014: 44), and the reverse also appears to be true. "Pride in heritage, ethnicity, and identity" in one study was "positively correlated with successful language acquisition" (Gómez de García et al., 2010: 122). Yet the incentives to learn Indigenous languages or to strengthen minority identity are not always clear, even for heritage-speakers. Moreover, there are few material incentives, as Indigenous language survival programs tend to be poorly resourced, with advocates spread across multiple organizations to earn a living and also do their language work (Jacob, 2013: 63).

Even so, attachments to Indigenous heritage languages are so connected to identity that people do language survival work anyway (McCarty et al., 2014: 41). This is certainly the case in both Oaxaca and California, where language activists do their work not because it is lucrative but because it is a part of their heritage they want to pass on. In fact, language teaching often operates as a proxy for identity teaching. While curricula may focus on animal or food vocabulary, the more ephemeral teachings of worldview are there alongside the quizzable words and conjugates (Gómez de García et al., 2010: 118).

Conclusion: Language Survival and Youth Identity in the Twenty-First Century

People are capable of vast complexity in their identities. Humans can have multiple overlapping identities based, for example, on their ethnic and national affiliations, political ideology, gender, sexuality, or occupation (Telles & Sue, 2019: 82). There is agreement across the social sciences that ethnicity is the result of shared social interactions rather than any sort of primordial identity (Telles & Sue, 2019: 44). Ethnic identity, which refers to shared cultural markers such as historical experiences, food, religion, customs, and language, is a marker of insider and outsider status in a given society (Telles & Sue, 2019: 121). Language loss for Indigenous peoples undercuts an important aspect of shared ethnicity, with considerable consequences.

In their study of the ethnic identity of Mexican Americans in the United States, Edward Telles and Christina Sue note that self-blame and shame over language loss were visible even among third- and fourth-generation respondents, which is to say that there are persistent psychological consequences of language loss over long time frames (Telles & Sue, 2019: 123). They further note that "psychologically, individuals who have lost their ethnic language can feel inadequate and . . . this dynamic may be particularly intense for women, especially those who are married and/or have children, because of the gendered expectations associated with the transmission of ethnic culture" (Telles & Sue, 2019: 125). While the cultural context of Indigenous youth heritage-speakers in Oaxaca and California is different from that of older Mexican Americans, Telles and Sue's research is helpful in documenting the real effects of heritage language loss.

Figuring out how to generate interest in the Yurok language continues to be an obstacle. To accomplish the goal of having Yurok survive and thrive, Mr. McQuillen notes that the language-learning population may need to include non-heritage-speakers as well as heritage-speakers (J. McQuillen, 2017). As he phrases it, "Non-Yuroks can become the champion folks to keep the language thriving and pass it on and support the effort, you know. They'll become as important as the Yuroks in keeping the language going so we need to offer it to everybody" (J. McQuillen, 2017). This point is critical for language survival; by encouraging non-heritage-speakers to learn the language, the Yurok Tribe allows language teaching to fit into the public school curricula. While heritage-speakers, especially in California, sometimes were surprised by or suspicious of non-heritage-speakers who wanted to learn Yurok, over time teachers have found that tension dissipates and that students appreciate non-heritage-speakers' interest in and validation of the Yurok language and culture (B. McQuillen, 2017). Similarly in Mexico, schools that teach Indigenous languages have made a point of accepting students from all backgrounds. Such language-access policy has widened the pool of speakers and enabled those who might otherwise have missed out to learn about Indigenous culture.

Prior to initiating data collection for this study, I heard anecdotal evidence, primarily from language teachers and administrators at each of the school study sites, indicating that language classes were doing something "good" for students, but the lines between correlation and causation were very fuzzy, as were the range of variables influencing youth identity formation and participation. As the following chapters will show, my analysis of an original mixed-methods data set, including interviews, focus groups, surveys, and participant observation in classes, schools, and communities, shows that language classes support healthy identity formation and consolidation among students and generate interest in, and in some cases facilitate, increased civic, culture, and political participation. The next four chapters look in depth at these issues in each of the case studies.

CHAPTER 4

Weaving Resistance: Zapotec Language Survival in Teotitlán del Valle, Oaxaca, Mexico

Introduction: Indigeneity in the Valley

The town of Teotitlán del Valle is well known on the Oaxacan tourist circuit as the must-see epicenter of traditional Zapotec loom wool-weaving. Because of this reputation, the town is more economically robust than neighboring communities, with newer solid-brick houses featuring weaving courtyards and galleries, and construction is a constant background noise. Passing through the town, one is as likely to see Canadian snowbirds or tall Danish visitors in short shorts with cameras in hand as one is to see short-statured grandmothers haggling over live chickens in Zapotec at the town's market.

Teotitlán del Valle is symbolic of globalization's tensions. On the one hand, facility with English has become vital for weavers and vendors to benefit from the rise of tourism. It is hard to sell a rug without a language in common with the tourists who hold the money. On the other hand, tourists come to Teotitlán del Valle precisely because it has remained a traditional Zapotec town, maintaining ancestral artisanship practices, although modernized with chemical yarn dyes rather than natural dyes in many weaver workshops.[1] Teotitlán del Valle has also upheld significant use of the Zapotec language, which goes hand in hand with its weaving traditions. Like many Indigenous communities, Teotitlán del Valle suffers from Zapotec language-use decline and disruption in intergenerational language transfer. And yet, the village is also at the forefront of efforts to revitalize the language and pass it to the next generation of speakers. From alphabet standardization workshops to cooking contests all conducted in Zapotec, there are multiple community activities to solidify and transmit language knowledge.

Although Indigenous language use in Mexico has declined over the last half century as a result of assimilationist state efforts described in Chapter 3, a significant Indigenous language-speaking population remains. As of 2015, 6.6 percent of the total Mexican population of approximately 126 million[2] five years of age or older identified as speaking an Indigenous language (INEGI, 2020a). Of those speaking an Indigenous language in Mexico, 6.2 percent speak some version of Zapotec (INEGI, 2020a). Of the Zapotec-speakers, roughly 6 percent are monolingual in Zapotec (INEGI 2015). Zapotec is part of the Oto-Manguean language family and contains at least fifty-eight dialects, which are generally grouped into three broad categories: Isthmus Zapotec (referring to the Isthmus region of Oaxaca); Sierra Zapotec (referring to the Sierra Juárez mountain region of Oaxaca); and Valley Zapotec (meaning the valleys surrounding Oaxaca de Juárez, south to Zaachila and east to Mitla). Teotitlán del Valle, as its name suggests, is part of the Valley Zapotec language cluster.

The state of Oaxaca has one of the highest populations of Indigenous language speakers in the country, with 1,165,186 people reporting Indigenous language skills (INEGI, 2020a; INEGI, 2015). The vast majority of Oaxacan Indigenous language-speakers are now bilingual; the portion of monolingual Indigenous speakers in Mexico as a whole is shrinking. Across the country, the rate of monolingualism has gone from nearly 20 percent of the population in 1930 to just 6.6 percent in 2015 (INEGI, 2015).

Roughly 45 percent of Oaxacans are Indigenous, 32 percent of whom speak an Indigenous language (Secretaría de Educación Media Superior, 2014: 66). Oaxaca is also one of the four poorest states in the country, alongside Chiapas, which has the second-largest number of Indigenous language speakers; Veracruz, which has the third-largest number of speakers; and Guerrero, which ranks sixth in number of Indigenous language speakers (INEGI, 2020a; Velásquez, 2020).

Much anthropological work has been done on the language and culture nexus in general. Yet despite such high numbers of speakers, there has been little research on what language use means for the identity formation and participation of the next generation in Oaxaca, meaning those coming of age in the 2010s and 2020s. This chapter charts access to the Zapotec language that high school students have at the Bachillerato Integral Comunitario numero 29 (Integral Community High School Number 29, or BIC 29), in Teotitlán del Valle. I examine how Zapotec language access at BIC 29 informs identity consolidation and impacts student decisions about civic, cultural, and political participation. I argue that the embrace of Zapotec by BIC 29 students constitutes a form of resistance to culturecide—the killing of culture—that would otherwise render them more and more mestizo with each passing generation and each step of their education.

Governance, Schooling, and Identity in Teotitlán del Valle

Teotitlán del Valle, like many predominantly Indigenous communities in southern Mexico, governs itself through *usos y costumbres* (traditions and customs), recently renamed *sistemas normativos indígenas*, or normative Indigenous systems. Both labels refer to the traditional system of Indigenous self-governance that serves as a local alternative to political party–based control. Indigenous governance systems include the standard provision of holding regular community assemblies where voluntary, uncompensated service works in the community, known in Spanish as *cargos*, are divided among residents. All members of the town eighteen years of age and older are expected to attend, participate, and graciously shoulder the responsibilities assigned to them.[3] Previously only men could hold cargos, and this remains the case for municipal leadership roles, though women now may also serve in some cargos.

The town did and still does maintain a primary and secondary (middle) school near the center of town. But young people had to travel long distances to attend alternate public high school systems[4] in neighboring, but not close, towns like San Jerónimo Tlacochahuaya and Santa María del Tule. These schools can take up to an hour to reach via public transportation, which is expensive for many families. Moreover, some community members wanted to promote schooling that was more in line with the cultural values of Teotitlán del Valle. In the 2000s, voting members of the community assembly that governs Teotitlán del Valle decided to grant land for the establishment of a public high school. They agreed that the BIC system would be the best type of high school for the community.

The BIC system was founded in Oaxaca in 2001 with the opening of twelve BIC schools. BIC 29 opened in Teotitlán del Valle in 2009. By 2020, forty-nine BIC schools operated in separate communities, with students speaking at least twenty variants of Indigenous languages (Secretaría de Educación

Media Superior, 2014: 66). As discussed in Chapter 3, Mexico's language regime has generally guided citizens toward assimilating into Spanish, and the public education sector played a major role in facilitating this assimilation throughout the twentieth century. In addition to general daily racism as a disincentive to being visibly Indigenous, much of the Indigenous language loss in places like Teotitlán del Valle occurred as a result of intense physical punishment and social castigation for using Indigenous languages in public schools (Anonymous, 2018p). In fact, being punished for Indigenous language use in schools is the most dominant commonality across all of the case-study communities. I heard numerous family stories about language-based school abuse in the grandparent generation, roughly defined as people born before or during the 1960s. The role of public education in coercing assimilation for Indigenous Mexicans was extreme (Maldonado Alvarado, 2000; Ramírez Castañeda, 2014). It constituted, and in some locations continues to constitute, a major factor in Indigenous language and cultural loss (Blancas Moreno & Vázquez Rodríguez, 2017; CNEI-UCIEP A.C., 2011; Maldonado Alverado, 2010).

Mexico now has laws that protect, at least on paper, Indigenous language rights, including Article 11 of the Ley General de Derechos Lingüísticos de los Pueblos Indígenas (General Law on Linguistic Rights of Indigenous Peoples) (Government of Mexico 2003). Article 11 mandates that federal educative officials guarantee Indigenous peoples access to bilingual intercultural education, as well as the protections to have a system that assures the dignity and identity of people, regardless of their language (Government of Mexico, 2003). However, ongoing problems with implementing and forcing compliance with this law, including the role of Mexico's biggest teachers' union, the National Education Workers Union (Sindicato Nacional de Trabajadores de la Educación, SNTE), and the Secretary of Public Education (Secretaria de Educación Publica, SEP), have meant that these protections remain lofty ideals (Gellman, 2017: 49). Moreover, newer laws that shift educational priorities from bilingual, intercultural education to inclusive education, in line with international norms, have deemphasized language rights in Mexican public schooling (Mendoza Zuany, 2017). While educational reform under former president Enrique Peña Nieto shifted power away from teachers' unions and toward the central government, in 2019 President Andrés Manuel López Obrador moved to undo those reforms and reprioritize educational unions, which have been the traditional agenda-setters for educational decision making in the state.

The BIC system attempts to reclaim language and cultural rights for Indigenous students. BIC schools are situated in communities that are interested in engaging young people in traditional community customs while also providing a standard high school education. Administered in its first year (2001) by the Instituto Estatal de Educación Pública de Oaxaca (State Institute of Public Education of Oaxaca, IEEPO), by 2002 the Oaxacan government authorized the creation of the Colegio Superior para la Educación Integral Intercultural de Oaxaca (Superior College for Integral, Intercultural Education, CSEIIO), a system separate from IEEPO and with the authority to design and implement culturally sensitive curricula within the framework of state high school standards. One of CSEIIO's goals is to help develop bilingualism in an Indigenous language and Spanish (Secretaría de Educación Media Superior, 2014: 69), but at the majority of the schools, the emphasis is on strengthening the Indigenous language, as it is the less-spoken language.

Today, the BICs operate under CSEIIO as an independent high school system that complies with Oaxacan state educational requirements, meaning it offers a general high school degree in contrast to some of the specialized vocational degrees in the Mexican system. High school education in Mexico is referred to as upper secondary level or preparatory (*preparatoria*), the equivalent of senior high school, as opposed to junior high school, education in the U.S. system.

The BICs adjust their curricula to reflect local cultural values: for example, teaching the language, arts, and culture of the region in which a given BIC is located. Such accommodations are a logical approach to educating Oaxaca's highly diverse population. As elsewhere in the world, measuring indigeneity is complex (DeLugan, 2012: 70), as some researchers allow for self-identification while others make judgments for respondents based on physical appearance, dwelling type, or brief assessment of language capacity.

Among today's Oaxacan youth, whether or not one identifies as Indigenous is muddy terrain without clear criteria. To illustrate, what follows is a sampling of the common interviewee profiles I encountered. Raul's[5] great-grandparents spoke Zapotec, but he grew up in an urban neighborhood near Tlacolula de Matamoros, where he did not experience any discrimination. Raul linguistically, physically, and in terms of lifestyle identified with the mestizo majority in Oaxaca, styling himself in urban teen fashion like he sees on television, speaking Spanish, and playing on his computer or phone in his free time. Yet his dark skin, black hair, and short stature identify him outwardly as being of Indigenous descent. Raul himself did not use the word *Indigenous* to self-identify because, as he put it, "our family lost the language and the culture" (Anonymous, 2018h).

In contrast, Laura,[6] an Indigenous-descent student like Raul who grew up near him, is part of a family that continues to be connected to the remote Sierra Juárez village of her great-grandparents, where Indigenous rituals and customs are maintained. Laura does not speak Zapotec, but she self-identifies as Indigenous. She and her parents return with her grandparents for annual festivals and life-cycle events to the village, and because the family continues to follow a small number of Indigenous cultural practices in their home, Laura's urban home base does not undermine her Indigenous self-perception.

While for many students at BIC 29 and elsewhere in Oaxaca, assessing their identity was a straightforward matter, for others it was not. In conversation after conversation with young people, they ran up against an inadequate vocabulary for identity in relation to indigeneity and intergenerational cultural loss. Few youth felt comfortable using the word *mestizo* to describe themselves, but a significant number also did not feel they were culturally connected enough to merit the label of *Indigenous* (Anonymous, 2018m). When I asked them what word I should use to refer to them, a few said, "I don't know, there isn't a good word" (Focus Group, 2018, 1.1).[7] One student asked me to create a new word, and then I in turn asked them to suggest a word, and neither of us could invent one on the spot (Focus Group, 2018 9.2). Such ambiguity around ethnic or racial categorization is similar to tensions experienced by young people with Afro-Mexican identities, who also wrestle with tensions over purity, mixing, and generational shift (M. Adams & Busey, 2017: 13–16).

In the absence of a self-generated term or conceptual framework from respondents, I refer to people like Raul in the example above as *Indigenous-descendant*. This term allows for ambiguity in terms of current self-presentation but acknowledges the heritage that may outwardly be identified or that parents or grandparents still identify with. Students with Laura's profile, on the other hand, are referred to as *Indigenous*. It is not my intention to offer a racial categorization framework for Oaxacan youth but rather to highlight the complexity of talking about identity in relation to indigeneity in a place where intergenerational identity shift has moved faster than the creation of vocabulary to describe it. While a deeper dive into the subjectivity of indigeneity is outside the scope of this study, I note it here because the ambiguity of identity and how it is formed, strengthened or weakened, and passed down is connected to how identity informs youth participation.

Data Profile for Schooling in the "Land of God"

When the community assembly of Teotitlán del Valle approved the creation of BIC 29 in 2009, they selected a plot of land to hold in trust for the school nearly a mile from the town center. Twice-daily buses serve the school to drop off and pick up students, teachers, and staff. Motorcycle taxis that hold three passengers shuttle people in canvas-covered seats to the school from the center of town. The road between the town and the school—which does not have transportation available during the school day itself—is dotted with local homes, most featuring a few big looms under covered porches and cactus gardens where people grow nopal, or prickly pear cactus, for home consumption. Teotitlán means "land of God" or "house of God" in Nahuatl, and walking the outskirts of Teotitlán del Valle, where the Sierra Juárez mountains in the distance ring the valley, it is easy to imagine how this valley was seen as such.

Local knowledge is integrated into BIC 29's curriculum in a plethora of ways. In its three-year curriculum, BIC 29 includes two years of mandatory Valley Zapotec language classes alongside two years of English, as well as classes like local and state history and traditional medicine. For example, the students learn to care for a cactus farm on site, which provides nopal, a staple food for the region. In Zapotec language classes, study topics include local gastronomy, dance, and weaving as themes that allow for teaching new vocabulary, or for heritage-speakers, for review of the vocabulary, in a formal way, including how to write the words. Students wear BIC 29 uniforms, and many students, teachers, and staff purchase breakfast on site from local vendors. Economically, the school is a boon for the local population, including the food vendors and transport workers who ferry students to and from the site, as well as other small businesses that meet school needs.

BIC 29 continues to grow in popularity even as most other BICs in the state saw their enrollment decline in the late 2010s. In spring 2018, BIC 29 had 180 students enrolled, and by spring 2020 that number had climbed to 230. I was told by several school directors and faculty throughout CSEIIO that this is because of BIC 29's location as the closest BIC to Oaxaca de Juárez, making it the most accessible for the largest amount of students. Many other BICs are in extremely remote areas and only serve local populations, which are shrinking from both out-migration and decreasing birth rates, while others like BIC 29 have enrollment boosted by internal migrant students from other parts of Oaxaca.

Roughly one-third of BIC 29 students come from Teotitlán del Valle; the remaining two-thirds commute from nearby towns and a few come from as far away as Oaxaca de Juárez. About one-third of the students are already speakers of, or at least have high exposure to, the Teotitlán variation of Zapotec; another third are familiar with other variations or other Indigenous languages. The remaining third of the student body comes from Spanish-only households, meaning they encounter Zapotec for the first time at BIC 29, or they may identify as distance heritage-speakers, meaning family members in their more distant, but not immediate, past (i.e., not parents or grandparents) were speakers.

In contrast to schools like CEDARTMC, which have created vetting processes to screen out students as demand overwhelms capacity, at the BIC, the school director and teachers take turns visiting communities and actively recruiting students to promote enrollment. However, in a February 2020 meeting of all the parents of students at the school, some parents questioned why the school would ask community authorities for funds to do school promotion when the enrollment was sufficient for a robust school. In fact, some parents were concerned that the school would get too big and exceed its capacity—indeed, just in the course of two years of fieldwork, from 2018 to 2020, BIC 29 had to build several new classrooms, a library, and a cafeteria to accommodate the increased student body. Two parents at the meeting suggested that promotion efforts should instead happen within Teotitlán del Valle and be undertaken by parents of currently enrolled students. The political tone of this conversation was uneasy, as it underscored concerns that BIC 29 was both growing too much and using too many community resources—and that too many students were coming from outside the village.

In fact, the student body includes students from a range of ethnic backgrounds, but the overwhelming majority identify as Indigenous Zapotec or Zapotec-descendant. At the time of my data collection in 2018, there were also a few Mixtec students and one Mixe-speaker. Overall, students report much satisfaction and appreciation for their school, with many stating that they are the only ones from their lower secondary school group to continue on to upper secondary (*preparatoria*) school. Education through upper secondary school became compulsory in 2012, with the goal of having all eligible students enrolled by 2022 (OECD, 2013: 4). Lower secondary school became compulsory in 1993, but many students still choose or are compelled by necessity to leave school after lower secondary (middle school) to enter the workforce, migrate, or marry because of a pregnancy. At BIC 29, from 2010 to 2020, nine to twenty-seven students failed out or left school for some reason each year between the start of the school year in September and the end of the year in July.

I invited students in the third-year Zapotec program to participate in the research, regardless of other demographic characteristics. At BIC 29, I conducted 21 surveys, 2 focus groups, 22 interviews with students, 9 interviews with teachers and administrators, and 30 classroom observations. I also collected data at the largest state university, at an educational NGO in Oaxaca de Juárez (Gellman, 2021b), and at an additional BIC school in the Sierra Juárez mountains in 2020 (my work at the last of these was interrupted by Covid-19) (Gellman, 2020a). I draw on a synthesis of these multiple field sites to inform some of the concepts of this and subsequent chapters, while highlighting student voices from BIC 29.

BICs are run by directors who are generally not from the host communities and are intentionally rotated through posts every three years at a minimum. Although the term-limit practice may prevent corruption or complacency, it is also quite distinct from the public school role of principal in the United States, which does not have term limits. I began my research at BIC 29 shortly after the arrival of the director, Francisco Martínez Covarrubias, and he was completing his third year at BIC 29 at the time of my most recent fieldwork in early 2020.

Every director works in cooperation with a Parents' Committee (Comité de Padres de Familia), though the composition of the committee and the dynamic between the director and the committee regarding how rights and responsibilities are defined vary at each BIC. At BIC 29, the Parents' Committee is composed of ten community members from Teotitlán del Valle who serve one-year cargos during a year they have a child enrolled at the school. One cargo-holder is selected as president of the committee, and this person is responsible for liaising between the director and the parents to ensure the smooth running of the school. The Parents' Committee office is located in a separate building from the administration office, where the director and the school secretary work, and is near the entrance of the school grounds.

Unlike in the United States where public school parent associations tend to only be involved in policy or curricular issues at schools, or projects like fundraisers, in the BIC system, parents do much of the labor that would be done in the United States by professional staff or outside businesses. For example, the BIC 29 Parents' Committee is responsible for unlocking and locking up the school each day, opening the locked school gate for any visitors (including me), maintaining a supply of clean drinking water for students by purchasing and delivering water jugs to dispensation points, making photocopies for students (one peso per copy), improving the physical infrastructure of the school by planting trees and organizing construction projects, expanding the well that brings water into the school bathrooms, and organizing community meetings and celebrations. Most importantly, the Parents' Committee is responsible for the financial well-being of the school, including collecting all school dues and tracking their use to cover school expenses. The financial profile of the school-going costs is discussed below.

Obstacles to and Support for Student Educational Success

In order to study youth identity formation in education, I spent a significant amount of time documenting the challenges that young people face in their lives, in particular, elements that they describe as being connected to school success. Given that all administrative stakeholders in each case-study community were particularly interested in examining factors in school success, I let the collaborative framing of the research lead and address these factors in some depth here. BIC 29 students generally cited economic resources, mental health, and motivation as their three biggest obstacles to school success, and I consider each in turn.

Paying for School

It is unsurprising that in rural Oaxaca, the most significant obstacle for students to complete their educational paths is a lack of financial resources. Over and over again in nearly every interview, when I asked students about things that made it hard to attend school, without any hesitation they would cite "*la economía*" (economics) as their number-one barrier to continuing their studies at BIC 29 and to pursuing future educational goals.

The vast majority of BIC 29 students come from low-income households. Many receive government scholarships to counter school abandonment or to partially cover transportation or inscription costs. To enroll, families must pay an initial inscription fee and then MX$450/US$25 each semester for those outside Teotitlán del Valle and MX$350/US$20 for those from the community, which can be waived for either group via a scholarship based on demonstrated need. The Parents' Committee uses these funds for the school's necessities; teacher and administrator salaries are paid by the government. While staff and parents did not indicate that the fees were barriers to attendance (Bautista, 2020; Esteban, 2020), some students did (Anonymous, 2018i). In addition, students must factor into their budget the purchase of mandatory uniforms, transportation, and photocopies. Most students also need money to buy their daily lunch at the school cafeteria, a series of food stalls run by residents of Teotitlán del Valle (Anonymous, 2018i; Bautista, 2020). BIC 29 is able to award a number of grants for transportation and food costs each semester; the exact number depends on school enrollment. For example, in spring 2020, the director allotted eight awards in consultation with the faculty during a meeting I observed at which the merits and needs of each student were discussed.

In addition, all students are eligible for discounts based on academic merit (Esteban, 2020). Students who achieve a grade-point average of 9.4 out of 10 get a 25 percent discount on tuition, and if students earn a grade-point average of 9.5 to 10, they get a 50 percent discount (Bautista, 2020). In 2019–2020, twenty to thirty students had earned each type of discount, according to the president of the Parents' Committee. Additionally, if a family has two students in the school at the same time, they pay fees for only one student (Bautista, 2020).

Finally, many families receive some sort of government support for low-income families, although the exact program name and range of benefits have changed with each new presidential administration. In 2020, the Benito Juárez Scholarship for Well-Being was the latest incarnation, and this amounted to MX$1,600/US$80 per month to low-income families with a student enrolled in high school (Martinez Covarrubbias, 2020). In sum, meritorious students and those with high demonstrated need are able to reduce the financial burden of their schooling, but the scholarships and discounts are often not applied until the beginning of each school semester, leaving families uncertain about how the economics will work out until the last minute.

In addition, even with all the scholarships, some families struggle to cover the costs.

Many students work to be able to pay for their schooling. The majority work at local businesses of friends or family; one student I interviewed commuted to Oaxaca de Juárez to waitress in a restaurant on weekends. The majority of students from Teotitlán del Valle and surrounding towns helped in some capacity in weaving industries, agriculture, or taking care of farm animals. Only one student out of eighteen interviews, who came from a remote town more than an hour away and boarded in Teotitlán del Valle with friends of his family during the week, did not mention money as a source of concern. In general, students talked about these paid jobs as separate from the regular family chores, including caring for younger siblings. Students at BIC 29 demonstrated a high degree of concern about the financial viability of their education, both at BIC 29 and in their college plans.

Mental Health and Physical Security

The second most frequently mentioned obstacle for students is their own mental health, sometimes in relation to their physical security. Students mentioned depression and anxiety as two factors that impacted their choices and behavior. Many students suffered significant emotional trauma for a range of reasons, including family violence and internal displacement due to community violence.

Mexico has a high level of physical insecurity and a culture of impunity for violence, where there is no meaningful justice for nearly 99 percent of crimes committed (Anaya-Muñoz & Frey, 2019: 3). This is particularly true of gender-based crimes (Tamés, 2019: 87–99). Mexican culture is deeply rooted in the practice of *machismo*, or male domination, where men and boys are socially prized and granted control over women and girls. Within the norm of machismo, boys are socialized to not show emotions considered to be feminine, such as empathy or pain, and they demonstrate their toughness through establishing turf, challenging anyone who questions their domination, and fighting to protect what they consider to be either their possessions or their honor (Gutmann, 2007). Socially embedded concepts of masculinity are reinforced at every stage of life, including in the media, educational opportunities, and in the treatment by state actors such as the police and judiciary of women and girls who may try to speak out about gendered abuse (Anaya-Muñoz & Saltalamacchia, 2019: 214; Wright, 2011).

Fear of gender-based violence was prevalent in numerous formal and informal conversations with students and community members both in Teotitlán del Valle and throughout Oaxaca (Anonymous, 2018c; Santiago Reyes, 2018). For BIC 29 students, there were high levels of physical insecurity in their transport to and from school, particularly when they walked from bus stops to remote homes (Anonymous, 2018i). A spate of robberies and murders had cast an air of insecurity over Oaxaca's small towns as well as its urban spaces, and young women were, and still are, particular targets. Female students' concerns about their physical insecurity, particularly fear of rape and robbery, were nearly unanimous, while most male students reported generally feeling safe, pointing to the clear gender divide in physical security within a male-dominated culture. However, one male student reported fear of physical insecurity when he heard about robberies and murders near him (Contreras García, 2018).

BIC 29 students who use the local Teotitlán bus service to get to and from school showed less trepidation about transportation. In contrast, students who lived far enough away from school such that some or most of their trip required public transport, particularly for Oaxaca de Juárez–based students, reported feeling very insecure while doing so. In the most dramatic case of physical insecurity at BIC 29, one Indigenous student had been displaced from her home community in another part of Oaxaca due to internal civil war there (Anonymous, 2018c). Her family migrated to Oaxaca de Juárez, and because this student had attended a BIC previously and felt most comfortable in the BIC system, she commuted to BIC 29 daily from the city (Anonymous, 2018c). During the course of my semester at BIC 29 in 2018, this same student was assaulted and robbed during her transport to school, compounding her already acute sense of physical vulnerability (Anonymous, 2018c).

There are also a few students at BIC 29 who have been traumatized by witnessing domestic violence (mostly mothers being abused by male partners) (Anonymous, 2020), and several other students who experienced real food scarcity remained physically insecure due to a lack of resources. One student, who is one of ten children and works after school and on weekends weaving, making tortillas, or pasturing animals to help her family, talked about the difficulties she experienced staying both motivated and alert at school given her economic pressures and her gnawing hunger (Anonymous, 2018f). In general, trauma from past violence, fear of future violence, and resource scarcity profoundly shape student identity and contribute to their participation choices.

Mental health care is scarce at BIC 29. Though there is one teacher who majored in psychology in college and is skilled in student counseling, she teaches a full course load and is not able to meet one-on-one with students as part of her regular duties (Anonymous, 2020). Nevertheless, she is generally the person students go to when they are dealing with difficult problems, and she keeps her classroom door open during all class breaks and transition times so students can meet with and confide in her, which they regularly do (Anonymous, 2020). No staff counselor position exists at schools within the BIC system, or indeed within most of the Mexican public high school systems. Without adequate care, childhood trauma manifests as depression, anxiety, and other mental health issues for BIC students (Anonymous, 2020). Many of these issues are carried into adulthood and factor directly into identity construction.

Motivation and Focus

The third most-mentioned obstacle to educational success is student motivation and focus. As is the case in the high schools in this study, and in many schools in general, motivation for educational success is somewhat personal and based on a range of factors including family and friend influences as well as clarity of vision for one's future. There are many highly motivated students at BIC 29. One of the most illuminative points of reference to upward economic and social mobility I encountered was that the majority of female students I interviewed have mothers who are housewives but they themselves are motivated to have careers outside the home (Anonymous, 2018j). While many of these young women have motivation and focus, they also expressed much self-doubt about their ability to succeed academically; for some it was because they struggled academically while for others it was because they were breaking societal norms by constructing such plans in the first place (Anonymous, 2018j).

At BIC 29, the two biggest distractions are dating and drugs. While high school flirting is a common global phenomenon, at BIC 29—where many students have friends who are already married with children, and whose parents may themselves have married and had children at a relatively young age—flirting can be more of a serious matchmaking endeavor in a context of limited birth control information and use (MICS, 2015: 15). The Catholic cultural backdrop of Teotitlán del Valle, and Mexico more generally, means that though some discussion of birth control does take place within the community development and health curricula of the school, each year at BIC 29 at least one student leaves before graduating due to pregnancy (Martinez Covarubbias, 2020). While pregnant students are not required to leave school, the cultural norm is that they do. Sometimes students will marry each other if pregnancy happens; oftentimes both students drop out of school, move in with one set of their parents, and the boy/dad goes to work or tries to migrate to the United States to provide for the young family (Martinez Covarubbias, 2018).

Drug addiction has also affected some BIC 29 students. In a few cases, the director has had to intervene with parents who were in denial about their child's situation to recommend that they enroll the student in a drug treatment program. In one case, a student attended a short-term treatment program, returned to school, and relapsed at school (Martinez Covarubbias, 2018). Such addiction continues to be a real issue even for rural communities in Mexico.

Most students are not verbally self-aware regarding the potential consequences of a lack of motivation or focus, though one stated "not getting pregnant" when I asked her about her near-future goals (Mata Moreles, 2018). Many students described seeing their friends leave school to work or marry, and their personal goals were therefore more in opposition to leaving school—"I want to keep going to school"—rather than representing a clear vision of what such a goal would yield. Obstacles to school success underscore the complex matrix of issues young people navigate as they form and consolidate their identities and make choices about how they will participate in the world.

Sources of Student Support

Lest I paint an overly pessimistic view of youth culture in BIC 29, it is important to mention the many sources of support that students described as well. Students cited their family members, administrators, teachers, and friends as people they could call on when needed. Some students did not quite understand that they could ask to talk to teachers outside of class or ask for extra help academically; however, this was not true in all cases. Students regularly said "I'm strong enough to deal with it" as a reason to not seek help for either academic or personal problems. While culturally logical behavior, this raises concerns about bottled emotions or increased potential for class failure.

In general, students turned to their families and each other—their peer group—for help before reaching out to non-familial adults. Parents in Teotitlán del Valle have completed a range of education levels, but in general the level of formal education in the community is very low compared to Mexico's more urban centers and wealthier states. For example, based on the total number of interviews I completed with students and community members at BIC 29 and in Teotitlán del Valle, the majority of mothers had completed some degree of primary school, the majority of fathers had completed at least middle school, and a smaller number of both mothers and fathers had completed high school. Very few parents of students and other community members hold college degrees, but nonetheless parents want their children to get ahead and try to support them.

School Climate and Youth Identity at BIC 29

BIC 29 is a physically vibrant space that continues to grow as student enrollment increases. Buildings, all constructed since 2009, are trim concrete structures that have been brightly painted, with several showing colorful murals on their outer walls, testaments to Indigenous identity as well as public health messages like maintaining positive relationships with family as part of caring for one's mental health. Many trees, though still small, have been planted around the grounds, as has a native cactus garden in the center of campus. Though most BIC students are low-income, compared to most other BICs in the CSEIIO system, BIC 29 is well resourced, with a robust library and full band, meaning that the school has the funds to purchase all the necessary musical instruments, which many BICs are not able to do.

All the students I interviewed spoke positively about BIC 29 in general, and their personal social groups in particular. However, the majority of students readily cited numerous examples when I asked about students being made fun of by other students. Several students described how teasing and insults were particularly rampant during a student's first year at BIC 29 and lessened by the final year as students, particularly boys, matured and learned the more respectful social culture of the BIC and left their middle school personas behind. Indeed, many students mentioned that they had found teasing and bullying to be much worse in primary and secondary school and that, in contrast, students at BIC 29 were much calmer and more amiable. Nevertheless, there is a culture of discriminatory "joking" that exists at BIC 29 that impacts identity formation and is worth exploring in detail.

Intragroup Racial Politics at BIC 29

Because most students at the BIC identify as Indigenous or as the children of Indigenous parents or grandparents, there is a strong sense of pride in Indigenous identity at the school. There is also a sense that Indigenous identity is a non-issue. Because everyone is Indigenous in some way (even though not all students self-identify as such), a person who says something demeaning about Indigenous people can't be held accountable for discrimination because he or she too is Indigenous. This permissiveness based on perceived shared Indigenous background regularly leads to microaggressions that highlight class and geographic fractures.

The majority of student examples about harmful teasing and joking concerned Indigenous identity, sexual orientation and gender identity, disability status, and physical appearance. Nevertheless, the microaggressions at play in BIC 29 illuminate larger patterns of internalized oppression and intragroup discrimination that have a bearing on youth identity formation and participation choices. Fissures of society became visible through discriminatory speech. For example, students heard discriminatory jokes directed toward students who came from more rural communities and spoke Spanish with accents (because it was their second language), or who didn't know some of the popular or mestizo cultural reference points that other students used in interactions (Focus Group 4.2 BIC 29, 2018; Focus Group 5.3 UABJO, 2018).

For example, students are sometimes made fun of for being "too Indigenous" and are the butt of expressions like "es un bicho raro," which translates to "he or she is a rare insect," or "es muy indio," meaning "he or she is very Indian," to refer to poorer or darker-skinned students (Anonymous, 2018c). This pattern of verbal discrimination continues Mexico's history of using the term "indio" in an entirely derogatory fashion, manifested at BIC 29 in the culture of teasing ways that students make fun of others. As in other case-study schools, these insults sometimes take the form of light joking, where students may be bantering with each other for the sake of engagement, but also in ways that are meant to be insulting (Anonymous, 2018c). Students said they thought such discourse was just part of life and didn't see it as an issue, but it demonstrates the thick skin students wear regarding historic discrimination toward Indigenous people in Mexico (Focus Group 4.2 BIC 29, 2018).

Interestingly, when I pushed students in focus groups about the use of nicknames like "gorda/o," "negra/o," or "güera/o" (translations: fatty, blacky, or whitey), they were all a bit bewildered that I thought such words were problematic (Mata Moreles, 2018). "Nicknames are just ways to show affection!" exclaimed one student. She then mentioned how she was called "güera" while her cousin was called "negra" by family, belying that her association with the historically more prized White characteristic was perhaps partly why she accepted its use (Mata Moreles, 2018). When I asked her what her cousin thought about the names, she, a usually verbose speaker, fumbled (Mata Moreles, 2018). In another instance, a dark-skinned girl in a focus group who was also nicknamed "negra" said she saw how it could reinforce certain negative ideas. Her fellow focus group participants avoided eye contact with her, and with me, when she said this. It was a moment of group self-reflection about how someone who is on the receiving end of these nicknames and comments might feel.

The notion of being strong enough to "take it" pervaded the interviews when discussing school climate. Students, when asked directly about mean things that might be said to them in the hallways or at breaks, even as part of "just kids joking around," would invariably follow their acknowledgment of the insult with the phrase "but I can take it" or, "pero soy fuerte" (Dionisio, 2018; Anonymous, 2018i). The element of personal strength was recounted with pride, as a way to excuse discriminatory behavior or to undercut my query about whether they had reported it to anyone. No anonymous reporting mechanism exists at BIC 29, but based on data from schools in California discussed in later chapters, anonymous complaint boxes do not seem to work as they are rarely used. Instead, the students' remedy for racist "joking" is to put on a thick skin and not talk about it.

Several students, particularly at the BIC, said that I was the first person they had talked to about the insults they heard (Anonymous, 2018c, 2018d), and this was one way that my positionality seemed to make me a safer bet for confessionalism than the teachers and administrators students saw every day. In my visible protocols as an outsider, including my guarantees of confidentiality if desired in interviews, some students opened up in ways that clearly demonstrated the lack of available mental health services, as well as students' hunger to have an outside adult to talk to. One student whose family had survived harrowing political violence said that besides me, only the director of the school knew her story (Anonymous, 2018c).

The clear need to talk about past trauma, and the lack of available resources to do so, made my role as an outside professional helpful at BIC 29. Students most likely censored themselves as well, but in general, once they saw that I was really interested, they were forthcoming with reflections about school climate. I also observed what they described over the course of my time in class with them, during breaks, and in transport to and from the school, which I frequently did with them on the Teotitlán bus.

Impact of Zapotec Language Access

Lorenzo Jiménez Martínez is the affable Zapotec language teacher at BIC 29. He is from Teotitlán del Valle, he married a woman from the same community, and they are raising their young daughter with Zapotec as her first language. Mr. Jiménez also teaches physical education and a research skills class, and tutors students, as most teachers do, during the weekly study hall classes. Students at BIC 29 take two years of Zapotec, and also two years of English, both during their first two years of the three-year high school curriculum. Throughout the BIC system, all BICs offer English alongside either the Indigenous language of the majority population—clearly Zapotec in the case of BIC 29—or a broader Indigenous languages class if the population is too heterogeneous to offer only one language.[8] While a few of the remotest BICs are situated in dynamic Indigenous language-speaking communities where the BIC emphasis is more on learning to write a language students already speak, in most of them and certainly in BIC 29 the task is to fill in some of the language lost through ruptures in intergenerational language transmission.

Many so-called mother tongues are just that—something passed down by parents in the home, usually by the mother, who in the context of patriarchal societies is expected to be the primary caregiver. Yet the potent histories of abuse and discrimination against Indigenous people in Mexico under the state's language regime have led many parents and grandparents to choose not to teach their children the Indigenous language of their family and encourage them to only focus on Spanish (Anonymous, 2018p). Below is an excerpt from an interview I conducted that illustrates this process. The interviewee is a student at BIC 29 who comes from the neighboring town of Santa Ana del Valle; she reflects on her own language pride in relation to the language shame of some of her classmates:

Question: Why are fewer people your age speaking Zapotec?
Answer: Because the parents didn't teach them, and because they feel ashamed to speak their [Indigenous] language.
Question: Tell me more about the shame. Where does it come from?
Answer: The shame can come because people fear being discriminated against. Some people say that to speak their language they feel less than others, or they are afraid to speak and be recognized [negatively] as Indigenous, or they are afraid to express themselves in their language because people will treat them worse, and also because they are ashamed they haven't learned enough [of their Indigenous language], because the elders no longer teach us.
Question: But you speak Zapotec, so you or your parents were not afraid to learn or teach it?
Answer: Well, because everyone in my family speaks Zapotec, and my father taught all of us [kids]. So no, I don't feel shame or fear to speak it, since everyone around me at home does.
Question: Tell me a little more about how it feels to speak two languages.
Answer: Here in school I use Spanish, and when I am in language class I use Zapotec and can help other students. And then when I am in my community and with my family, we all communicate in Zapotec. And I feel good to speak my language [Zapotec] because I identify with it more than anything, and because my family has been speaking it for generations. And the truth is I feel very content and happy to speak my language, because I feel it is my identity.
Question: Have you had a moment in your life where you felt discriminated against for speaking your language or being identified as an Indigenous person?
Answer: No, so far I haven't suffered any discrimination. To the contrary, many students say they want to learn to speak my language and so I help them so that they can better understand [what is happening in Mr. Jiménez's classes].

Question: Has anyone in your community talked about feeling ashamed or being treated differently because they are Indigenous? Answer: Of course. Some of my classmates who do speak Zapotec have said that other students who don't speak it have criticized them for speaking [their language] because they [the non-speaking students] didn't understand what was being said and didn't like that. And when I talked to the students who were saying mean things, the ones who can't speak, they told me that they had been discriminated against in their primary schools because they were speaking their language [Zapotec]. And when they told their families about it [the discrimination], the families said, "Why should we keep speaking Zapotec if they [society] tell us it is backwards? We have to speak Spanish." And so they [classmates] didn't keep their language and tease the ones who did. And others say, [Zapotec] language, it doesn't serve us at all, why should we speak it? (Anonymous, 2018f)

This exchange touches on multiple themes. First, it shows how past generations experienced discrimination because of Indigenous identity and that such discrimination is not currently experienced by someone who identifies as Indigenous, indicating a societal and institutional shift toward greater acceptance of indigeneity. Second, the student also shares how among students, embedded racism and internalized oppression continue to pervade social dynamics through the teasing of Indigenous language speakers. Third and more broadly, this interview highlights the complex social dynamics at play for young Zapotec-speakers in the public school setting where Indigenous language access is both an identity-validating mechanism for speakers and a potential source of shame for those whose families have not passed on the language in attempts to protect their children from further stigmatization.

Many students at BIC 29 had pride in their abilities as Zapotec-speakers, which is a testimony both to their families and communities who continue to emphasize the importance of the language and to the school's role as a source of institutional validation for language ability. Another student told me:

To speak my language, it does not cause me to feel intimidated—I feel pride to speak. I don't feel that it is something ugly, but rather it is part of my personal development. Speaking doesn't threaten me.

In my town [a few towns over from Teotitlán del Valle] we speak almost the same variant as here, with just some words different, so I am doing well in the language class. But I know so many parents and grandparents in my town who talk about being hit at school when they spoke [Zapotec] so they either stopped going to school or stopped speaking their language. (Anonymous, 2018g)

Intergenerational transmission interruption due to the discrimination-based shame of a previous generation of speakers was one of the most common points of overlap in interviews with heritage-speakers across Oaxaca and California. Dozens of interviewees offered similar versions of the same story; they didn't speak their Indigenous language because their predecessors had been discriminated against or physically abused for speaking it, and to spare their children the same experience, they chose not to pass down the language. For example, another BIC 29 student from a neighboring valley town remarked: "I would like to learn Zapotec. Only my grandparents speak, but they speak to us in Spanish because neither my parents nor my brother speaks Zapotec. They didn't want my parents to learn, and to suffer like they did. So I am taking as much advantage as I can of the Zapotec class at school, to learn new words and a new culture" (Anonymous, 2018j). Even though this student is a heritage-speaker, meaning she has Zapotec-speakers just two generations back in her family, because of intergenerational transmission interruption, she is approaching the Zapotec class as if it is a whole new culture. Her own parents raised her with a more assimilationist identity, viewing mestizo culture and the Spanish language as things that would benefit their children more than their Zapotec roots.

The potential for the formal education sector, through curriculum selection and implementation, to play a formative role in supporting positive Indigenous identity formation is evident from the examples thus far. What is more subtle is how processes of youth identity consolidation may translate into civic, cultural, and political participation choices. Students talk about being simultaneously drawn into the ongoing patterns of family identity; for example, many see weaving and selling weavings as a viable economic future, as did their parents and grandparents before them. At the same time, the impact of globalization, particularly through media consumption, clothing, and an interest in English, diminishes the formation of Indigenous or "traditional" identities. Formal education by no means influences this alone but instead is one of many variables for young people, albeit one that constitutes a significant portion of their daily routine.

Intervening Variables in BIC 29 Student Identity Formation and Participation

Many variables contribute to the identity-formation process and participation choices that young people make, including family norms, community climate, school climate, cultural relevancy of teaching, migration legacies, and the regional political context. Each of the chapters addresses a variety of these variables in relation to the case studies. In the section below, I single out two variables that are particularly salient for understanding Oaxacan youth issues: the way that migration patterns inform youth identity, and the influence of Oaxaca's highly political environment on participation choices. Migration has changed and continues to change the value assigned to language repertoires, as high emigration from Oaxaca to the United States creates a cultural incentive to prioritize English over Indigenous languages in schools and communities. The second variable, Oaxacan politics, is a volatile backdrop of protest tactics that disrupt daily life and may lead to highly polarized opinions about the merits of political participation, yet this backdrop affects people in a range of ways depending on their profiles and locations. Each variable is explored in turn below.

Migration Legacy Impact on Students

Oaxaca as a state has a deep history of migration both to the United States and internally from rural to comparatively more urban areas or to other Mexican states (Cohen & Ramirez Rios, 2016: 223–228). Of all Oaxacan migrants, 96.5 percent go to the United States, and alongside Mexico's other most Indigenous and poorest states like Chiapas and Guerrero, Oaxaca has a negative net migratory balance, meaning that more people leave the state than enter it (INEGI, 2020b). While Oaxacan migration to the United States has declined in recent years, first-generation migrants' decisions to stay in the United States, combined with lower fertility rates and higher internal migration, have changed many Oaxacan village demographics (Robson et al., 2018: 299–323), including Teotitlán del Valle. A discussion of the impact of such migration on local participation for communities as a whole is outside the scope of this book, and the effects of migration on Indigenous governance and cultural survival have received serious consideration elsewhere (Barabas, 2016: 81; Robson et al., 2018: 299–323; Stephen, 2007).

In my ethnographic work, students and adults from valley communities including Teotitlán del Valle, Santa Ana del Valle, and Tlacolula de Matamoros estimated that roughly 30 percent of their town's members were currently working in the United States or elsewhere in Mexico, beyond Oaxaca. I also queried self-estimates from people in other Oaxacan communities such as San Pablo Guelatao in the Sierra Juárez mountains and Huajuapan de León in the Mixteca region, who responded similarly. Respondents were asked to first imagine their street with ten houses on it and to estimate how many people from their street had a long-distance family member, and then to imagine a subsection of their community, such as a school or neighborhood of one hundred people, and similarly estimate the number of migrants. While by no means statistically sound, this line of questioning helps illustrate the perception of many young people I interviewed that migration is ubiquitous. This loose accounting for migrant numbers serves to inform students' notions that migration is one of several viable options for their future, which in turn may shift the matrix of considerations for school success as well as for local participation. Students who imagine they will soon be working in the United States may have less motivation to both achieve excellence academically and get further involved in their local communities.

The issue of migration is particularly salient for one growing number of students in Oaxaca—those whose families have returned after living for a period of time in the United States. Some of these students had family members deported, while others chose to return of their own volition to care for a sick relative, trading the financial benefit of working in the United States to honor familial ties. Students' citizenship is also heterogeneous. While some were born in Oaxaca, taken to the United States by parents when they were young, and brought back to Oaxaca by their family members for a range of reasons, others were born in the United States and now hold dual citizenship. This issue was brought to my attention in a roundabout way when I was collecting data at BIC 29 on how many students held a national scholarship to support them financially to stay in school.

In spring 2020, there were eight BIC 29 students who had been born in the United States to Oaxacan parents who had since returned. Because these students' Mexican national identity cards[9] had an "Ex" for *extranjero*, or foreign-born, on it, they were unable to receive their federal well-being scholarship for at least a semester, while the school director worked with the federal agency to address the problem. Bureaucratic snafus such as this one, which are highly significant for families who count on scholarships to keep their kids in school with requisite funds for school fees, uniforms, and transport, highlight the role technical obstacles may play in youth identity formation, participation choices, and school success.

There is another population of students affected by migration at BIC 29 and many other schools throughout Oaxaca: those who said at one time, if not in the present moment, their father worked in the United States. While some had a father who had since returned, after being absent much of their childhood, a few interviewees talked about not having seen their father since they were infants and held back tears as they described what this meant for them and their families. Many students talked about having aunts, uncles, or cousins in the United States who would send back remittances but said that they would rather have the family member back, though the students said they knew their families appreciated the money.

This type of economically based family fragmentation can affect the well-being of the whole family. While materially beneficial, family fragmentation can underlie depression, anxiety, and negative behaviors that manifest because of a sense of abandonment, isolation, or identity fragmentation for those who hold dual citizenship or feel connected to the United States as well as Mexico. The majority of students I spoke with at BIC 29 talked about wanting to migrate themselves, either internally for further study or work or to the United States. While some students who come from Teotitlán del Valle weaving families described their plan to study in Oaxaca's capital and then return to help run the family business, others just wanted to leave to find better opportunities.

Migration might decrease but it will not disappear. Oaxacan schools will continue to host students with a range of migration legacies, from those who have returned from time spent in the United States to those who have a migrant parent or parents. Understanding the effect of migration on identity formation and participation choices, as well as school success, is vital not just for the scholarly community but for the teachers and administrators on the front lines of student engagement. Migration as a part of globalization will continue to form social and linguistic realities for Mexicans, in addition to economic and political shifts. As an intervening variable, migration wields tremendous power to shape the identity and participation choices young people make every day.

Effects of Oaxacan Politics on Student Learning

Students at BIC 29 interface with politics in a variety of ways, all of which contribute to their sense of what is politically possible for themselves and their communities. Oaxaca is a highly politicized state in Mexico, with a history of intense social protest movements including strikes, roadblocks, and sit-ins, and from all sectors of society, from teachers and health workers to rural Indigenous communities (Davies, 2007; Gellman, 2017; Indigenous Peoples of Oaxaca Forum, 2006; Oaxaca, 1992; Pye & Jolley, 2011; Stephen, 2013: 59, 64–67). And yet in Teotitlán del Valle, politics mostly refers to usos y costumbres and the community assemblies that are the site of most governance decision-making in the town. While in some ways Teotitlán del Valle is a model of usos y costumbres, with regular voluntary service meeting the needs of community members, the town is now regionalized (people move there from other parts of Oaxaca) and globalized (migrants return or families have members living abroad). Many students, teachers, and staff come from outside Teotitlán del Valle and are therefore more exposed to wider political contexts than town locals might be.

However, even those locals, as described above, may have migratory links with family elsewhere, or have migrated themselves. In addition, the politics of allowing migrants to pay people to serve their cargos if they are living elsewhere has taken on a political life of its own. Though for years a topic of much debate, this practice of cargo substitution has become widespread in many Indigenous villages in Mexico, where the migrant selected to do the cargo pays approximately US$15 per work day to the person serving as their substitute, thus allowing the migrant to continue working elsewhere and providing an income for the substitute who may have to leave their regular job to shoulder the cargo responsibilities.

Students and families who live in the town are somewhat insulated from the state-level politics raging in the capital, although not entirely. Most teachers at BIC 29, as well as the director, live in Oaxaca de Juárez and make the forty-five- to sixty-minute commute daily to the school. The highway leading into the city is periodically blocked in either direction, making those commuting either late for school or, on the way home, late picking up their own children from school. Though BIC 29 students predominantly come from surrounding communities and are generally not affected by political road-blocks, usually one or two students per term commute from Oaxaca de Juárez.

The displaced BIC 29 student I interviewed in 2018 described what it was like, after fleeing extreme political violence in her village, where rival po-litical factions were assassinating each other, to arrive in Oaxaca de Juárez and have to navigate the roadblocks and other protests. Though she was frus-trated by the fact that she was usually late getting to school because of the roadblocks, she also saw first-hand why people protested. She works in a restaurant on the central plaza in Oaxaca de Juárez on the weekends, right in front of the displaced Triqui encampment,[10] and she commented that she thought it was important that they were asking the government for help (Anonymous, 2018c).

Most BIC 29 students do not describe being at all engaged with or in-formed about state-level politics or urban issues. However, in contrast to students I interviewed at an urban high school, featured in Chapter 5, BIC 29 students demonstrate much higher levels of knowledge about, and par-ticipation in, local-level civic, cultural, and political happenings. This is in line with cultural expectations of village life—that people will all participate to keep the community functioning, as usos y costumbres systems have en-abled since long before the invention of the modern state.

For example, BIC 29 students mentioned accompanying their parents to community assemblies at some point and knew that they would become vot-ing members when they turned eighteen, although girls frequently men-tioned that they didn't expect their voices to really count until they were married. A few female students mentioned not feeling welcome at assemblies, while others showed little interest. The exclusion of girls and women from political and civic forms of participation in traditional Indigenous commu-nities continues to haunt human rights advocates in southern Mexico. In fact, gender discrimination has long brought to the forefront tensions over respect for Indigenous governance methods versus liberal values of inclusion (Dan-ielson & Eisenstadt, 2009). In this case, gendered exclusion is one more factor that contributes to an understanding of participatory trajectories. Overall, political participation for BIC 29 students was low, with more involvement at the community level and almost none beyond the village level.

For students who had grown up in traditional communities like Teotitlán del Valle and Santa Ana del Valle, civic participation was higher than it was for political participation. Numerous students mentioned participating in some aspects of *tequios*, or special voluntary community service projects that usually last a day or two at a time. Female students described taking part in domestic tasks like helping their mothers make tortillas to feed the men doing physical labor, and both male and female students mentioned participating in community cleanup projects like street cleaning or clearing fields. While not explicitly civic participation, because it takes place within individual family homes, it is worth noting that most students commented that they spend their free time helping to cook, clean, or take care of younger siblings, with only one boarding student saying that he rarely helps with housework either at home or where he boards. In other words, students are participating significantly in family and community labor, but in forms that may not be immediately recognizable as participation to an outside observer.

Cultural participation for students at BIC 29 engaged the broadest number of students in a wide range of ways. Female students and a few male students mentioned participating in local dance groups, and one student had been a representative of Zapotec language continuity at cultural events for two years. Many students reported helping their families with aspects of traditional artisan production, from carding, spinning, and dyeing wool to learning to weave themselves. Unsurprisingly, given the strong Indigenous cultural profile of Teotitlán del Valle, cultural participation was generally robust for female and male students from the town and from other nearby artisan towns. For students who came from the *fraccionamientos*, or government-sponsored housing projects, which tend to host heritage-speaking families at least a generation or two removed from more rural Indigenous lifestyles, cultural participation was lower.

Students from the *fraccionamientos* did not exhibit the same level of civic participation as students from traditional towns in no small part because basic custodial tasks like street cleaning and brush clearing there are performed by paid employees rather than as part of community service projects that require community volunteerism to function. In addition, though generally low for all BIC 29 students regardless of place of origin, political participation is generally higher in the traditional villages where students see their family members perform cargos and participate in community assemblies, while students from elsewhere did not have this kind of political participation role-modeled to the same extent.

Overall, it is clear that the high accountability in traditional village frameworks promotes higher levels of civic, cultural, and political participation, although some students from outside these communities have still found meaningful ways to participate. Each student, based on their family and geographical base, interacts with the curricular opportunities at BIC 29 in different ways. Oaxaca's segmented politics—with political parties controlling the *fraccionamientos* and less Indigenously rooted towns and cities, and usos y costumbres governing Indigenous villages—play a role in determining the self-identity patterns that inform participation choices for young people.

Conclusion: BIC as Mother Tongue Celebration

The BIC system was designed to deliver culturally respectful education that strengthens the language, culture, and communality of Indigenous communities in Oaxaca (Secretaría de Educación Media Superior, 2014: 13–14). In numerous articles of the State Education Law, protections for preserving Indigenous language access are laid out alongside a commitment to value and promote political, economic, and social systems of Indigenous communities (Secretaría de Educación Media Superior, 2014: 16–17). The 2003 General Law on Linguistic Rights of Indigenous Peoples recognizes sixty-three Indigenous languages as national languages, alongside Spanish, and cites their importance in a healthy democracy (Government of Mexico, 2003; Secretaría de Educación Media Superior, 2014: 65). While like all legal documents these laws are aspirational and do not deliver in practice what they espouse, they are important because they demonstrate a legal recognition of Indigenous language access as intertwined with pluriethnic democracy.

The CSEIIO system that oversees the BICs tries to put the above-mentioned values into practice by offering Indigenous language access to students from a range of backgrounds. Challenges abound. Indigenous students at BIC 29 wonder how speaking Zapotec will benefit them; English might appear to be a better use of time if students intend to migrate or work in the tourist industry. And yet at the same time, it is clear that speaking an Indigenous language is valuable, not just in monetary terms (for example, students are eligible for special college scholarships as Indigenous language speakers) but also in terms of cultural connectedness.

One powerful example of an identity-forming experience for BIC 29 students that I observed in both 2018 and 2020 was the International Mother Language Day celebration. In line with the United Nations Educational, Scientific and Cultural Organization (UNESCO), February 21 is a day of celebration of the mother language, which in Mexico is interpreted to mean Indigenous languages. Under the enormous arching laurel tree in the urban plaza that is considered the heart of Oaxaca's capital, each year a stage is set up and students from each of the BICs are bused in to perform original poetry and music in Indigenous languages, with live transmission on local television. The performance is preceded by a traditional *calenda*, or parade, featuring the many BIC high school bands that weaves through the city's main downtown streets. In both 2018 and 2020, the *calenda* and performances included hundreds of students and their family members and officials from each of the BIC communities, along with a smattering of tourists and a few people like me, White-skinned and taking notes. Students were giddy with excitement, their families were proud, and BIC administrators and teachers saw their purpose reflected back to them.

Events like the Mother Language Day celebration embody a hybrid identity encompassing both indigeneity and globalized modernity that has been long noted by postcolonial scholars (Canclini, 1989; Guerrettaz, 2019; Shlossberg, 2018). Students, teachers, staff, and community members embrace a certain degree of folklorization, being photographed by tourists and lauded for Indigenous cultural and artistic practices. Such folk performance coexists with modernist practices. Many students change from jeans and sneakers into their celebration *huipils*,[11] and nearly all of them had phones tucked into pockets or, for girls, purses added to their outfits just for the sake of keeping phones close. Students, both at the event and in life, switch back and forth between Indigenous languages and Spanish in a fluid, code-switching manner that allows them to occupy multiple worlds at once. They can chat with their grandmothers in Zapotec while helping make tortillas, fight with siblings over whose turn it is on the computer in Spanish, and watch Hollywood movies in English with Spanish subtitles all in the course of an afternoon. Simultaneously, they can dream of taking over the family weaving business or emigrating to the United States. Many of the young people I spoke with see themselves as separate from previous generations of their family while still identifying as Indigenous.

The hyperpublic presentation of Indigenous language skills, alongside traditional clothes, music, puppets, and other Indigenous artistry, parading along Alcalá street, the pedestrian-friendly tourist vein of the city, and into the central plaza, shows students both the institutional and social legitimacy their Indigenous identities can hold. While students may go back to lives where they feel ashamed or limited by their Indigenous identities some of the time, interviews and ethnographic data clearly show a simultaneous and burgeoning pride in Indigenous self-hood. This is part of identity hybridization— after all, even the Zapotec teacher at BIC 29 texts with me on WhatsApp, and most of his students are on social media daily via their phones, all in Spanish. Most lack the written skills in Zapotec to hold forth on Facebook in the language.[12]

As students find the balance of assimilation versus tradition that works for them, they have the ability to be intercultural translators for their older family members, and for their extended communities. The Mother Language Day celebration featured not just Zapotec heritage-speakers but students from many other Indigenous communities as well, including those who had mostly stopped using Indigenous languages in their families. Even as students are folklorized by external audiences, they post videos of themselves dancing in *huipils* on Facebook and claim a multitude of ways of living as legitimate. Who gets to determine what indigeneity is? Ultimately, they do.

Access to Indigenous languages in the BIC system shows students that Indigenous language and identity are valued. This is true not just in the world of adults and institutions but informally in their interactions with classmates, as students experiment with gossiping in Zapotec or posting to social media in Mixe. The true impact of Indigenous language access for high schoolers may be unknowable, given the number of intervening variables at play in identity formation and participation choices. This case study has documented a snapshot of the complicated process by which young people at BIC 29 form the selves that will follow them into adulthood.

CHAPTER 5

"My Art Is My Participation": Language and Rights in Oaxaca de Juárez, Mexico

Introduction

The Miguel Cabrera Center for Artistic Education (Centro de Educación Artística "Miguel Cabrera," CEDARTMC) sits in an elegant former government administrative building in downtown Oaxaca de Juárez. Visitors and students enter through a wrought-iron gate and down a hall lined with posters announcing upcoming poetry readings and performances. The hall opens onto a Spanish architecture–style courtyard, in which trees share space with brightly decorated student-created puppets and scene paintings. Concrete classrooms and administrative offices ring the courtyard and contain few noise reduction elements to quell the student enthusiasm that bounces off the walls.

Stepping off the street and into the school feels like entering a counterculture den of the city. Students here are decidedly more pierced, tattooed, and fashion-savvy than the general population. Their dyed hair and flamboyant makeup are less common among age-mates elsewhere in Oaxaca, and virtually nonexistent within the BIC system. CEDARTMC's encouragement of individual expression is most visible in the lack of uniform requirement, which lets students dress as they choose, in contrast to the mandatory uniform policy in most other public and private schools in Mexico.

In general, the school emphasizes personal agency and creative expression. This is also visible in the generally egalitarian and humane approach of teachers and administrators toward students. Students are treated as autonomous young adults who have to make their own choices, for example, to arrive at class on time without a bell system or to complete an assignment by creating a dance, painting, play, or story (Anonymous, 2018s; Cárdenas González, 2018; Navarro Tomás, 2018). The freedom at CEDARTMC is exhilarating for many, and those with the ability to self-regulate thrive, while some who struggle with self-discipline do not (Anonymous, 2018r; Cárdenas González, 2018; Osorio Méndez, 2018; Sánchez Martínez, 2018).

CEDARTMC plays a special role within the four high schools featured in this book because it is the only one that does not offer an Indigenous language class. It is included to serve as a control, in order to better define the role that language access, or its absence, plays as a mechanism in identity formation and participation processes. Because CEDARTMC students take English classes for a comparable number of years as students in the other schools are required to take either Zapotec or Yurok, this case study helps unpack the way that youth identity is built across languages and cultural frames.

To foreshadow the CEDARTMC case-study findings, this chapter shows that while Indigenous language access is not necessary to build engaged youth identity—English language access appears to facilitate such identity formation too—the familial, cultural, and curricular context of schooling is meaningful for considering how young people want to participate in the world. CEDARTMC's academic and artistic foci lead students to prioritize cultural participation and interest in international issues. They devote less attention to civic participation and community issues than do their counterparts at BIC 29.

CEDARTMC Data Snapshot

From a hallway bench I can see into CEDARTMC's dance studio, where a lanky fifteen-year-old pulls a pair of ballet slippers out of his backpack decorated with band patches and counterculture pins. Pushing a shock of fuchsia hair out of his eyes, he turns to a fellow student who has her own slippers on already and is reapplying black lipstick in the studio mirror. "Bailamos!" he says, with hand extended to her. "Let's dance!" She tells me later the dance they created is about identity and what it means to be stretched across many worlds, from the Indigenous rituals of their grandparents to the technology they use to stay connected to their fathers who are working in the United States. Both students are dance majors, and their opus is for a student project they will perform for their class.

CEDARTMC is part of the National Institute of Fine Arts and Literature (Instituto Nacional de Bellas Artes y Literatura, INBAL) education system, which provides an upper secondary education referred to as *preparatoria* or *bachillerato*, equivalent to high school in the United States. There are twelve CEDART schools throughout Mexico, with only this one in Oaxaca. Unlike the BICs, which actively recruit students and are open to anyone, entrance to the CEDARTMCs is highly competitive. To be eligible to apply students must have at least an 80 percent attendance rate at their secondary school (Sánchez Martínez, 2018). As part of the admissions process, students participate in a weeklong period of exams and evaluations where faculty and administrators determine whether a student's abilities and profile are a match for the school. This holistic approach allows evaluators to consider academic performance, creative expression, and socioemotional student profiles in the selection process. In 2016, there were 240 applicants to CEDARTMC and 135 were accepted, and in 2017, 300 students applied. In spring 2018, when I conducted the majority of my CEDARTMC fieldwork, there were 350 enrolled students in the entire school across the equivalent of tenth, eleventh, and twelfth grades.

Admitted CEDARTMC students at any of the twelve schools must fulfill INBAL's general education requirements for a high school degree, which emphasizes competencies in arts and humanities. Although they do adhere to minimum shared curricular standards with Mexico's SEP, faculty have significantly more autonomy in designing curricula than they would at another type of high school program in the country. Some faculty and staff are CEDARTMC alumni themselves (Anonymous, 2018s; Sánchez Martínez, 2018). Many faculty either practice as or were artists in their youth and share an affinity with their students for innovation and creative expression.

In their third semester, CEDARTMC students choose a specialty track, or artistic focus, from dance, music, literature, visual arts, and theater options. For their remaining three semesters, students take specialized classes with others in their chosen track. General education classes mix specialties, enabling students across program tracks to continue to work together. One such general education requirement is English, which serves as the required foreign language requirement, and is taken for two years of the three-year program.

Compared to other public high school systems in Oaxaca, CEDARTMC students are generally from more middle-class families, with only 10–15 percent described as having high economic needs (Sánchez Martínez, 2018), although parents' educational backgrounds vary considerably. There is also a high proportion of legacy students, those whose parents, siblings, or other family members attended CEDARTMC before them (Cárdenas González, 2018). This means students have an awareness of the uniqueness of CEDARTMC prior to enrolling (Cortés Reyes, 2018). The 2017–2018 student body included young people from a range of ethnic backgrounds, with the majority listing their place of birth as Oaxaca de Juárez and surrounding areas, but more than a dozen students were born in traditionally Indigenous-identifying villages (Sánchez Martínez, 2017). In a CEDARTMC survey of the 131 incoming first-year students who completed the school guidance counselor's survey in fall 2017, only 3 listed that they spoke Zapotec, 22 listed speaking English, and 106 responded that they only spoke Spanish (Sánchez Martínez, 2017). The school's survey does not capture the significant ambiguity about Indigenous self-identity among young people in Oaxaca. Only a small number of CEDARTMC students speak an Indigenous language themselves, but many have grandparents or great-grandparents who do. In contrast, at BIC 29 parents or grandparents tended to be the Indigenous language-speaking generation, so Indigenous identity was a generation closer.

While the majority of students commute from some part of the urban capital, students also hail from many of Oaxaca's regions. Some students commute daily from small towns like San Jerónimo Tlacochahuaya, and others travel from more distant locations and board either on their own or with relatives in the city in order to attend school (Cárdenas González, 2018). In a testimony to the desirability of attending CEDARTMC, in 2017–2018 thirteen students said that they changed their address to facilitate their access to the school, including seven students who came from great distances in other parts of Oaxaca, and two from out of state; one student boarded alone in the city and seven students lived with brothers or sisters there (Sánchez Martínez, 2017). The school guidance counselor confirmed that these numbers are generally consistent year to year, and this speaks to the sacrifices students and their families make to ensure attendance once admission has been gained (Sánchez Martínez, 2018). At CEDARTMC, I collected 25 surveys and conducted 18 interviews, 2 focus groups with students, 4 interviews with teachers and administrators, and 40 classroom observations. I observed multiple levels of English language classes as well as Mexican Art History classes one to two times a week from March through June 2018, and I checked back in with teachers and administrators in 2020.

CEDARTMC School Climate

School climate is a major factor in each of the case studies in determining the social context in which identity formation is taking place and participation choices are being made. As one of many variables in this research puzzle, school climate runs the gamut from more inclusive to less inclusive. For example, CEDARTMC is a particularly inclusive school in terms of sexual identity but more hostile toward culturally conservative students, and these dynamics are visible in how students treat each other and talk about coexistence in their school.

All of the students I interviewed spoke positively about the school in general, and about their social groups—clustered within their specialties—in particular. However, numerous students readily cited specific examples when I asked about students being made fun of by their peers. The majority of the examples were about tensions across specialty tracks at CEDARTMC, with several students commenting that everything was fine within their specialty but that when specialties overlapped in classes and activities, students would frequently tease or insult each other. This meant that general education classes, including the two classes I regularly followed—English and Mexican Art History—were more fraught than the artistic practice classes.

Many students stated that teasing and bullying were much worse in primary and secondary school and that, in contrast, they found CEDARTMC to be much calmer and more amiable (Anonymous, 2018u; Martínez Martínez, 2018; Osorio Méndez, 2018). This was particularly true for students of nontraditional sexual orientations and alternative gender performances. Students who identified as LGBTQI+ talked about teasing in previous schools based on their sexual identities and how relieved they were to get to be themselves at CEDARTMC (Martínez Martínez, 2018; Osorio Méndez, 2018). One student who presents as female but introduced themselves as Juan said that they were miserable before coming to CEDARTMC but now have a strong friend group and feel like they can be themself. For LGBTQI+ students, CEDARTMC's alternative atmosphere and celebration of creative expression is a refuge.

This refuge is sometimes complex. In one interview the school counselor described an annual tradition at CEDARTMC, a party at which the students award prizes to each other for "biggest slut," "gayest student," and the like, and this is supposed to showcase that sexual diversity is accepted and that having sex and enjoying sexuality are good (Huerta Córdova, 2018). Though the prize party is intended to be funny, descriptions of it reveal the same underlying conservative values in Oaxaca as a whole, namely that the girl who sleeps around gets the "slut" prize and the boy who presents most feminine gets the "gay" prize; each of the prize categories is laden with social conflicts (Huerta Córdova, 2018). Though CEDARTMC presents itself as sexually inclusive, the prize category example shows how culturally conservative stereotypes are still at play at the school, sending messages to young people about what is and is not acceptable in terms of identity performance.

The school's reputation as an alternative cultural space is mired in the social judgment of a country, state, and society that remain largely Catholic and conservative. Even as many creative social movements and artistic events take place regularly in the city, in public spaces, and among childhood friends and their families who have gone to other high schools, students are judged for being at CEDARTMC (Huerta Córdova, 2018). Sometimes CEDARTMC's promotion of critical thinking and expression places children in conflict with their parents; for example, one student began questioning the existence of God after taking a philosophy class and refused to keep going to church with their religious family (Anonymous, 2018s).

The lack of uniforms, along with the high proportion of students with dyed hair and tattoos, leads people from outside the school to characterize CEDARTMC students as lazy. Even many parents who send their children to CEDARTMC see the arts as a pastime and not as a viable career path (Cárdenas González, 2018). In fact, students take fourteen subjects at a time and the academic standards are quite rigorous (Cárdenas González, 2018). But even within families there is tension with regard to CEDARTMC students' appearance—long hair, piercings, black clothes—and parents worry that their children will start using drugs and alcohol or reject Catholicism (Huerta Córdova, 2018; Sánchez Martínez, 2018).

One of the ways the counterculture tension is revealed in the school climate is in discrimination toward more conservative students. There have been problems between more liberal students and those who hold conservative political opinions, for example, with artsy students saying to conservative students "you are a sheep," calling them "slaves of the system," or criticizing the fashion choices of more mainstream students (Huerta Córdova, 2018). Nicknames meant as a rebuke, like "*fresa*" (preppy) or "*ñoña*" (teacher's pet), delineate mainstream students from "*los alternativos*" (alternative/counterculture people) and "*los hipsters*" (Cárdenas González, 2018; Huerta Córdova, 2018). One student in plastic arts who self-identified as being religious said she was mostly quiet and didn't feel like she fit in at school, though she was a good student and enjoyed her studies, and wasn't teased so much as overlooked (Méndez Vera, 2018).

However, in contrast to BIC 29 and general Oaxacan society where nicknames, both affectionate but frequently loaded with sociopolitical implications, are ubiquitous, at CEDARTMC faculty members have had some success in confronting this issue by asking students what they want to be called and encouraging people to honor students' choices (Anonymous, 2018s; Navarro Tomás, 2018). This may be connected to the LGBTQI+ solidarity framework of the school, where the presence of transgender students makes name politics especially pertinent. One teacher also mentioned trying to call attention to the gendered nature of words in Spanish in his classroom in order to raise awareness about how machismo is ubiquitous (Anonymous, 2018s). Overall, attempting to eliminate the culture of labeling students through nicknames that they don't affix to themselves helps reduce teasing.

Indigenous Identity

Indigeneity is mostly invisible at CEDARTMC. Those who identify as such are discreet about this part of themselves and tend to assimilate into the mestizo-dominant identity of the school to avoid stigmatization (Huerta Córdova, 2018; Navarro Tomás, 2018). To be sure, the Indigenous renaissance in Oaxaca has affected CEDARTMC students as well; there is certainly a pride in and revalorization of Indigenous culture in Oaxaca that CEDARTMC students are tuned into. When asked how they felt about not having an Indigenous language class, some students said that they wished they spoke an Indigenous language or that they wished their family hadn't lost their Indigenous language (Anonymous, 2018u). However, there continues to be a danger in romanticizing indigeneity in general, while not taking into full consideration the responsibility of this identity.

Academic success for Indigenous students who commute long distances to attend school, or who are renting a room and living in social isolation far from their families, is a matter of concern to the school counselor, though students who fit these profiles are generally highly motivated (Martínez Martínez, 2018; Sánchez Martínez, 2018). According to the counselor, Indigenous students who move to the city to attend CEDARTMC follow one of three paths: they spend a lot of time alone in their rooms if they have moved to the city to attend school; they are too adventurous and exploit their new-found freedom; or they are too fearful to explore the city and rely on the counselor to help them with directions about where to get what they need (Sánchez Martínez, 2018).

Also, the pressure students feel to assimilate culturally and act in similar ways as other students who don't face such additional burdens is real (Martínez Martínez, 2018). The tension between appreciating indigeneity in Oaxaca's Indigenous renaissance and the desire for a smartphone-laden urban, mestizo lifestyle reveals a gap between the Indigenous realities and deep inclusionary practices. This tension informs the way that Indigenous students navigate identity consolidation and participation choices as they try to straddle multiple social worlds and family commitments, as well as survive economically.

While this book mostly centers around student voices, the CEDARTMC English teacher Ms. Navarro, a graduate of the school herself, offers a particularly poignant reflection on her ethnic background. I quote our exchange below to illustrate the social context of Indigenous identity navigation that is shared across students and teachers in Oaxaca:

> I identify as an urban resident with Zapotec roots, because [my] mother is from the Sierra [Juárez, a Zapotec region], and my father's mother is from Huatla [de Jiménez, a Mixtec region], but she doesn't like the idea of saying she is from there; for her, she is from the city. In my family, no one speaks another language. My mother knows how to speak Spanish and Zapotec, and she keeps speaking Zapotec with her family, but with us [her children] she didn't want to teach us, because she decided that it wouldn't serve us to learn Zapotec. Well, later I told her it would have been a good idea, but when we were little she would only speak to us in Spanish. But I feel very close to the culture of my mother, or rather, to its customs, and traditions, which we still have at home. And when we go to community celebrations in the village or in our neighborhood, we participate, so the culture is not so close, but it also isn't so far away.
>
> I would have liked to learn to speak Zapotec, but I know I couldn't . . . my mother doesn't know how to write it, but she speaks and understands it. She wasn't educated in a mother tongue system, where she could learn it in school, and so she didn't want to teach it to us, so that is how Zapotec was lost in my family. (Navarro Tomás, 2018)

This portrayal of hybrid-Indigenous and urban identity, along with a common pattern of language loss, is shared by Ms. Navarro and some of her students and fellow teachers, and with many Oaxacans who have Indigenous roots but urban lives.

A third-year student has grandparents from the Sierra Juárez region close to where Ms. Navarro's mother is from, but neither she nor her parents ever learned any Zapotec because her grandparents wanted to avoid further discrimination against their children in what this student describes as "a little bit of a classist society" (Anonymous, 2018r). Like Ms. Navarro, she describes Indigenous-based customs as important to her family, despite their lack of Indigenous language knowledge (Anonymous, 2018r). This same profile is held by another teacher, whose grandparents are also from the Sierra Juárez and who also was not taught Zapotec. A student whose grandparents spoke Chinanteco also said they didn't teach her mother or her because they didn't want anyone else to go through the discrimination they had experienced (Anonymous, 2018u). This was echoed by a student whose grandfather spoke Nahuatl but did not pass the language on to his children or grandchildren (Anonymous, 2018b).

Esteban, a first-year student, commutes from a small, majority-Indigenous town and has Zapotec-speaking parents but does not speak it himself. He aspires to a career in theater or politics, and he is also the transitional generation in his family (Martínez Martínez, 2018). Some Oaxacans use the term *transicional* (transitional) to refer to the generation that is the first to leave major traditions of indigeneity behind, whether language, dress, occupation, or place of residence. This is similar to the notion of Indigenous-descendants discussed in the previous chapter. Esteban could have gone to BIC 29, much closer to home and his own Indigenous identity, but he wanted both a theater program and an urban lifestyle and sought out CEDARTMC to achieve these goals.

Esteban's and Ms. Navarro's family histories in relation to their own realities paint a picture of intergenerational language loss coupled with a reduced cultural continuity that is shared by many. Yet Oaxacans descendant from Indigenous families don't always have the vocabulary to define themselves in relation to shifting language and cultural practices. Ms. Navarro elaborates about the role of language as a key ethnic identifier: "People ask if you speak the language to know if you belong to a group, because if you don't speak the language, it doesn't matter how many other customs you adopt, you aren't in it. It was like that when I asked about scholarships at the university—they told me, 'it doesn't matter if your mother speaks it [an Indigenous language], if you don't, you aren't eligible.' This is also true of federal programs [for aid to Indigenous people], to be included in them, you have to demonstrate that you speak the language" (Navarro Tomás, 2018). Ms. Navarro shows that regardless of other aspects of indigeneity, if people do not speak an Indigenous language, they are not considered Indigenous per se but rather inhabit a more fungible space of identity hybridity that is not as lucrative in terms of scholarships yet easier in terms of gaining the benefits of mestizo social assimilation. This Indigenous-descendant identity in Oaxaca is pervasive and exemplifies a twenty-first-century hybrid sense of self that fits within traditional Indigenous cultural practices as well as operates within cultural, economic, and political globalization frameworks.

Effects of English Language Access at CEDARTMC

CEDARTMC does not include Indigenous languages in its curriculum but instead offers English. In my data collection, I was especially interested in the similarities and differences in how students and teachers at CEDARTMC talked about the role of English in their lives, versus how teachers and students discussed the role of Indigenous languages in BIC 29 and the California high schools. The similarities are, simply put, that access to another language—particularly one laden with socioeconomic benefits and cultural complexities like English in the context of Oaxacan migration to the United States—pushes students to consider intercultural contexts and other perspectives that help expand their ability to relate to others. However, as expected, English language access does not serve the identity-strengthening role for Indigenous and Indigenous-descendant students that Indigenous language access does. Instead, English language access serves to further assimilationist plans for students, who are more interested in gaining scholarships to study abroad than they are in connecting with the culture of their grandparents.

With her classes at CEDARTMC, Ms. Navarro hopes that English language access, whether it is a second language for Spanish-only speakers or a third language for those who also speak an Indigenous language, can be a tool that opens more global communication (Navarro Tomás, 2018). Navarro recognizes that for her students, English classes help them to be more tolerant of expressions, cultures, and languages of other people and to be respectful of the different inner workings of those cultures. In other words, the level of tolerance and respect for the "other" increases greatly with the acquisition of another language, regardless of what language that is. This is because for both those who do and do not have Indigenous language skills, all are able to better relate to other perspectives introduced through language frameworks. CEDARTMC students are frequently called by other schools to come teach English workshops or help with English classes because they are perceived as having advanced English skills and as being professional (Huerta Córdova, 2018). Such work experience exposes students to other social contexts as they participate educationally, and they gain intercultural information through the English curriculum itself (Huerta Córdova, 2018).

In addition, by becoming versed in English CEDARTMC students may better understand what is happening in the online world. The internet sites many students use are at least partially in English, and with English skills they also have more opportunities to share their art or craft with the world. Ms. Navarro describes how she discusses these themes in class as students learn the language:

> Students begin to understand the things they already see every day, as some read some small news texts on the internet, or watch videos, especially on Facebook, which are in English. Well, before [learning English] they say, "I only saw the images, but now I understand what they say."
>
> I also have students who do not see the meaning of learning English, who say, "Why do I learn English if I am going to dedicate myself to something else?" So I use examples, for dance students, look at Anna Pavlova, she was Russian, but she had to learn to speak English, because if not, she was not going to be able to do everything she did! With any artist that you tell me, they need the language, because if not, they cannot do more, they cannot leave where they are, and look for other possibilities.
>
> So little by little, students are assimilating the idea that language is a tool that will serve them, in order to expand their horizons, and that they will not only have access to what is here. They learn to appreciate the "other" as part of the things that are in the world that we have to live with and that can help us. (Navarro Tomás, 2018)

In this way, Ms. Navarro helps students see the real-world practicality of learning English in terms of both their social media consumption and their professional aspirations. Juan, in their[1] final semester of study at CEDAR-TMC, commented that they have always liked learning English and hoped it would let them continue on to a foreign exchange program where they could spend time abroad and learn more about their art (Osorio Méndez, 2018).

While BIC schools include English alongside Indigenous language instruction, the majority of Mexican public schools offer only English as the non-Spanish language option, thus presenting a narrow scope of what multilingualism can be. The notion of English as the necessary second language in Mexico carries with it some of the assumptions about the benefits of assimilating into the majority for upward socioeconomic mobility. There are benefits to learning English, given Oaxaca's tourism economy and the larger Englishization of the world, but such prioritization also has significant political implications.

Some students explicitly do not want to learn English because it is the language of imperialism. Ms. Navarro recounted an example of this that shows the link between language and political participation: she responded to a student who made the argument about imperialism by saying, "Good, protest in Spanish, but there are more people in the world who understand English, so even if you don't like it [the imperialism of English], it is the way we communicate with the world" (Navarro Tomás, 2018). By encouraging this student to make their protest bilingual, Ms. Navarro is rightly citing the broader reach of the message if done in both languages. At the same time, the implications of such cultural globalization are fraught. Students in the music track at CEDARTMC tend to come from outside Oaxaca de Juárez, where traditional Oaxacan music is often a core value of more Indigenous and rural communities, and these students frequently have family members from their villages living in the United States (Navarro Tomás, 2018). For these students, conveying the importance of English is less necessary, as they already knew how useful it could be from talking to their migrant family members (Navarro Tomás, 2018).

What, then, about the impact of the absence of Indigenous languages? CE-DARTMC students and teachers exhibited high degrees of trauma from colonization and assimilation processes in their reflections on interrupted intergenerational transmission of Indigenous languages. The number of students, teachers, and administrators who identified as second- or third-generation Oaxacans of Indigenous descent, and who felt some kind of cultural connection to their Indigenous heritage even in the face of language loss, was high. What could it mean to such a school to bring Indigenous language teaching into the curricula? Several members of the CEDARTMC community mentioned wishing they spoke their family language, but the gaze toward the national and international artistic community keeps English firmly in place as the language requirement.

In light of this reality, it is important to mention the many ways that the school does promote Indigenous culture and identity. Many interviewees cited Day of the Dead rituals at school, which feature their own artistic creations, as Indigenous-based and meaningful to them personally based on their family legacies. Others spoke of learning about Indigenous art and artists in their Mexican Art History classes, and how powerful it was to see people with whom they could ancestrally identify represented in formal educational spaces. Though the absence of Indigenous languages in the curriculum does silence—especially as it is paired with the prioritization of English—CEDARTMC students continue to explore ways to resist culturecide through their art.

Oaxacan Politics as a Factor in Identity and Participation

Oaxacans live in a hyperpoliticized environment. For decades, the state has had a domestic and international reputation as a place with low state capacity and high levels of political grievances (Cook, 1996; Métais, 2018; Ornelas, 2008). A range of groups, from labor unions to Indigenous peasants, routinely use extra-institutional mobilization tactics such as strikes, blockades, sit-ins, and boycotts after exhausting their institutional means of protest (Gellman, 2017: 64–67; Stephen, 2013). Such contentious political tactics provide a visual and auditory rallying point for grievance-holders that sometimes has pushed governments to change their own agendas. But along the way, these tactics also cause significant inconveniences for Oaxacans trying to go about their daily lives.

Dozens of people I interviewed from a range of locations and schools, including CEDARTMC and BIC 29 students and teachers, as well as Autonomous University "Benito Juárez" of Oaxaca (Universidad Autónoma "Benito Juárez," UABJO) students and faculty and alumni from academic support programs throughout the state, complained about the strikes and roadblocks along their commutes. Contentious political strategies negatively impact student learning most significantly when roadblocks cause delays in punctual arrival to school and when increased transportation costs for students or family members stress the household (Anonymous, 2018t, 2018u, 2018v). To illustrate, when commuters encounter a roadblock, they have to exit public transport—a bus or collective taxi—at the blockade, find a way through it on foot, and then reenter transport on the other side, when normally the first vehicle would have taken them all the way to their destination. This means commuters have to pay twice, which quickly adds up if one regularly encounters blockades, which is very possible on a weekly or monthly basis across Oaxaca de Juárez and its many arteries.

Juan, who commutes from Santa Cruz Xoxocotlán, mentioned that usually a few times per month they have to cross blockades and that some protesters have attacked commuters with machetes when they try to get around the blockade on foot (Osorio Méndez, 2018). A first-year student talked about the many fights he has seen between transportation union members at the blockades, and about how generally violent the protests are in his neighborhood (Anonymous, 2018t). Another student said that her mother sometimes has to cross roadblocks to get to her job in the Administrative City, on the outskirts of Oaxaca where many government offices are located, that her neighbor who works in a restaurant has her pay docked when she is late because of the roadblocks, and that she herself is frequently late to school because of them (Anonymous, 2018r). She expressed how she is frustrated that the roadblocks affect regular people much more than the government and showed no interest in the protesters' issues, just annoyance at how they affected her community (Anonymous, 2018r). Another student told me that "the roadblocks are a mess—it is poor people preventing other poor people from getting to work or school. It isn't changing what those in power do" (Anonymous, 2018v).

Esteban, who commutes an hour each way from Tlacochahuaya, estimates that he has to cross road blockades seven to eight times per month (Martínez Martínez, 2018). The extra expense, in addition to the emotional stress of having to navigate protestors who often scream at or threaten commuters for crossing the roadblocks, is one negative way that Oaxacan politics impact CEDARTMC students. At the same time, Esteban, who described himself as a politics junkie and the most politically engaged person in his social group, says he wants the government to actually deal with poverty and its many issues, and he would be okay with the blockades if they worked but he wasn't sure they did (Martínez Martínez, 2018).

One major effect of Oaxaca's political disfunction is a sense of general disappointment in, and disengagement from, political systems. One student commented that "it is all corrupt, and you never know if what politicians say is the truth" (Anonymous, 2018t). Juan noted that "people are tired that things just keep staying the same as always" and so they disengage (Osorio Méndez, 2018). Saúl, an eighteen-year-old theater student, declared that politics "isn't something that has interested me much; in fact sometimes it seems like a waste of time. The candidates don't interest me, but the system at the base, democracy, does, but it has not been well-implemented" (Cortés Reyes, 2018). Saúl offered an astute analysis of Oaxaca's political situation, even while perceiving himself to be distant from it: "It is lamentable to see that in our society, protest is so normalized that people don't even really see it, like, 'oh, they are blocking the road again, like always.' But sometimes we don't even make ourselves think about what is behind it, like, 'what is provoking all these problems in the first place?' And we don't look for a solution. It's funny because in Oaxaca there are many types of people, but the most typical think 'those others are to blame, not me'" (Cortés Reyes, 2018).

On a more optimistic note, some students are able to gain a broader understanding about collective action as a political participation option from these experiences. Juan worked with a group of students after the 2017 earthquake to document damage to the school and demand that the authorities send an engineer to review it, because there were visible cracks in the building but the authorities had not made plans to inspect the buildings (Osorio Méndez, 2018). The fact that CEDARTMC students took it upon themselves to advocate their cause to the government may be partially based on their exposure to a range of ways for grievances to be aired, alongside an expectation that people can and should speak up when they want the government to take action.

Such participatory behavior has also taken place on the local scale. CEDARTMC students drew up a petition to reduce disposable bottles and cups on campus, and students continue to run the campaign for environmentally conscious consumption within the school, including collecting money to purchase refillable tanks of water for students to use to fill their water bottles (Anonymous, 2018s). In other words, while political participation may not happen all the time, for some students, the politicized environment of Oaxaca lends itself to the formation of identity that includes political action as one of many viable behaviors.

Saúl's parents are retired teachers, which gave him an inside look at Oaxacan politics at his own kitchen table: "I listened to my dad all my childhood about political problems, about reforms that teachers wanted to be approved in secret, about protests so that the government would not take away certain rights, on protests to make books free, on protests to give vouchers for uniforms, on protests because they [teachers] were not paid, on protests because the government did not give them [teachers and schools] the infrastructure. Protest, after protest, after protest, after protest, my dad was rooted in the arguments about protests" (Cortés Reyes, 2018). Students with friends or close family members who were part of unions and had discussed the strikes with them had much more informed perspectives on what the issues were, or at least general support for them. These interviewees either had participated in strikes or blockades or were usually educated about the conflict and sympathetic to the protesters because members of their family were participating. One student, whose parents are both teachers, stated, "It is good that they protest for their ideals. Usually they strike when the government doesn't pay them. But I don't really know what it is all about" (Anonymous, 2018y).

Varied awareness about Oaxacan politics due to family member involvement was also true for teachers, one of whom has a father and sister in the National Education Workers Union (Sindicato Nacional de Trabajadores de la Educación, SNTE) and saw both the pros (like health insurance) and cons (like corrupt mafias) of Oaxacan union organizing (Anonymous, 2018s). One student said a friend was paid MX$100 to wave a flag at a rally, and he thinks politicians' promises are empty and that democracy doesn't really exist, just the idea of it does (Anonymous, 2018b). Esteban, the commuter from Tlacochahuaya, doesn't have political family members but said if he didn't pursue a career in theater, he wanted to study law or investigate political candidates. He cited corruption in his local community as inspiration, saying that "for two years there has been no public transport in my village, but where did the funds go? This makes me want to investigate and tell people about it!" (Martínez Martínez, 2018). Mónica, from out of state, said she thought the politics in Oaxaca were in some ways better than where she was from because at least in Oaxaca the government was providing some services—in her home state "local officials didn't really do anything" (Méndez Vera, 2018).

When asked during our interviews, most students seemed to feel that extra-institutional protest in Oaxaca had not inspired increased political participation. The vast majority of student interviewees could not cite what the roadblocks were about or relate to them politically at all. Such contentious tactics also disrupt public education at many levels. Teachers who are part of the SNTE strike in May and June each year as union leaders enter nego- tiations with the state government about better pay and working condi- tions. Some years, the strikes cause school to be canceled for only a few days here and there, but many years, strikes last for weeks, disrupting life for the working families who rely on public schools, as well as minimizing the con- tact hours of educational time.

Obstacles and Support for Student Educational Success

Youth identity formation and participation choices are impacted by a vari- ety of factors, and this book specifically documents the larger context of the formal education sector in each case-study school, with special attention given to the challenges and sources of support young people articulate. At CEDARTMC, students report much satisfaction and appreciation for their school, including their courses, teachers, and classmates (Martínez Martínez, 2018; Méndez Vera, 2018). Students who are accepted to CEDARTMC worked very hard to get there, but this doesn't mean they all thrive once in the midst of a demanding curriculum and a socially intense environment. There are significant obstacles to academic success that also impact identity formation and participation choices. As at BIC 29, the three most common obstacles to student success are motivation, mental health, and finances. However, un- like BIC 29 students, overall, CEDARTMC students rank finances as an ob- stacle less frequently than either mental health or motivation. Each of the obstacles are addressed below, followed by the sources of support that stu- dents discuss.

The obstacle to educational success most mentioned by CEDARTMC stu- dents, faculty, and administrators is personal motivation to take coursework seriously. Many students described enjoying and being engaged in the class- room during in-person classes, and particularly enjoying their specialty classes, where they were able to dive deeply into expressing themselves in their preferred medium (Anonymous, 2018r; Méndez Vera, 2018). But students and teachers simultaneously cited "distractions" like partying, drugs, or hanging out with friends as activities that often took precedence over school- work for either themselves or others they observed in their classes (Anonymous, 2018r, 2018s; Sánchez Martínez, 2018). Students were self-aware regarding the potential consequences of this lack of motivation. The school director also mentioned that when students come to school intoxicated or having committed other transgressions that affect motivation or performance, there is a non-punitive, dialogic process to address the situation (Cárdenas González, 2018). Students also mentioned problems with time management (Anonymous, 2018r; Méndez Vera, 2018).

The second obstacle most frequently mentioned by students is their own mental health. Students discussed depression and anxiety as two factors that prohibited them from attending or participating in classes from time to time or from absorbing information when they were in the classroom (Méndez Vera, 2018; Osorio Méndez, 2018). Some students seek help from the CED-ARTMC counselor, who is tasked with helping first-year students adjust to CEDARTMC. The counselor also supports students with special profiles such as those who are renting housing on their own, living with non-parental family members, or commuting long distances in order to attend school (Sánchez Martínez, 2018). These three student sub-populations include the majority of students who identify as Indigenous.

While a few students mentioned seeking psychological counseling, more said they spoke with family members when mental health episodes occurred. Other interviewees mentioned fear of the stigma that continues to silence mental health issues in Oaxaca and in Mexico more broadly. One student described a negative experience when they tried to talk to the school counselor and family members about their issues, but this was an outlier.

The third most significant obstacle for CEDARTMC students is a lack of financial resources. Even at CEDARTMC, whose student body is more affluent than those at other public preparatory schools, many students shared concerns about being able to pay for both high school and college (Anonymous, 2018u; Martínez Martínez, 2018). I spoke with students who have paying jobs outside the home, from weekend shoe shining, to restaurant work, to helping family members run their small businesses (Anonymous, 2018v, 2018w). One teacher commented that students were not judgmental of those who had to work to pay their school fees, noting that two students in spring 2018 brought yogurts and sour mangoes to sell to other students at break times and that students would introduce themselves to each other based on their family's working-class identities, such as "I'm from the cheese booth" or "I'm from the juice booth," referring to their family's shops in the public markets (Anonymous, 2018s). One student I spoke with agreed that this lack of stigma generally prevailed but that there were a few cliques of more well-off students who were judgmental of those who were less so (Anonymous, 2018w).

Students in the visual arts specialty were the most likely to comment on economic hardship, as the cost of purchasing class materials for required projects was difficult for them (Méndez Vera, 2018). One of the CEDARTMC staff members, who works with faculty and students to reduce conflicts, mentioned that sometimes teachers would punish or look down on students who couldn't afford class materials but that she was working with teachers to increase understanding about these situations and design alternative solutions (Huerta Córdova, 2018). Navigating bureaucracy to access funds for schooling also posed a barrier. For example, one student was supposed to have a monthly government scholarship to counter school abandonment, but the money hadn't materialized in several months and she didn't know how to resolve the problem (Anonymous, 2018v).

The lack of smartphone, laptop, or home internet access were also cited as logistical barriers to staying on top of coursework (Cárdenas González, 2018). One teacher said that approximately 15 percent of her students needed to stay late at school to use the computer lab for class assignments or paid to go to an internet café (Navarro Tomás, 2018). This is roughly the same figure the school director cited as being in perilous economic circumstances (Cárdenas González, 2018). When students let this teacher know that they didn't have internet access, she was sometimes able to provide them with a photocopy of the assignment instead, but some preferred to not say anything to avoid drawing attention to their circumstances (Navarro Tomás, 2018). Although members of Generation Z are thought to be highly networked, I found that at least one student in each case-study school in both Oaxaca and California did not have a phone; a few more in each location had only a basic call-and-text-only phone. Given that most courses at CEDARTMC rely on some internet-based mechanism to communicate or access assignments, this financial and technical limitation is a significant one.

Whereas at schools like BIC 29 where nearly all students placed economic hardship as the top barrier to their academic success, most, but not all, students at CEDARTMC ranked it last. The exceptions (where finances really did seem to be the most influential determinant of student success) were clustered in particular demographics. These include students with high-cost specialties like plastic arts and students from rural and frequently Indigenous backgrounds who had to commute long distances (Anonymous, 2018u), those who rented a room or helped a family member with rent in the city, or whose non-legacy family did not have the capital to help them with school costs (Cárdenas González, 2018).

The class difference between students was also evident when I talked to students about how they used their time after school. Many CEDARTMC students commented that after finishing their homework, they spent time with friends, participated in cultural events like watching movies or going to poetry readings, and helped out at home (Anonymous, 2018r). For those with fewer economic resources, time after school was spent working at paying jobs. In addition, because CEDARTMC does not require uniforms, the visual ability to assess each other is a social liability, as students can tell who is wearing the same clothes they wore earlier that week and who has tattered or out-of-fashion clothes they can't afford to replace (Navarro Tomás, 2018). These obstacles to educational success are important for understanding the context of youth identity formation and participation choices.

Effects of Physical Insecurity on Students

The high level of physical insecurity students experience in their transport to and from school, as well as how daily insecurity shapes their extracurricular choices, was a strong and nearly unanimous theme of this research. Though it was not mentioned by students when I asked them about obstacles to their academic success, in a separate line of questioning about their own physical security, students indicated they were very scared of being harmed moving to and from school. Even those who live technically within the city limits, or just outside it, have arduous commutes made in multiple stages of public transportation every day; some leave home in the pre-dawn darkness in order to get to class on time. Other issues of physical insecurity such as domestic violence and gang violence also arose in these conversations. One student lives near the school in an area with gang violence and takes a taxi to school to avoid walking by gang members on his block (Anonymous, 2018t).

The vast majority of students, as well as some faculty and staff who take public transport to go to or from CEDARTMC, reported feeling unsafe in some aspect of their commute. Sources of insecurity include drivers or fellow passengers, as well as the need to cross roadblocks where violence frequently breaks out. Female students mentioned fear of assault, sexual violence, or robbery in public transport; several said that such an incident had happened to a female relative, friend, or neighbor or that they had witnessed such an act happening to a fellow passenger (Anonymous, 2018r, 2018u, 2018v, 2018y; Sánchez Martínez, 2018).

Many female students mentioned not wanting to attend evening classes or activities because they would then have to take transport at night and modify what they might like to wear to avoid male attention (Anonymous, 2018r, 2018u, 2018v, 2018y). One student, who lives on the outskirts of a rough neighborhood, pays to take a motorcycle taxi the last two hundred meters to her house if she returns at night because there are so many assaults on pedestrians on the unlit streets (Anonymous, 2018v). Male students reported generally feeling safe in their commutes in terms of fellow passengers and drivers, but they knew from their sisters or female classmates that women were regularly harassed and that fellow classmates had been robbed and assaulted, and that crossing political roadblocks was especially dangerous (Anonymous, 2018w; Cortés Reyes, 2018).

While numerous CEDARTMC students described the kind of physical insecurity mentioned above, two interviewees in particular were significantly traumatized by having witnessed family violence. In the case of one student, his family had relocated to avoid continued gun violence in another state; his mother feared for his safety to the extent that he was required to go home each day after school and lock himself in the house alone, as his mother works long hours, his father lives elsewhere, and he is an only child (Anonymous, 2018t). While this is an extreme case, the majority of students described returning home from school and locking themselves in their houses to ensure their physical security (Anonymous, 2018u).

However, there are also cases of parental fighting and domestic violence, rendering homes less of a refuge and more of a liability (Sánchez Martínez, 2018). In the case of a second student who had migrated within Mexico, she described Oaxaca as feeling safer than where she lived before, where she had seen dead bodies in the street more than once, although she still felt very unsafe in the city. In general, student trauma from past violence, or fear of future violence, significantly shapes student behavior because it limits their participation in a variety of ways. Students make logistical calculations to not attend workshops or events that take place at night because of increased risk of assault on their commutes home. They live with a general sense of vulnerability that translates into choices to be as invisible as possible by not participating and therefore not risking increased targeting. In sum, human security undeniably affects youth identity development and informs the participatory choices they make.

Sources of Support for Students and Professional Goals

Students cited their family members as supportive confidants and as people who might push them, but in helpful ways (Anonymous, 2018r, 2018u; Cortés Reyes, 2018; Osorio Méndez, 2018). Some students named administrators, teachers, and the school counselor as sources of support when they needed someone to talk to, as well as their social groups. Many teachers and administrators were perceived as truly caring about students and being willing to spend time with them—some teachers had been students at CEDAR-TMC themselves and this extra ability to identify with students helps them empathize (Anonymous, 2018s). Teachers made time before and after classes and during break periods to be available to students, who in turn were not intimidated to seek out academic help. CEDARTMC has also instituted a "homework workshop" staffed by faculty, where students can get more personalized help on whatever they are working on (Cárdenas González, 2018).

However, during the school day from 7 a.m. to 2:30 p.m., most teachers are in front of students the whole time and have few free moments. In addition, because teacher pay is low, most work additional jobs in the afternoon as private tutors or teachers in other programs (Huerta Córdova, 2018). As is common in many schools, CEDARTMC teachers are not professionally prepared to handle the range of student needs beyond their disciplinary expertise, including psychological, emotional, and social conflict issues. When students bring these issues to teachers, they are referred to one of the counselors, although most students were reluctant to admit they needed help (Huerta Córdova, 2018).

Some CEDARTMC students have relatively clear and pragmatic visions of their path to professional success beyond high school. Several of the students I spoke with are interested in pursuing artistic careers in line with their specialties, and they named the departments at different universities where they planned to go for further training (Anonymous, 2018r; Osorio Méndez, 2018). Other students identified three or four potential careers in mind and were unsure which path they would take (Anonymous, 2018u). Several interviewees, having realized upon their engagement with the CEDARTMC curriculum that they did not want to pursue a career in their specialties, talked about how they could use CEDARTMC training in critical thinking and expression in other careers.

The students' clarity and sophistication in relation to their academic and professional path plans stem from both inside and outside the school. The faculty who themselves followed similar career paths no doubt serve as positive role models, and their high-quality teaching and encouragement give students a narrative they can emulate (Anonymous, 2018s). A portion of the CEDARTMC student body is cosmopolitan, with college-educated parents and social groups who have helped students learn about their professional options early on, and being based in the state capital means they can explore those models in ways not available to rural students (Anonymous, 2018r; Méndez Vera, 2018). At the same time, many of those parents work long hours, and many young people are unsupervised and on their own for much of their adolescence (Cárdenas González, 2018). There are also some students who are the first in their families to attend upper secondary school and who do not have the social capital of their schoolmates, although the school does not gather this data explicitly. Roughly 70 percent of CEDARTMC students continue on to college (Cárdenas González, 2018).

Family economic status is the number one factor that determines whether students will pursue their artistic paths, according to the students themselves. As one student told me, "I want to be a sculptor, but I am afraid of failing, so going to school to be a nurse is my backup plan" (Layna Sarmiento, 2018). A student with more economic resources told me he was planning to take a sabbatical year after graduating CEDARTMC to consider what he really wanted to do and then apply to college (Anonymous, 2018b). In contrast, students with few economic resources talked about trying to go to college to pursue a degree in practical fields like accounting or science (Anonymous, 2018u). Some students said they wanted to be artists even though their families were worried they wouldn't be able to make a living (Anonymous, 2018r; Osorio Méndez, 2018). One student said he wanted to study psychology but his parents, a taxi driver father and street merchant mother, wanted him to study orthodontics to try to get ahead (Anonymous, 2018w). A few students with more economic options mentioned using their arts training to be a good team player and critical thinker in a more math- or science-oriented career if their artistic careers didn't take off (Cortés Reyes, 2018).

Migration as an Intervening Variable at CEDARTMC

The international literature on migration, and especially urbanization, coincides with a devaluation of ethnic identity and Indigenous or minority language (K. A. King & Haboud, 2014: 143; Tacelosky, 2018: 63–67). Oaxaca as a state has a very high level of migration both to the United States and internally from rural to comparatively more urban areas. While remittances are economically vital for many families, the list of social ills that accompany emigration, including depression, loneliness, and loss of traditional cultural values, makes migration more than just an economic phenomenon (K. A. King & Haboud, 2014: 144–145; Tacelosky, 2018: 75).

At CEDARTMC, migration operates fairly similarly to how it operates for BIC 29 students. Many students have fathers who have migrated for periods of time, and depending on the student's age, duration of parental absence, and circumstances of migration, this is more or less traumatic (Sánchez Martínez, 2018). The CEDARTMC counselor confided that one student's father had been in the United States since he was three, and his mother recently left to join the father, leaving the student alone and feeling rejected (Sánchez Martínez, 2018). Another student's father had been in the United States from when she was seven to eleven years old, and once, when he tried to return to the United States after a family visit, he was detained and deported; he now sells ice cream in the streets of Oaxaca and the student works to meet her school expenses (Anonymous, 2018v).

Esteban disclosed that he had a family member living in the United States, that his father had been deported, and that for every twenty people he knew in his community four or five had gone to the United States and had either been deported or returned on their own (Martínez Martínez, 2018). Other students had extended family members living in the U.S. that they talked to occasionally on the phone or on video chat, but they didn't really feel connected because the family member had been gone for so long (Anonymous, 2018b, 2018u, 2018y). When asked if he thought about migrating, one student from an economically difficult background on the urban periphery responded: "Staying here is easier than migrating—here you know where you can sleep at night" (Anonymous, 2018w).

Of particular concern for all Oaxacan schools is the management and support of *retornados*, students who have returned from time spent in the United States. Students return for a variety of reasons that influence their behavior in school. Some return with their families because their parents chose to return, others had parents deported and so the student returned as well, and in other cases students themselves were deported. The scenario of return informs the degree of trauma a given student may be experiencing.

Vilma Huerta Córdova, a school counselor and education scholar, identifies five major issues for returned students. First, returned students tend to have difficulty with Spanish language proficiency, especially in writing (Huerta Córdova, 2018). Second, they lack the social and cultural knowledge of how to operate in the Oaxacan context, making their ability to socially integrate more challenging (Huerta Córdova, 2018). Third, some returned students have a sense of superiority based on their spoken English level that leads to exclusionary or haughty behavior in the classroom—indeed, some may speak far better English than their teachers (Huerta Córdova, 2018). Fourth, returned students may be dealing with trauma based on family separation and relocation or the trauma of deportation (Huerta Córdova, 2018). Fifth, returned students may struggle with a sense of non-belonging in Mexico, in relation to the duration of time spent in the United States (Huerta Córdova, 2018). Although CEDARTMC does not collect statistics on returned students in a formal sense, more information is needed to determine how to best support this particular student population that brings unique challenges and resources to the high school.

Art as Participation for CEDARTMC Students

Regardless of rural or urban location, young people everywhere are navigating how they develop identities, individuate from family members, and make choices about how they want to participate civically, culturally, and politically in the world. While the formal education sector is only one of many influences on these processes, students spend at least half of every waking weekday during the school year within institutional purview. There are some universals across Mexican formal education institutions, but the influence of each individual school climate is significant as well.

CEDARTMC students do not necessarily participate in the same way that their age-mates at BIC 29 do. There is the sense that for CEDARTMC students, "art is their salvation" (Huerta Córdova, 2018), their way of expressing themselves and existing in the world in a way that is meaningful to them. Rather than taking explicitly political stances, students describe making art as a way to raise consciousness and educate others about a range of issues, including violence, migration, and Dr. Huerta Córdova describes CEDAR-TMC students as "young people who take risks of creating, who consume the state culture, and who involve themselves" (2018).

A theater-focused student described the role of art among his peer group:

What art always does is sensitize you, give you ideas, and you get to know history as well. Because without history you cannot know your background, so you cannot have a current perspective. . . . If we do not seek, if we do not inform ourselves, we cannot have arguments or grounds to say this [violence, corruption] is wrong. If we are not interested in art, in humanity, this [society] does not work. . . .

Theater leads you to many questions that I think frees you, and makes you a better person in your environment. Because in theater, you have to get along with your peers, it is collaborative, collective. . . . It is like a body, if one part of my body begins to go wrong, to not work, my whole body begins to feel bad. . . . The essence of an artist is a great accumulation of euphoria, of anger, of "I do not agree," . . . that is what makes people's minds change. Because they see it [a work of art, of theater] and they see something from another perspective and they say "I'm touched," and it helps them change, and that is very good. (Cortés Reyes, 2018)

The role of the artist is thus to convey emotion and perspective, and that can help wake other people up. Artistic expression for CEDARTMC students is a way of participating in the politics of the world in an indirect way.

Art can help foment political participation, and Oaxaca has a rich tradition of using graffiti, street art, theater, music, and other visual and aural displays to describe injustices in the world. For example, one student talked about the context of violence against women in Oaxaca, which activists decry through messages on posters and stencils on walls across the city. Another student reflected that he feels somewhat powerless as a citizen of his country, but he recognizes the way his role as an artist in the theater can help awaken audience members by creating plays about migration.

Whereas BIC 29 students see themselves as local actors but detached from the larger sphere of Mexican politics, CEDARTMC students, in part because of their artistic ambitions to have their work recognized in a broader sphere, tend to envision multilayered participation more focused on national and international issues. However, the urban lifestyle in an era of physical insecurity means that there is much lower civic participation by CEDARTMC students than at BIC 29. CEDARTMC students participate culturally, and in politics indirectly, but they are not active in their local communities because when they go home, they tend to lock themselves in to remain safe. In addition, the political party system by which Oaxaca's capital is governed does not provide the same mechanisms that normative Indigenous systems do, such as *tequios*, that allow for robust youth participation.

Despite these limitations, CEDARTMC also has many strengths in producing a next generation of young leaders. The school director cites self-structured learning and personal initiative, both required for artistic creation, as things that the school's curricula and pedagogy excel at promoting (Cárdenas González, 2018). Leadership qualities are expected of CEDARTMC students, and alumni have been selected for high-level civic roles in society, including as the arts and culture directors for several regional municipalities and in the capital, in part because of the school's reputation for producing capable leaders (Cárdenas González, 2018). In this way, CEDARTMC students move through their studies knowing they may have opportunities to actively participate in civic, cultural, and sometimes political roles.

Conclusion: English as Assimilation and Art as Resistance

From CEDARTMC, students gain employment opportunities based on their English language skills and leadership qualities in the classroom. Students are generally willing to embrace English because of the professional doorways they hope it can open. Few students showed real interest in the work of repairing Indigenous language loss, which the BIC system is designed to do.

Instead, CEDARTMC is a high school system that conceptualizes resistance and participation more globally than locally. Its dynamic counterculture of politicized artistic expression is harmonious with inclusionary values surrounding LGBTQI+ rights, economic diversity, and physical appearance. Young people's professional goals of "making it" as artists inherently look north to the United States rather than to local Indigenous culture. With high rates of migration from Mexico to the United States, and the dependency on tourism for the city's economic growth, the focus on English is pragmatic. After all, why shouldn't students flock to a language designed to facilitate upward socioeconomic mobility? And yet, what is lost in the process? While Indigenous culture is drawn upon in art, Indigenous languages have become a thing of the past for most of CEDARTMC's community members.

CHAPTER 6

Like Water Slipping Through Cracks in a Basket: Teaching and Learning Yurok at Hoopa Valley High School, California

Introduction: Yurok Language Access in California

The Hoopa Valley in far Northern California is home to Yurok, Hupa, and Karuk peoples who, despite the ravages of settler colonialism and forced assimilation, persist in cultural survival and continuity. From the coastal college town of Arcata, itself six hours north of San Francisco and two hours south of Oregon, the drive to Hoopa is another hour on a good day, when one has avoided roadwork (to keep the mountain from sliding down to cover the road and the road from sliding down the mountain) or fire closures. Wind up stuck behind a cargo truck on the one-lane highway that connects Arcata to Hoopa, and it can easily be ninety minutes. This makes the Hoopa Valley, known as *Natinook* in the Hupa language,[1] a remote place even in relation to remote places.

Seasonal tourism, hunting, and fishing are the main on-reservation economic options; otherwise, people make the long drives to coastal towns for work (Kessler-Mata, 2017: 53). Employment in the on-reservation schools allows local people to work in the community they live in, but family expectations of responsibilities (time) and financial assistance (money) with both time and money sometimes place a heavy burden on people with the credentials to give back in the Valley. In part because of its distance from urban coastal life, the Hoopa Valley Tribe (*Natinixwe* in the Hupa language), alongside Yurok (*Oohl* in Yurok) and Karuk people, have managed to maintain cultural continuation in numerous ways. Tribes have tried to further

Indigenous language transmission as part of a cultural survival process, bringing languages in danger of disappearing back from the brink by growing the speaker base through instruction to young people.

This chapter explores how the context of life on the Hoopa Valley Indian Reservation, a nearly ninety-thousand-acre space surrounded by privately held land and non-Indigenous towns, shapes community resistance to culturecide. In particular, I focus on techniques of culturecide resistance employed by high school students and community members connected to Hoopa Valley High School (HVHS), where both Yurok and Hupa languages are offered as part of the formal high school curriculum. Because my permission for the study comes from the Yurok Tribal Council, I only follow the Yurok language classes at HVHS, although the impact of Hupa language access remains a significant area of study for future research, ideally in partnership with the Hoopa Valley Tribal Council.

The hypotheses laid out in Chapter 1—that access to Yurok language classes in public high schools promotes increased self-esteem and well-being and ultimately seeds the possibility for civic, cultural, and political participation for heritage-speakers, and that Yurok class access boosts intercultural competency and allyship for non-heritage-speakers—are tested at HVHS. To foreshadow the findings presented below, Yurok language class access appears to serve a universally positive role for students from a range of backgrounds at the school, even for those not enrolled in the class. The presence of Native culture integrated into the formal curriculum at HVHS helps students from a range of backgrounds better understand and appreciate the role of Native people in the local community and situate them as significant actors more broadly. Causal patterns, as will be shown below, contain numerous feedback loops and intervening variables. Indeed, the ability of the research puzzle to account for complexity is tested, as factors such as poverty, family violence, drug addiction, isolation, and migration are all intervening variables in how young people construct their identities and imagine their own participation in the world.

HVHS predominantly serves Native American students and has offered Yurok and Hupa language classes since the late 1990s due to interest from both tribes and communities. Though the school is technically on the Hoopa Valley Indian Reservation, the close border of the Yurok Indian Reservation combined with historic population overlap and contemporary blended families across ethnic lines mean that there is a large Yurok population in the Hoopa Valley as well. Total tribal membership for Yurok people is approximately 6,000, and enrolled membership for the Hoopa Valley Indian Tribe is around 3,500, though there are others of mixed ancestry who, for example, may be enrolled Hoopa members with one Yurok parent. The Yurok Tribe is the largest Native American tribe in California, with the majority of the enrolled population living either on the Yurok Reservation around the small coastal town of Klamath, in the Hoopa Valley, elsewhere along the Klamath River, or in regional towns such as Eureka.

Although Yurok is no longer used in extended daily exchange by most people, the Yurok Tribal Council encourages its use in work meetings, and it continues to be used in ceremonial and intentional cultural spaces, especially by language-keepers. A language-keeper is someone who has had a language passed down to them, either from family usage or by seeking out elder language-keepers and asking permission to learn from them, or through a combination of ways to expand language repertoires. A distinguishing characteristic of language-keepers is their sense of responsibility to participate in the survival of the language, namely through teaching it, whether formally or informally. During my collaboration with the Yurok Tribe, roughly a dozen people were identified as having the level of Yurok fluency sufficient to bear this honorific title. As this book went to press in 2022, twenty-four people were identified as advanced Yurok-speakers.

Indigenous (In)visibilities and Curricular Politics

Cal Poly Humboldt professor of child development Kishan Lara-Cooper, of Yurok, Hupa, and Karuk background, writes about healing within Indigenous communities and about the way in which White students are valued within education systems in the United States while Indigenous students are not. She shares the vignette of Ijo, an Indigenous child, who brings a carved model of a Yurok *auth wayach* (a canoe) to one of his first show-and-tells at school (Lara-Cooper, 2019: 31). Another student calls the *auth wayach* a boat and the White teacher misses the teachable moment and does not validate the Yurok culture identity Ijo was trying to share (Lara-Cooper, 2019: 30). The result of this exchange is that by the second day of school, Ijo understood that aspects of his Indigenous identity were not valued at school, and he therefore chose to self-censor by leaving other indications of his indigeneity at the schoolhouse door (Lara-Cooper, 2019: 31).

The formal education sector has long operated as a mechanism of forced assimilation for Native Americans. Adrienne Colegrove-Raymond, a Hoopa tribal member on staff at the Native American Center for Academic Excellence at Cal Poly Humboldt in Arcata, California, comments: "Students have to be cognizant to never forget that the American educational system was based on providing leadership skills for a capitalistic society and it was used as an effective form of assimilation. A capitalistic society, where members seek personal wealth with little to no regard for community or the environment, boldly conflicts with tribal value systems" (Colegrove-Raymond 2019: 279). Some learners are able to navigate the system to their own benefit. Colegrove-Raymond notes that in her own family, her grandmother had said, "I learned early on that we need to learn the White *system*, not their *ways*, because it is then that we will beat them at their game" (Colegrove-Raymond 2019: 279). However, many learners are not able to distinguish the difference and, in order to succeed in the system, end up assimilating into the ways of dominant culture.

Such identity undermining happens both within and across racial and ethnic groups. Across case-study schools, I found that Indigenous-descendant students taunted other Indigenous-descendant students about physical appearance or capabilities in school activities (Focus Group 4.2 BIC 29, 2018), and those students were in turn taunted by those who were not Indigenous (Anonymous, 2018ab). The majority of discriminatory speech across all schools was racially or ethnically based, and these insults were also directed at minority students over and over again, leading to silencing, insecurity, and self-doubt, even as students tried to put on tough facades.

Indigenous youth grapple with the legacies of genocide and culturecide every day. In nineteenth-century California, eighteen treaties signed with Indigenous tribes were supposed to have set aside nearly 7.5 percent of the state land for Indigenous use, but all treaties were broken following settler outcry, leaving Indigenous people dispossessed of promised lands (Risling Baldy & Begay, 2019: 50). There have been scant apologies for the abuse of Indigenous people in the United States, and most have been local or specific to one massacre. For example, in 1990 Congress issued a statement of "'deep regret'" for the 7th Cavalry's 1890 massacre of three hundred men, women, and children at Wounded Knee (Norton, 2019: 125). In 2019, the Eureka mayor offered an apology for the Duluwat/Indian Island massacre during the ceremony returning Duluwat to the Wiyot Tribe (Greenson, 2019). Yet even in the face of these moments of recognition, the larger machines of culturecide—what Yurok scholar and activist Jack Norton calls "the rudimentary policy to assimilate Indian people and resources into the fabric of the American society"—have not stopped working (Norton, 2019: 125).

As inheritors of broken treaties, today's Indigenous youth in California navigate the physical and psychological trauma of betrayal and human rights abuses. Many have been caught in vices such as alcohol and drug abuse, but Indigenous communities continue to find ways to resist ongoing erasure through forced assimilation and assert their contemporary presence. Though the traumas are serious and many require intervention, some Native scholars explicitly reject discourses of victimhood and other negative aspects of Native life circumstances because such discourses pin people into tragic tropes from which there is little recourse. Cutcha Risling Baldy describes how this plays out for Native people, with a satirical engagement of the White gaze:

> We are always losing something: our languages, our futures, our traditions, and our cultures. In this story, if we haven't lost these things, we are on our way to losing them, one step away from an extinction that seems inevitable and also, improbably, accidental. Native peoples are always in the last stages of existence. This is to solidify the settler colonial desire for an eventual inheriting of this land, a rightful, uninhabited, ahistorical passing of ownership from the poor, dying Indigenous to the stronger, healthier, more vibrant settler colonial society. This becomes the narrative that many are taught in classrooms, that is reflected in popular culture, and it remains ever so stubbornly central to much of the scholarship written about Native nations-scholarship that now builds the foundations of law, policy, history, and acceptable rhetoric about Native culture and societies. (Baldy, 2018: 5)

Risling Baldy acknowledges many ways in which such losses may be real but does not allow those realities to turn into logical narrative trajectories toward settler-colonial domination. Instead, she catalogues Native resistance to such silencing and pushes readers to see how silencing is a means to finalize questions of power and domination: "The language of 'giving up' or 'losing' that is perpetuated in the rhetoric of history and ethnography completely ignores the lengths to which Native people went to survive and resist the continuing attacks on their cultures and peoples. It also denies any sort of culpability or responsibility; it makes the founding of the state of California benign, removes any lasting or residual trauma, and pretends that ownership or rights to land and resources in this state are settled and beyond reproach" (Baldy, 2018: 58). Affirming Native presence therefore is not only part of an ethical imperative to recognize contemporary Native existence but also contributes to decolonization by reopening questions about rights to land and culture that White people previously considered settled or in the past.

The Impact of Victors' History

Even though California is progressive compared to other parts of the United States in terms of commitment to including Native history and culture in the public K–12 educational curriculum (Foxworth et al., 2015: 956), like many states, it still scores poorly in terms of the adoption and implementation of the Native American education curriculum put forth by the National Congress of American Indians (National Congress of American Indians, 2019). Curriculum committees at the state and local levels have notoriously perpetuated the status quo (Vizenor, 1994: 8). This is significant considering that more tribes live in California than in any other state.

The cliché that victors write history means that the United States' history of genocide and culturecide against Indigenous people remains obscured for most students. Jim McQuillen, the director of the Yurok Tribe's Education Department, writes: "There are many other community groups that have monuments of healing for the historical loss they experienced, including the monuments for the Jewish holocaust and the September 11th World Trade Center loss. Tribal people need these same monuments, symbols, and dialogue for healing to occur. School curriculum can assist in this understanding and healing potential" (J. McQuillen, 2019: 286). Curricular reform is a logical place to include the lived trauma of Indigenous people, in order to foster an accurate understanding of the past in ways that will promote healing and understanding. Moreover, the power of curricular decision making is the power of identity formation or negation. Indigenous students have for far too long been subjected to the most violent condemnation of their identities in school and daily life. Curricular intervention can disrupt the silence.

Melanie Gensaw, a Yurok Tribal member who worked in cultural competency capacity-building at the time we spoke, said:

We're still in that place where we're taking the dominant curriculum and trying to add in. And that's great. It's better than where we were in the 1960s and it cannot possibly be the end. We're not at the end of this journey of how to incorporate cultural-ness, for lack of a better term, into our systems. We're just starting, I think in this community especially, we're just starting to recognize we have to do things a little bit differently. . . . That's something to celebrate and to constantly remind people like, no this isn't the end. I'm not *the* solution. I'm part of *a* solution that has to continue that momentum. (M. Gensaw, 2017)

Of course, developing culturally relevant and Indigenous-focused curricula takes time, as does its implementation. Teachers may have concerns about fulfilling state requirements if they deviate from standard textbooks. But changing the script is vital not only for Indigenous students but for settler-descendant ones, as well as students of other backgrounds. Jim McQuillen writes: "History lessons are necessary to explain how the aboriginal tribal lands were lost through the 1887 General Allotment Act, how familiar relationships and family bonds were systematically broken due to the boarding school era, and how genocidal acts exist here locally in recent history. A trauma-informed approach such as this has potential for community self-awareness for the community and its members" (2019: 286). Like awareness of trauma-informed care, momentum around Indigenous language and culture in the United States is growing in the twenty-first century. Tribes across the country are promoting language use in a range of arenas, including in films, books, and official tribal spaces.

Native American language inclusion is seen as one of many factors that can contribute to increased school success for Native students (Proudfit & Myers-Lim, 2017). In California, the Yurok Tribe has navigated the public school bureaucracy to get the Yurok language classes accredited to meet official state requirements. High school students in California need to fulfill what are called "A to G" requirements[2] to be eligible for the California State University (CSU) system, as well as for the University of California (UC) system (Carpenter IV, 2018). These requirements include taking two years of the same language course, with more than two years of coursework preferred for the UC system.

In many public high schools, language class offerings generally include widely spoken or prestige languages like Spanish, French, German, and—at more urban schools, increasingly—Mandarin. Indigenous language offerings tend to be relegated to community language classes, often held at night or on weekends, and attended mostly by older community members—parents or grandparents who either learned some language or didn't get to learn when they were young people. Thanks to advocacy by the Yurok Tribe's Education Department, as well as funding from the Yurok Tribe, Yurok is regularly offered at three other regional high schools in addition to HVHS: Del Norte High School in Crescent City (the closest high school to the Yurok Indian Reservation in Klamath), McKinleyville High School (just north of Arcata), and Eureka High School (the case study of Chapter 7). Inserting Yurok language study at the high school level, where its continuity as an offering can affect a student's college application, raises the stakes for the continued availability of the language.

Yurok language is also offered intermittently in K–8 schools, with language-keepers driving long distances for low pay in order to maintain language presence at several primary schools with higher numbers of Native students (Anonymous, 2018z). Yurok language instruction is also available to younger students in early childhood development programs in multiple Head Start daycares in the region (Anonymous, 2018z). Yet teacher availability and funding continue to inhibit efforts to expand language offerings, which often lead to ad hoc teaching schedules and job insecurity (Anonymous, 2018z). To address this situation, the Yurok Tribe's Education Department created a grant-funded five-year teacher training program. The program helps Yurok people interested in teaching in the public school system to complete their California teacher credentials while at the same time acquiring a level of fluency in Yurok that would allow them to teach the language, in addition to other subjects. The rationale for this is important. Teaching Yurok alone is not a full-time job that allows for economic security, but a Yurok language position for someone also credentialed to teach additional subjects could be.

The Hoopa Valley and HVHS

Native American communities in the United States are underserved and economically marginalized, with legacies of broken treaties, genocide, and culturecide. The Hoopa Valley claims some of the highest poverty rates in California. To address food insecurity, all high school students are provided with free breakfast and lunch. For years, the only food store in town was a small branch of a White-owned grocery chain. When it closed due to health code violations (California Freshworks, 2020), the community of approximately 3,500 residents was left without a grocery store within a forty-mile radius for almost three years—officially qualifying it as a food desert. The community overcame this challenge robustly, opening the Iłwai Kiliwh shopping center—meaning "where they sell things" in the Hupa language—including a grocery store committed to providing healthy products as well as locally produced food and managed by the Hoopa Valley Tribe (California Freshworks, 2020). Nevertheless, the food desert experience of the Hoopa Valley is indicative of the economic and infrastructural challenges that contextualize any discussion of education and community resilience.

HVHS is part of the Klamath Trinity Joint Unified School District (KTJUSD) and provided secondary education for 267 students in 2018–2019. It is the only high school in the district, though it shares its campus with Captain John's Continuation High School, which serves students who usually have failed out of HVHS and are working toward a GED. The community of Hoopa is 78 percent Native American, 8 percent mixed race (most commonly Native and Latinx), 7 percent White, and 5 percent Pacific Islander, with a minute number of Latinx and Black-identifying residents (World Population Review, 2020). These statistics loosely match the demographics of HVHS, which vary from year to year, but the school is overwhelmingly attended by students from Native American backgrounds.

The majority of students identify as Hupa, Yurok, and Karuk, and 92–95 percent are to some degree Native American. Students as well as staff and faculty identify as part of other groups as well, such as Tolowa, Sioux, and Tohono O'odham, and there are several students who identify as mixed race, including both Mexican American and Native American students. The percentage of White students is small, somewhat lower than the percentage of White residents in the Hoopa region as a whole.[3] This is because White parents with the means to do so often send their children out of the Valley to the coast to attend high school if logistically viable, although this happens less now than in previous decades (Anderson, 2018).

Boarding School Legacies in Hoopa

Precolonial contact estimations of California's Native American population range from 300,000 to 1 million (Lara-Cooper & Lara Sr., 2019: 2). In the 2020 census in California, around 1.4 million people, or 3.6 percent of the popula-tion, identified as Indigenous in some way (America Counts Staff, 2021). While settler-colonial contact took place in parts of California beginning in the late sixteenth century, in the more rural northern part of the state it did not occur until the mid-nineteenth century (Lara-Cooper & Lara Sr., 2019: 3). Indigenous death from assassination, enslavement, disease, and starvation perpetrated by White settlers reduced the population to 17,000 by the turn of the twentieth century (Norton, 1979).

Much has been written about the boarding school experiences of Indig-enous peoples and the physical and cultural destruction that ensued (D. W. Adams, 1995; Lindsay, 2015; Norton, 1979; A. Smith, 2009). HVHS is located on nearly the same physical footprint as the Hoopa Valley Indian Boarding School, which operated from 1893 to 1932 in the former location of Fort Gaston (Risling Baldy & Begay, 2019: 52). The maxim of "kill the Indian, save the man" that pervaded racist colonial thinking at the time was a culture-cide mechanism that encapsulated the bedrock philosophy of the schools, where students were punished for speaking their languages or engaging in anything related to Indigenous culture (T. King, 2018: 122; Risling Baldy & Begay, 2019: 52). The Bureau of Indian Affairs, which historically managed Hoopa Valley Tribe matters, sold the land to the school district for a small amount of money after determining that the sale was in the best interests of the Tribe. The boarding school was converted into a day school and then was eventually subsumed into the present-day KTJUSD public school system.

In Hoopa, the boarding school was used by White settlers and their descendants to separate Native children from their families and attempt to "civilize" them by forcing them to follow the customs of White people in terms of clothing, religion, language, food, and daily routine. The boarding school provided a generation of Native laborers and servants for the White community by proletarianizing them into mechanisms of an industrial economy (Moorehead Jr., 2019: 68). The schooling experience also system-atically destroyed Native family bonds and many aspects of cultural con-tinuity. The legacies of genocide and culturecide toward Native peoples in the region contribute to high rates of trauma, cultural PTSD, and cultural loss.[4]

In addition, there are significant contemporary physical repercussions connected to historical trauma. According to Indian Health Services, as cited by Kishan Lara-Cooper:

Indigenous people have the highest death rate in all of th e following categories: heart disease, cancer, diabetes, stroke, liver disease,
kidney disease, and influenza. Alcoholism rates are 510% higher
than the general population; Indigenous teens experience the
highest rate of suicide, ten times the national norm; and violence
accounts for 75% of deaths for Indigenous youth ages 12–20. . . .
Indigenous adolescents have death rates two to five times the rate of
Euro-American adolescents in the same age group. . . . High school
dropout rates are double the national average and 50% higher than
any other ethnic group in the State of California. (Lara-Cooper,
2019: 16)

Many Native students at HVHS have grandparents or great-grandparents
who were coerced into the Hoopa Valley Indian Boarding School or another
boarding school in California. Some of those students cited the loss of Yurok
or Hupa language in their families as a result of their grandparents' internment; others mentioned a parent's drug abuse as the result of growing up in
an emotionally dysfunctional home, impacted by an interned grandparent's
post-traumatic stress disorder.

Mr. Cornelson, the then-vice principal and athletics director who has
Karuk heritage, spoke with me in his office and pointed toward the HVHS
football field. He commented, "We have a 1960s photo of the football field,
and those were the old boarding houses still up there" (Cornelson, 2018). This
was personal for him. "My grandmother didn't speak her Native language
because she was separate from it, but she was also not willing to acknowledge
who she was because of the racial discrimination she experienced down on
the coast" (Cornelson, 2018). The forced boarding school era deeply impacted
the Hoopa community in terms of language loss, cultural separation, and
intergenerational trauma. Yet no plaque stands to recognize this; no museum
documents the role of the boarding school for contemporary residents.

The absence of formalized memory for an immensely traumatizing institution like the Hoopa Valley Indian Boarding School is endemic of the hidden memories of White violence toward Indigenous people in the United
States. As one White teacher at HVHS put it, "We have to own it, we have to
say, 'this was a boarding school.' We don't have a word for institutionalized
widespread child abuse and neglect. We don't have that language, but we need
to make it" (Anderson, 2018). The history of the boarding school is important

context for studying both the invisibility of Native people in contemporary curricula and the significance of Indigenous language courses being offered at HVHS.

Contemporary Schooling "on the Rez"

Concrete data on Native American public K–12 enrollment is challenging to locate or capture accurately, but in the twenty-first century, the population has generally constituted 1 percent of total student enrollment (National Center for Education Statistics, 2019: iii).[5] In 2016–2017, approximately 1 percent of students in the K–12 system in the United States identified as Native American (Hussar et al., 2020: xxi). Native American students are the lowest-performing students of all racial and ethnic categories across all school disciplines. For Native American students, the national high school dropout rate averages 50 percent, and Native American students have the highest rates of suspension, absenteeism, and expulsion (TEDNA, 2010).

In 2018, there were 267 students at HVHS. Most students who attend HVHS do so because it is the closest high school to their homes; two students reported they opted to switch to HVHS from Happy Camp[6] in order to fulfill their A to G requirements. Students who have the option of commuting to coastal high schools tend to do so, leaving the HVHS student population composed mostly of those who are there because of geographic relevancy. Some students—there is not clear numeric data on how many—go on after graduation to attend the College of the Redwoods (CR) Hoopa branch campus, CR in Eureka, or other regional community colleges, with the goal of then transferring to a four-year university. A smaller number go directly into a four-year university such as Humboldt State University or occasionally places like Stanford, UC Davis, or UC Berkeley. As students describe what they want to do after high school, self-goals for education appear to be weighed in relation to family obligations and economic viability.

Economically, HVHS provides jobs for many people who live in the area, especially the administrative support staff, which is mostly made up of Hupa, Yurok, and Karuk locals. The overwhelming majority of teachers are White, in line with national averages (National Center for Education Statistics, 2019: 10). While some administrators and teachers have long-term connections to the area through family ties and background, others do not. Sometimes the insider-outsider relations lead to tension, as local context and relevance may not be as readily accessible for the outside group of administrators and teachers, while innovation for change may not be as available to the inside group because of habits and path-dependent practices. In general, administrators, teachers, and staff seem aligned in the common mission to help the students under their charge.

KTJUSD schools emphasize Native and local culture and rights; this is particularly visible at the K–8 level through the Indian Land Tenure Curriculum. HVHS has also integrated local history and knowledge into the curriculum, with teachers from a range of demographic backgrounds working to balance the state requirements with content that has the most local relevance for young people. For their language electives, students can choose from Hupa, Yurok, and Spanish. Many who opt for Hupa or Yurok language classes do so because they identify with it personally. Other students cite being placed in Yurok or Spanish although it wasn't their first choice, saying they would have preferred a different language.

As with the other case studies, data for this chapter comes from a range of sources. I collected 23 surveys and conducted 24 interviews with students, 3 focus groups with students, 10 interviews with teachers and administrators, 40 classroom observations, and a dozen interviews with Yurok Tribal members unaffiliated with HVHS but involved in cultural survival in some way. In general, response rates at HVHS were lower than those of the other California high school but still sufficient to be representative of the larger student body.

"Speaking Indian": The Politics of Yurok Language Access at HVHS

Carole Lewis is a Yurok language-keeper and elder who has taught Yurok for years at HVHS and in other schools and community settings, including the first Yurok language class at the Hoopa branch of the regional community college.[7] She described the barriers she overcame to become a Yurok speaker:

When we were young, my grandmother was very much a fluent speaker, my mother spoke the language as well, my aunt spoke too. But we were really encouraged to learn how to live in the White world. We were really encouraged because [my grandmother's generation] had suffered a lot because of their cultural ties, because

of their inability to speak [English]. And they'd seen how things
were going and said we need to learn [English]—they wanted their
children to learn how to survive in this modern-day non-Native
world. And so we did. We did that really good. (Lewis, 2017)

Because Ms. Lewis's mother and grandmother experienced intense physical
punishment in school for speaking Yurok, they did not pass on the language
to Ms. Lewis as a child (Lewis, 2017). But as an adult, Ms. Lewis had a strong
yearning to learn the language; she sought out elders and community classes
and eventually became a proficient speaker (Lewis, 2017).

As a Yurok language-keeper, Ms. Lewis initially taught community language classes, which were mainly for other Yurok heritage-speakers who
wanted to learn more of the language than they had in their own families.
These classes were not controversial among Yurok people. But some tensions
arose in the Yurok community when the Yurok language class was added to
the HVHS curriculum in the late 1990s:

> I've had comments made—"Why are you teaching White people our
> Yurok language?" And I think, "Why not?" It doesn't matter who
> knows the Yurok language. Whoever knows it can go teach other
> people. 'Cause we do have some White people, well, our linguist,[8]
> who can speak the language, you know, he's pretty doggone good.
> And they can teach other people. . . . When I first started working
> with language, I worked a lot with elders, and they wanted anybody
> who wanted to learn it. They wanted to give them access to the
> language—they actually took votes on it that, as far as learning
> the language, they were very open to it. (Lewis, 2017)

Opening up the language to anyone who wants to learn is an important part
of the language's survival. While secrecy pervades a significant portion of
Yurok cultural ritual, the choice of Yurok elders to make Yurok language
learning available to all has been a significant step toward its preservation.

The majority of Yurok students in Ms. Lewis's classes at HVHS are ethnically Yurok, and some are White or of mixed ethnic backgrounds. In Yurok
classes at Eureka High School and McKinleyville High School, classes (especially at the introductory levels) are often half White and include students
from other minority backgrounds. The Yurok classes at Del Norte High

School tend to attract students who are ethnically Yurok or Tolowa. Tolowa is not offered as a language, so those students take Yurok instead. The integration of Yurok language classes into high school curricula has had many benefits for these communities. The mainstreaming of Native culture in a public and institutionally recognized venue contributes to the destigmatization of Native peoples for students from all backgrounds as well as their families.

When asked what being a language-keeper means to her, Ms. Lewis replied, "I just love talking language" (Lewis, 2017). She does not see it as a vocational attribute connected to upward economic mobility: "Our people know the value of language has nothing to do with making money or living in a nice house. It has to do with something that's more important, deeper, and more spiritual than that" (Lewis, 2017).

While language is an element of culture in the academic sense—meaning the traditions, food, religious practices, shared history, and norms of a given people—the language-culture connection is not always straightforward. Ms. Lewis's sister, a retired Yurok language teacher who taught at HVHS for many years, said: "Well, there's a lot of people totally involved in culture who have no language. And maybe there's people who are involved in language who aren't really participants in cultural activities, ceremonial activities. But you got it all when you have both" (Inong, 2017). The idea of "having it all" as a culturally connected language-speaker resonates with some Yurok heritage-speakers at HVHS and holds promise for Yurok cultural and linguistic continuity.

Yurok Language Class Impact

One day while observing Ms. Lewis's Yurok III class, I had the chance to facilitate an informal focus group with students. We all stood in a circle while each student introduced themselves in Yurok and then said in English why they were taking the class. Some of their reasons were as follows: "It's dying out, I want to know it. I don't know why else"; "My family is really involved in the Yurok Tribe. I'm enrolled [as a registered member in the Tribe]. I want to know more language since I'm involved in [tribal culture]"; "Talking Yurok reminds me of my grandma who was a speaker"; "We are the only ones who can learn it, us Yurok. My family is really involved [in Yurok ceremonies], and I want to learn it"; "My family speaks it. I can joke with them and say, 'what's the weather?' and they'll say, 'hey, are you cussing me?'" (Focus Group, 2018b).

For the five students quoted above, their motivations to take the class come from a feeling of personal connection as heritage-speakers. They have families who are active in Yurok cultural continuity in a variety of ways, and they understand that there are high hopes for them to become the next generation of speakers.

There are also a few students whose responses showcased more pragmatism than cultural motivation. Two students in the informal focus group responded to the question of why they were taking the class as follows: "It's fun. It doesn't feel forced, and isn't as much work as other classes," and "This is the only class that fits in my schedule" (Focus Group, 2018b).

The first response (that Yurok is less work than other classes) is worth addressing head-on. To a cultural outsider like myself who is not used to Ms. Lewis's teaching methods, which weave cultural knowledge and storytelling with Yurok word usage, these classes may appear unwieldy. This, combined with the lack of standard textbooks that usually accompany Language Other Than English (LOTE) courses, makes the classes sometimes feel like casual conversations with an elder rather than a typical language class, replete with grammar worksheets and quizzes.

In fact, students at HVHS, as well as those at two of the other high schools where Yurok is offered, talked about the perception that Yurok classes were easier than other language alternatives like Spanish because Yurok instruction was more oral and interactive, whereas Spanish had more worksheets and tests. However, it is important to note that this perception of Yurok classes at both HVHS and EHS is at least partially rooted in different pedagogies rather than actual level of difficulty. While non-Native observers might superficially see such classes as unstructured and perhaps undisciplined, the non-lineal and personal style is culturally resonant with Native students, in contrast to the structure of traditional Spanish classes.

However, there are downsides to less regimentation. The permissive classroom atmosphere allowed for rampant non-curricular cell phone use by students, including several who sat watching videos with headphones on during class, ignoring Ms. Lewis and their fellow students. One diligent student in Yurok III talked about her frustration with her peers who behaved like this: "I mean . . . they're losing a good opportunity to learn a really important fact and skill that they can learn . . . and provide to other people" (Anonymous, 2018aa). Ms. Lewis was not unaware of or unresponsive to the phone distractions, but she remarked that a coercive "put the phone away or I'll take it" approach was inconsistent with the values instilled in her class. This points toward deeper pedagogical clashes between Native educators and White systems, something beyond the scope of this book.

As discussed above, there are many challenges for students at HVHS. Sometimes these challenges manifest in the students' inability to pay attention in class—a struggle that has been exacerbated by screen addiction and constant phone use during class. Some teachers and administrators, however, recognize that allowing students who are likely dealing with a range of traumas to focus on their screens without punishment may offer a safer and more soothing alternative than ejecting students from the classroom setting and sending them to the principal.

The vast majority of students in Ms. Lewis's Yurok levels I, II, and combined III/IV classes are at least partially Yurok, with several describing mixed ancestry and tribal enrollment across Yurok, Hupa, and Karuk tribes.[9] Lelencia, a Yurok II student who identifies as Hupa, Karuk, and Yurok, conveyed her gratitude for her own cultural survival both inside and outside the classroom: "It's really amazing, like how . . . most of us got [killed], or that we're even still here. Standing. And breathing and living and still practicing our ceremonies and our language and everything along those lines" (Pole, 2018). This sense of wonder related to survival was a dominant theme among HVHS students, who did not take their own survival for granted given the history of their communities.

Despite the classroom control and cell phone issues, students were overwhelmingly glad to have Yurok classes offered to them, and they related to Ms. Lewis like a trusted elder. One student, who was enrolled in both Yurok III and Spanish I to connect more deeply with her Yurok and Mexican heritage, was a disciplined student in both classes. She was culturally connected before arriving in Ms. Lewis's Yurok class, as her family had helped put on some of the annual Yurok dances. This student saw herself as playing a role in the continuation of both culture and language: not only was she a dancer, regalia-maker, and community helper who cared for small children and helped in the kitchen, but through her studies at HVHS, she was also a steward of the language.

She related a moment when she felt particularly grateful for what she had learned in Ms. Lewis's classes: "I remember when I was at a summer camp for Native Americans, like, we all had a circle, everyone was introducing themselves in their Native language, and since I took the Yurok class, I knew what to say. . . . And if I didn't take Yurok, then I wouldn't have known. . . . It'd have been embarrassing. If I didn't know my language, I don't know, I'd hate that feeling" (Anonymous, 2018aa). This student's Yurok language skills allowed her to introduce herself to other culturally connected young people in a way that made her proud and to assert her Native-ness in a space where she was socially rewarded for doing so. At the same time, this student's mixed background meant she extended across multiple cultural worlds and was interested in learning more about all of them. Her grandmother, who came to California from Mexico, lived in the area and spoke mostly Spanish. The student, referring to her grandmother, said: "She's one of the ones that inspired me to take Spanish. 'Cause, like, I asked, 'Hey *abuela* [grandmother], if I take Spanish, can we, like, practice together and stuff like that?' and she's like, 'Of course.' So yeah, she inspired me to take it. And, like, every time she talks, she speaks Spanish, and someone else kind of understands, but, I understand mostly what it is, and if I don't, I always ask her questions" (Anonymous, 2018aa). The interest in engaging cross-generationally has helped ground this student in both sides of her identity, through Spanish as well as her active cultural participation as a Yurok girl learning the Yurok language.

None of the students in HVHS Yurok classes who identified as White or from non-Yurok Native backgrounds returned signed permission forms to be interviewed, so I was unable to speak formally with them. However, non-Yurok students whom I interviewed in other classes, including Spanish, made illuminating comments about what being at a school that offers multiple kinds of exposure to Native culture, including language, means to them. Esmerelda, a Mexican American student in Spanish I, lives near Weitchpec and comes to HVHS on a bus that takes an hour each way, around curves that hug sheer drops into the river valley below. She says, "Even though I'm not, like, Native or Yurok, I still like learning about the culture. I mean, I love how they make the baskets, so pretty. And I actually learned a bit about how to do it, . . . the bear grass braid, I did that and it was pretty cool" (Aruaz, 2018).

Taylor, a White student in the same Spanish I class as Esmerelda who grew up in Orleans and commutes to school with her father (a teacher at the school), sees the availability of Yurok and Hupa languages as a "neat" feature of HVHS. When I asked her about how it felt to be an ethnic minority at the school, she commented that she has "friends that will be like, 'You're Native to us' and, like, they're really accepting so that's pretty cool" (T. Cole, 2018). For both Esmerelda and Taylor, having Native culture and Native classmates all around them appears to have a positive influence on their ability to appreciate and relate to Native people even though they themselves opted to take Spanish rather than Yurok or Hupa.

Locally Relevant Curricula and Youth Engagement

Joe Marshall, a Hupa tribal member who is also Karuk, Yurok, and Tolowa, teaches Civics and Physical Education, coaches basketball, and runs a non-profit wellness and Native culture-focused afterschool program, the Warrior Institute. He grew up in the Hoopa Valley and graduated from HVHS himself. Mr. Marshall went to college on a basketball scholarship and returned to local acclaim to raise his family in the Valley and get involved in both the school and the community.

Talking about the role of HVHS in identity formation for young people, and his own aspirations for the Warrior Institute, he observes: "The whole school system is set up for socialization, assimilation, you know, conformity, compliance. . . . The whole system is set up to separate, isolate. To be more engaged, to be more aware, raising an awareness, raising the consciousness, would be ideally, you know, like, for me the end goal" (Marshall, 2018). Recognizing the limitations of the institution he is a part of—not HVHS specifically but formal public education in general—Mr. Marshall is trying to find ways to do consciousness-raising with the young people in his charge, both in his Civics classes and on the basketball court. He is not alone in this endeavor, as the school district leadership also wants to promote Native culture as something that can facilitate healthy identity development:

The school board is, like, they've identified culture and identity as . . . helping people be successful in school . . . I totally agree, identity is huge. Like, sixth through eighth grade, if you look [to Hoopa Elementary School, across the parking lot from HVHS], once they hit sixth grade, that's when they are searching for identity, that's where rites of passage kind of come in. And so they're searching for their identity, who they are. I did the same thing, you know, and you're kind of like searching for it and you get connected to, you know, some negative kind of identities at that time. It's easy, there's a negative peer group at that point, you know what I mean?

And then, you come here learning about all this stuff, British literature, you know, economics, physics, civics, and that has nothing to do with you; it's never anything you identify with, that anchors you in your identity. And I think that's one thing that helped me, I was more anchored in my identity, even going through college, I went through history, but, like, everything I was learning, I was like, *how can I relate this back to what was happening at home*? You know, constantly trying to make it relevant to me. And I just think the education system, the school system, is maybe not relevant, and . . . things are changing, society is changing. (Marshall, 2018)

For Mr. Marshall, the irrelevance of the White-oriented public education curriculum that he grew up with and is now, to some extent, expected to replicate in his Civics classes (with a state-sanctioned textbook on White political institutions) is a source of frustration. Mr. Marshall knows that lessons on local civic engagement would be more motivating to his students, but to develop those lesson plans and get them to meet state standards is a tall mandate, particularly when there are few resources to support that work.

Still, Mr. Marshall believes there is a need for culturally informed curricula.

We're losing so much culture, [there is] so much, like, loss of things. . . . One idea is this basket holding water, and it was just seeping through, there's cracks, holes in it. So like, how do you mend that basket and have the institution to, like, reverse the systematic effects of colonization, genocide, all those things? How do you systematically, you know, include cultural knowledge, leadership, different things? Before, I had to go see different elders, see different people, I didn't have that big cultural teacher in my life, so I had to go find it out. I was like, man, if all that kind of knowledge was concentrated, you know, in our sweathouses, in the natural classroom where elders and men got together and they shared information, and they transmitted that to the youth, what potential! (Marshall, 2018)

As a Native teacher at HVHS, Mr. Marshall is navigating the many cultural and political currents of the local community to make school a safe and meaningful place for young people. His identification of cultural loss as water slipping through the cracks in a basket draws on Pacific Northwest Native stories that often use the basket as metaphor for cultural integrity in communities where basket-weaving was and remains a prized skill (Lara-Cooper, 2017). The idea of repairing the cracks of cultural loss by reversing the systemic effects of genocide and culturecide is a huge mandate and a worthy goal for high school curricula.

White Teachers, History Curricula, and School as Safe Haven

Most of the White teachers at HVHS commute daily from the coastal towns of Arcata and Eureka. Robert Anderson is one of a few White teachers at HVHS who lives locally. His two eldest sons graduated from HVHS and his youngest child began there in 2019—in this way, he has local credibility for showing commitment to the school. He teaches U.S. History, Civics, Economics, AP U.S. History, and AP Government, when there is sufficient enrollment. Mr. Anderson is sensitive to his role as a White person at the school and made many disclaimers with me about only speaking from his own point of view. He postulates: "If you want to have a useful role in a postcolonial world or want to heal the injuries caused by colonialism, the first step you have to do is decolonize yourself. Or you have to have a decolonizing experience, because I don't think it's actually something that you arrive at, it's a practice" (Anderson, 2018). He centers his own practice on the content of his classes.

KTJUSD's superintendent during the 2018–2019 period was not supportive of centralized development of culturally sensitive curricula but did agree on the utility of the Indian Land Tenure Curriculum, which works to promote understanding of Native history and culture in schools (Indian Land Tenure Foundation, 2020) and is implemented at Hoopa Elementary School. Mr. Anderson, as the history teacher at HVHS, has experimented with ways to mainstream local issues into his syllabi:

> Particularly for social studies, I've made specific reference to this [Native] community. Because if I've given you [students] the skills that you will use to succeed in this community, you can succeed in other communities as well. But if I build it around a standard, middle-class, middle America approach, then I've missed some really key things that are essential for surviving here. . . . So I reached out to tribal experts, I reached out to the Indian Education Resource Center with Margo Robbins,[10] and in great humility, 'cause I'm trying to do something as an outsider to this community. I need to bring the community into the classroom. It doesn't exist in the standards, it doesn't exist in the texts . . . especially when we get closer to local history, my students may well be the experts in the room. And I defer to them. . . .
>
> I've had to write units that are missing from the standards. And that's ok. I'm not really leaving any of the standards out to do that,

which has often been the fear of administrators [who say], *We have a standardized test coming, how are they going to do with the STAR[11] test?* Honestly better, 'cause if I woke them up with a question on Native Americans, then they stayed awake when we're talking about Napoleon. . . . But to talk about the genocide of the gold rush, for example, was a threat to the dominant model, and a threat worth ending careers over. [Administrators would operate like] "We'll just start farming you out to the bad classes until you burn out and leave." That had been done. (Anderson, 2018)

Today, there remains a serious need for locally relevant curricula. Increasing flexibility at the district level has made it less risky for teachers to advocate for such relevancy, and there is more work to be done.

The biggest priority for many HVHS teachers is to help students feel safe. This requires recognizing the history of abusive education in the Hoopa Valley during the boarding school era and that, for many students, educational goals will not immediately line up with personal goals. Mr. Anderson draws on examples from numerous students he has taught to expand upon this:

[Becoming] an effective adult may be for some kids not perpetuating five generations of physical abuse. That's a huge win. Or being the first person in their family to not go to jail. Huge win. And those [kids] get left out when we're measuring successes. We [only] want to look at how many kids we send to college. God, that pisses me off . . . because we don't follow how many of them don't make it. The attrition rate in the first year of college is around 88 percent. They don't make it. We send them [to college] ill-prepared, and then they've got the culture shock as well. And it's cruel, because it added to their experiences another failure. It's just wrong. (2018)

Mr. Anderson's observations demonstrate that the metrics for success in the Hoopa Valley are complicated by many factors. As he suggests, for some students it is a victory to simply not follow the self-destructive paths of their parents; but this is also a woefully low benchmark for the public education of minority students.

Ultimately, if students' basic needs for safety are not being met first, it is unreasonable to expect that they will succeed academically—and it's possible that, by setting them up for failure in this way, feelings of defeat can compound into an overall dislike or disregard for education. Both the Reflection Room and now the Wellness Center at HVHS provide safe physical spaces so that students can address personal issues away from the classroom without disrupting other students. The high usage rate of both spaces speaks to the prevalence of stress and trauma in the HVHS student population. Administrative and faculty recognition of these issues is vital to set students up for success as much as possible.

There is one additional factor that is unique to schools with high tribal-enrolled populations. Many tribes in California hold what is called "eighteen money" in trust until young people turn eighteen, and many require a high school diploma as a stipulation to release the funds. Mr. Anderson describes the role of this money on student academic engagement:

> What many families want is diplomas. They don't want skills. They don't want personal development. They want the diploma so that they can gain access to their deferred per capita payments that have accrued over the years, that's called "eighteen money." The Hoopa Valley Tribe and to a degree the Yurok Tribe saves the money from per caps for all of their tribal members from the moment that they were born, and then when they're eighteen and have a high school diploma, it's handed to them in a lump sum. Twenty, thirty thousand dollars in the hands of an eighteen-year-old. And families descend upon them. (2018)

It is common for family members (both nuclear and extended, including parents, cousins, aunts, and uncles) to ask for cuts of the eighteen money when it is distributed; because Native culture places a high value on family as well as reciprocal responsibilities, that eighteen money is spent quickly. It isn't saved for college, as a general rule, because such an individualistic approach is not in line with the cultural practice of sharing.

With eighteen money, there is incentive to at least finish high school. Thus, the challenge for schools like HVHS is not simply to ensure that kids graduate but instead to make curricula as engaging as possible. That way, students might really absorb their education rather than simply check off the boxes en route to a diploma and eighteen money. The more locally and culturally relevant curricula that is available, the more students may gain from high school along the way.

Obstacles to Student Educational Success

In 2018–2019, administrators, staff, and faculty at HVHS met to devise a school plan where they listed barriers to student success. According to then-district superintendent John Ray, such barriers include "student mobility and transportation, social and emotional issues, trauma affecting students, low income and poverty, high percentages of discipline problems, access to healthy meals and holistic nutrition, relevant curriculum for all students, and the historically oppressed colonization boarding school history" (2018). When students were asked to identify barriers to their school success, some of their responses overlapped with those of the HVHS staff and faculty. When asked to rank the biggest obstacles to their own educational success, students at HVHS generally agreed that motivation, mental health, and economic resources were their greatest challenges, in that order. I look at each of these obstacles in turn.

The first significant obstacle for HVHS students is motivation and academic focus. Sometimes this is related to individual behavior and personality, but frequently the lack of motivation is connected to deep, familial patterns of dysfunction that reframe student priorities away from academics. Lack of motivation most frequently came up in interviews when students mentioned how hard it is to care about content that feels so disconnected from their own lives (Pole, 2018), or how difficult it is to maintain a focus on homework and studying when faced with co-parenting siblings and finding ways to feed and clothe them.

It is worth noting that no students who reported coming from self-described functional households reported feeling this lack of motivation or conflict of priorities. Rather, students who held responsibilities beyond what might be considered customary childhood chores were those who struggled to prioritize or be motivated for school. Although students indicated that motivation was their biggest obstacle to academic success, in fact, the underlying reasons for the lack of motivation were nearly always resource scarcity, dysfunctional home life, and culturally irrelevant curricula that made it difficult for students to see the point of studying something that appeared to have no bearing on their own lives.

At HVHS, students, teachers, administrators, and staff all cited the lack of designated mental health care providers as the biggest hindrance to their work and to student success. Students mentioned depression and anxiety as two factors that impacted their choices and behavior. Many students indicated that they had suffered some form of significant emotional trauma; without adequate care, this trauma manifests as depression, anxiety, and other mental health issues. In 2015–2016, the Yurok Tribe declared an emergency based on the high number of Native youth suicides—there were seven in a fifteen-month period (Moorehead Jr., 2019: 70). The mental health of Indigenous youth is an urgent public health crisis that should be understood in the context of historical trauma that affects the present (Moorehead Jr., 2019: 71).

In considering positive additions to the school, some students mentioned the Reflection Room (a space staffed entirely by teachers without mental health training) where students can go to have a private, calm space on campus during class time or break times. Some of the teachers who staffed the Reflection Room in 2018 felt overwhelmed by the responsibility given their own lack of counseling training. The need for mental health professionals to serve in a counseling role was acute during the 2017–2018 school year. When I returned for subsequent fieldwork in fall 2019, Angie Brown (the only district nurse serving hundreds of students across multiple school sites), had successfully obtained a major grant to construct a Wellness Center. The Center, a health clinic that includes mental and physical wellness services and is located on the HVHS campus, is designed to meet the physical and emotional needs of HVHS and Hoopa Valley Elementary students as well as their families. When I toured the facility, the equipment was still in boxes and staff positions were not yet filled, but it is poised to be a major boon for a community that suffers from a shortage of wellness services.

The third most mentioned obstacle to educational success is a lack of financial resources, including for planning next steps after high school. Students struggle with a range of resource-related issues that are a problem for the Hoopa Valley community in general, including the high burden placed on older siblings to care for younger siblings, food insecurity, and homelessness. In the Hoopa Valley, as on many American Indian reservations, drug addiction in one's family and domestic abuse frequently correlate with poverty and intergenerational trauma. All HVHS students are eligible to receive free breakfast and lunch at school, and the school and nearby community organizations also run a supper program and bag food for students who need it to take home on weekends (Ray, 2018). The staff also works to provide students with adequate clothing and school supplies.

The aforementioned HVHS Wellness Center may also be able to address poverty-related physical health issues, including malnutrition, that affect the local community, as both students and their family members will be able to use its services. The need to support low-income, food-insecure, and housing-insecure students is perpetual. Students spoke positively about things like school meal services and clothing distributions that addressed both physical challenges and stress-related mental health. The school's function as a safe portal for multiple services is a vital one given the community challenges and the prerequisite to meet students' basic needs so that they have enough energy for higher-order learning.

For many students, school is an escape from chaotic or dangerous home environments, and HVHS operates as a safe space where basic needs can be met and students can receive a meaningful education. Several students I spoke with at HVHS have been traumatized by witnessing family violence, namely that of male partners toward their mothers, and several others experience real food scarcity. One student, the oldest of more than a dozen siblings and step-siblings, talked about raiding her foster family's freezer to find food to give her siblings when her mom was using drugs and how she worked a whole range of jobs to clothe and provide basic necessities for her siblings (Anonymous, 2018ae).

Another student who transferred from Happy Camp talked about how she lives out of her car Monday through Thursday so that she can attend HVHS, because she can only afford to drive home on the weekends. Students who face such physical and structural insecurities have difficulty staying motivated and alert at school. All students seemed generally appreciative of HVHS's efforts to give them a safe place and provide food for them. The student who lived out of her car wished she could do an expedited high school diploma, since she was college-motivated and didn't want a GED, the only credential available if she left high school early.

Given the remote location of HVHS, the need for a car and the lack of access to jobs during high school are real barriers to earning money before college. For those interested in attending college while living at home in the Valley, the only option is CR Hoopa, a tiny, one-building campus that offers very limited classes toward an Associate of Arts (AA) degree. Some of the barriers students face when considering schooling beyond high school are a lack of knowledge about college in general, about how financial aid packages work, and what it would actually mean to attend a school beyond CR Hoopa. Many students are overwhelmed by the financial and logistical responsibilities that moving away from Hoopa would entail. This is especially true for students who are preoccupied with significant responsibilities at home and don't have the time to fully research the implications of different college options.

There are some resources available to help students navigate the college application process. The Johnson O'Malley (JOM) Program[12] supports Yurok educational success at HVHS, alongside its counterpart program for Hupa students. While there are two JOM college counselors at HVHS, their caseloads are high and the context of the school makes their jobs particularly complex. Other available academic and life success programming at HVHS includes TRIO, Gear Up, and Upward Bound. These college-knowledge-and-readiness programs are cited by students as playing a key role in helping them go to college beyond Hoopa.

Many students at all four case-study schools identified numerous options for themselves after high school without a clear idea of what they actually wanted to do. At HVHS, students named viable potential career paths for themselves (wildlife management, teaching, counseling, logging) but were still very much exploring ideas. Only some HVHS students mentioned definitive plans for college in ways that showed they were invested in their grades in order to gain admission somewhere beyond CR Hoopa. A few students were highly motivated to go straight to a four-year college and had made significant efforts to get the information they needed and their A to G requirements fulfilled. For others, college was mentioned as a default next step, but they lacked the conviction and academic success to actually make it happen. It is clear that the college tours for Yurok students facilitated by the JOM staff have fostered interest beyond the Valley. Several students articulated a desire to go to places like Lane Community College, which they would not have had information about or a realistic impression of without JOM counselors arranging an in-person tour.

The three primary obstacles to school success were ranked based on how the majority of students responded in interviews, as well as on the perspectives of teachers and administrators. However, these obstacles did not have the same degree of influence for each student. One high-achieving student said that the obstacles she faced were, in order of magnitude, money, mental health, then motivation, but when asked about the challenges for most of her peers, she said they were motivation, mental health, and then money. As these are subjective assessments, the obstacles themselves may be more relevant than the order in which they are ranked by students in understanding youth identity formation in context.

Additional Challenges at HVHS

While HVHS students face socioeconomic challenges in their own homes, infrastructure and administrative challenges have plagued HVHS. While students did not mention these problems, nearly all of the staff and teachers I spoke with did, both on and off the official record. For example, numerous incidents of arson have damaged parts of the school, and a mold problem led to an extensive renovation. During my fieldwork from 2017 to 2019, the school's physical site itself was in constant flux. Numerous teachers talked about the physical instability of the school environment as something that was a subtly stressful influence on student behavior at school.

In 2019 a new wing of classrooms opened, as well as new administrative buildings, reducing the construction site feeling of campus. Nevertheless, the mirroring of instability for students in the very infrastructure of their school, signified through the years of construction and demolition happening all around them, was poignant. Instead of experiencing a visually appealing school landscape, HVHS students were confronted with the wire fencing, machine traffic, dust, and chaos of a large construction site.

Similarly, school leadership has rapidly turned over, creating a sense of administrative upheaval. In the four years I conducted my study, from 2017 to 2020, I sought permission from four different HVHS principals, two of whom served only one year. In addition, the KTJUSD superintendent who granted me permission for the study in 2018 left his post in March 2019—under mounting pressure from parents and the American Civil Liberties Union of Northern California (ACLU NorCal)—and was replaced with an interim superintendent who stayed for more than a year after the hired replacement backed out of the job at the last minute (Mukherjee, 2019).

Nearly all the teachers I spoke with talked about the difficulties posed by a constantly changing principal. Not only were their own work plans repeatedly reinvented under new leadership, but such turnover made long-term planning for the school virtually impossible, especially given the turnover at the district level as well. Teachers also found this instability to be a major stressor for students. They shared anecdotal observations that the number of student fights increased whenever principal transitions took place—presumably the students' response to the insecurity at school, leading them to demonstrate their stress in negative, physical ways. In short, when students sense that the school itself is unstable, they act out that instability themselves. As of this writing, former athletics director and vice principal Craig Cornelson (Karuk), is the principal, bringing some consistency to the office, and the renovated campus is in good shape.

Sources of Support for Students

Students cite their family members, administrators, teachers, and friends as sources of support. One straight-A student commented: "I have a really good support system. Like, my family supports me and like, I have a lot of friends that are on the same track as me, so it's good to have a good close friend group 'cause . . . I don't know how I'd make it without my support system. . . . Like, if I'm ever feeling down, they'll always give me like, a motivation speech, and it really helps me get through it. Say I was having a down day, they're like 'it's okay, we're here for you, anything you need'" (Anonymous, 2018aa). While this student and others cited family as a positive support system, they also noted that other students do not necessarily have the kind of family that they do—one full of college graduates who are employed and living functional lives (Anonymous, 2018aa).

Students with more complicated family lives turn elsewhere for support. Many students spend significant time talking to teachers, staff, and administrators outside of class. Students, teachers, and administrators in general said that one of the greatest strengths of HVHS is that the students are "like family" and "all in this together" (Cornelson, 2018), and there seemed to be camaraderie between some students both in the halls and in classes. Given Hoopa Valley's size, some students are related to school personnel, and may turn to them for on-site support. However, the frequency of fights between students also shows that chronic stressors don't go away even in a close-knit environment.

River Politics as Resistance for Yurok Youth

Despite all the challenges described above, Native students at HVHS exhibit resilience and resistance to assimilation into dominant White frameworks. Some young people continue to resist assimilationist schools by running away (physically or through escapism) (Risling Baldy & Begay, 2019: 50). Others craft a range of resistance strategies. Resistance to culturecide through taking Yurok or Hupa language classes is a form of asserting Indigenous presence. It is one of many ways that Indigenous peoples advocate for recognition in the institutions that have usually excluded them. Scholars have documented the role of language revitalization as an inherently political form of Indigenous resistance. In the classroom, the very bodies of youth become sites of "critical pedagogy" (Jacob, 2013: 45).

Learning to critique standard assumptions about identity and education in Indigenous language classes could lend itself to fostering political critique as well. The efficacy of political participation is not easily measured (Centellas & Rosenblatt, 2018: 643), but I argue that building a solid identity-rooted foundation for participation, regardless of the outcome of that participation, is key to building engaged democratic actors. While HVHS students described being culturally connected in a range of ways, much of those connections were expressed through food provisioning—such as fishing, hunting, and gathering—or dance participation. Several interviewees said they were part of the Associated Student Body (ASB) and served various elected posts within HVHS. In this way, students had exposure to what it takes to govern on a small scale. Yet no student mentioned being involved in local politics, and several students openly said they stayed away from tribal politics because it was so fraught and divisive between families.

The line between wanting to participate in the world to make a difference, and paralysis in the face of the world's problems can be very thin. Given the many structural barriers facing Native American youth, political participation can be a means to channel young people's energy in a positive direction and away from drugs, alcohol, and other means of self-medicating. Virgil Moorehead Jr. (Yurok and Tolowa), the behavioral health director at a local Northern California health center, writes about empowerment as an alternative to overmedicating Native young people who have mental health issues: "Specific interventions might include teaching Indian children advocacy skills by engaging in local politics and activism via broad social movements (e.g., Standing Rock), and community organizing skills and critical media literacy in order to diminish the power of the pharmaceutical industry" (Moorehead Jr., 2019: 77). In the context of a culturecidal regime in the United States, his is a radical idea. Rather than channel depressed or anxious patients toward medication to overcome the burden of their historical trauma, intervene to teach them how to resist and survive.

Resistance as part of survival is critical to youth identity formation for many Native American youth. Vizenor's notion of survivance as "active presence" (2010: 1) discussed in Chapter 1 is visible in the testimony of a seventeen-year-old HVHS student:

> I know well the stories of rape and killing of my people, the cap-
> tured family members that were sent to government boarding
> schools, the countless fathers killed in front of their children. . . . As
> I stomp my heels into mother earth as I dance, I am saying I am
> here, you are here, and we will not be in conflict with ourselves, but
> remember how this prayer has survived. . . . I have spoken out and
> my voice will only become stronger. I have assisted in organizing
> cities to stand against police brutality, and shut down state capitals
> to stand against the dams so that rivers can flow healthy. Being an
> "activist" is to stand against what is wrong and stand up for what is
> right. (Joseph, 2019: 307)

Joseph's politicization comes in part from being raised by parents who themselves were active in the Fish Wars (Joseph, 2019: 307).

To provide some brief context, the Klamath River, which is sacred in Yurok, Hupa, and Karuk cosmology, runs through the Yurok Reservation, and has provided the fish and fresh water that all three tribes depend on for survival, was dammed to provide water for ranchers and farmers further north. The dams prevented salmon migration and reproduction, raised water temperatures, and dropped water levels. This led to algae blooms, fish die-offs, and crises of sustenance, economic survival, and spiritual distress for Indigenous communities. There have been decades of controversy stretch-
ing back to the 1970s over who has the right to the river water. Shaunna Oteka McCovey describes more recent events:

> The biggest fish kill in Yurok memory thrust the Klamath River and
> its water crisis into the national media [in 2002], pitting farmers in
> the upper Klamath basin against fishermen, Indians, and environ-
> mentalists in the lower basin. The loss of salmon, both chinook and
> coho, was estimated upward of 60,000, and those of us dependent
> on the salmon runs were completely devastated. What happened is
> what I refer to as an attempt at cultural genocide. Cultural genocide
> is just as appalling, if not more so, than physical genocide because
> its form appears benign. From this standpoint, the perpetrators of
> these acts can evade responsibility for the demise of a group of people

because the people are, in fact, still living and breathing. (McCovey, 2006: 290)

The culturecide resulting from damming the Klamath taps into a much larger story about genocide and culturecide perpetrated by White people against Indigenous people in the United States for centuries.

> As the Yurok tribe and other affected citizens collected and counted dead salmon carcasses we received no government apology, no compensation, and certainly no claim of responsibility or promise to change the undoubtedly ineffective water use plan. But should we have expected any of these things? Certainly not. We've never been apologized to for the loss of our people during the gold rush, we've never been apologized to for the theft of our land under the General Allotment Act of 1887, we've never been apologized to for the loss of language, and the attempted extinction of our culture by the boarding schools, and on and on and on. (McCovey, 2006: 291)

After mass Indigenous protest, the PacifiCorp company that owns the dams agreed to the 2016 Klamath Hydroelectric Settlement Agreement, which was supposed to have removed the dams by 2020, but was delayed. In 2019 the Hoopa Valley Tribe hired a Yurok contractor to remove the dams (Orcutt, 2019: 211), but only in 2021 did the Federal Energy Regulatory Commission approve a license transfer from PacifiCorp to the Klamath River Renewal Corporation that would let dam removal begin in 2023.

However, removing the dams and restoring the Klamath River water levels to what the salmon need to survive is only one step toward address-ing the violations of Indigenous peoples' human rights. This includes the right to cultural continuity. Apologies for the genocide and culturecide that have decimated Indigenous populations have been few and far be-tween, even as Indigenous communities demonstrate resilience in the face of overwhelming odds. River politics offer a culturally relevant case study that could be used across a range of classes to encourage student empower-ment and participation on the issue. Yet I found that while numerous stu-dents were interested in the river, or water use and access more generally (Anonymous, 2018aa; Aruaz, 2018; T. Cole, 2018), most were not versed in the river's politics.

Other Political Interests of Students

Though by no means the majority, there were some HVHS students who were politically astute and showed a predilection for political engagement, broadly defined. These included Joseph (mentioned above) and Estalita (quoted below).

> I actually really enjoy discussing politics and arguing and stuff, like that's like one of the things I used to do a lot in Happy Camp, and during Government class. It's different here. A lot of kids—at least in History class, when [Mr. Anderson, the teacher] asks us questions, a lot of kids, almost every class, stay quiet, they aren't super responsive. Which is interesting. Whenever I'm home, I watch *PBS NewsHour*, and then I watch all the satirical kind of political shows like *The Daily Show* and stuff like that. . . . Then I, like, argue with my brother, then I argue with my mom, then I argue with anyone else who wants to argue. (Galindo, 2018)

Estalita is one of the only students who shows significant awareness of political issues, and she is frustrated by the apolitical attitudes exhibited by her classmates.

While most students seemed tuned out to issues beyond the Valley, whether because their personal situations are all-consuming or because they just aren't interested, other students responded to questions about how they wanted to change their community in ways that were inherently political, even though they did not use such a framework to define it. Some students said they weren't involved in politics but demonstrated an awareness of and involvement in things that political scientists might broadly classify as political. When I asked one student how she would change her community if she had three magic wishes, she responded: "Get rid of drugs, get rid of Styrofoam plates, and save the water. . . . We're in a drought, like a really bad one, and our salmon, it's really bad, poor salmon. Our salmon is one of our main foods that we have, and, like, back in the day, that's what our ancestors ate. And they're really important to me. Our salmon is really important to us [Yurok people]" (Anonymous, 2018aa). This response shows that, even though the student does not connect her desires for her community to a larger political landscape, the sort of social and environmental reform she hopes for is political at its core.

The drug problem in their community was often mentioned by students as an issue they wanted to see addressed (T. Cole, 2018), and one that, within the context of both the opioid crisis and California's marijuana cultivation and legalization, is also intensely political. Native language classes—which offer a path to cultural connectedness within a safe classroom environment— may decrease the need to use drugs as an escape mechanism. Such classes also instill values, such as caring for community and the environment, that are embedded in Native cosmologies.

Conclusion

Schooling in the Hoopa Valley is no easy task. Many students travel long distances over perilous roads to get to school each day, and a few students cross the Klamath River by boat to get to their bus stop. From basic access issues to the community history informed by the trauma of genocide and culture-cide perpetrated by White settlers and their descendants, education at HVHS is fraught. However, the teachers are dedicated and, along with the staff and administrators, appear to keep their students' best interests at the forefront. Through creating spaces for personal wellness and encouraging a culturally connected curriculum, educators and students together are trying to redirect the story of the Hoopa Valley. While poverty, drug abuse, and gender-based violence plague Hoopa as they do many American Indian reservations, there is also a tremendous cultural connectedness that leaders in the school and community foster and hope to channel to inspire more positive futures for young people. Many students want to leave the Valley as soon as possible (Focus Group, 2018b), but others dream of acquiring useful skills in college so they can return home to serve their community (Anonymous, 2018aa).

At HVHS, it is clear that Native students benefit from the availability of Yurok language classes, and non-Native students are positively affected by the integration of Native culture at the school more broadly. For students enrolled in Ms. Lewis's Yurok classes, the curricular inclusion of Yurok as a formal subject validates Native identities and creates new incentives for cultural pride and survival in the next generation. Curricular inclusion of Native culture, through units that range in subject matter from basket-making to the history of boarding schools, also builds intercultural understanding for non-Native and Native students alike.

Moreover, in rural areas such as the Hoopa Valley, the potential to use language and cultural skills in everyday life allows language learners to see the immediate applicability of their studies in ways that more urban learners may not have. As one student stated when I asked how she engaged in any traditional Native cultural practices, "I mean, I got, like, twenty fish at home right now in a smokehouse, but that's just food, man!" (Pole, 2018). The blurring of lines between daily survival and cultural survival speaks to the high level of integration between different forms of cultural traditions in the Hoopa Valley. Such blurring also opens doors to conversations about the interconnectivity of physical survival and cultural survival, and how language access and identity intertwine as young people explore how they want to participate in their communities and the world.

While the civic, cultural, and political participation of HVHS students cannot be neatly divided into separate categories, the use of cultural practices, including language, constitutes a form of resistance to cultural assimilation into dominant White culture. Yurok students, and students at HVHS more broadly, are carving out a space for themselves in the world that does not require them to be White, although some Native students benefit from White-passing privilege along with White students. Instead, the family culture of the school can be seen as a respite from the challenging social environments of surrounding communities, even as it struggles through its own moments of dysfunctionality. What matters most is that young people are encouraged to go forth into the world as themselves without the oppressive effects of whitening.

CHAPTER 7

"We Are Still Here": Navigating Cultural Rights and Discrimination at Eureka High School, California

Introduction: *Aiy-ye-kwee* as Hello

"Aiy-ye-kwee, everybody, skue-yen' 'ue-koy!" "Hello, everybody, good morning!" Eureka High School (EHS) Yurok language teacher James Gensaw greets a room of Yurok III/IV students. While some of them look distractedly at their phones or out the window, many of them look back at him shyly and reciprocate, "skue-yen' 'ue-koy." The students who have made it this far, meaning they are in their third or fourth year of taking Yurok at EHS, have shown commitment to the language, though their actual speaking and comprehension levels vary quite widely. So do their ethnic compositions and reasons for taking the class.

While the majority of students in the upper-level Yurok class are ethnically Yurok or Yurok and another ethnicity, there are also White students, a Latina student, and a Hmong American student. The upper-level class combines two language levels due to lower enrollment, but in Yurok I and Yurok II, nearly every one of the thirty-five seats in the room is full. In these classes, closer to half of the students are Native American, predominantly Yurok but also Hupa and Karuk, or with multiethnic family backgrounds, while the other half are White, Latinx, or Asian American.

This chapter explores the different effects that Yurok language access has on students with a range of identities at EHS. The Yurok language classes at EHS are attended by the most ethnically diverse group of students in any of the case-study schools in this book. EHS is also the most ethnically diverse of the four schools. Therefore, EHS is a particularly important case to explore how non-heritage-speaker students, both White and from other minority backgrounds, experience Indigenous language access. This chapter will show that for Native students, engaging in Yurok language study is part of a larger repertoire of resistance to culturecide, while for White students, Yurok language access helps undo myths about Native people they have learned both formally and informally. For non-heritage students of other minority backgrounds, the Yurok class empowers them to consider ways in which they too can advocate for their own curricular representation.

Eureka and Eureka High School Snapshot

The city of Eureka sits, enshrouded in fog or rain much of the year, on gorgeous Humboldt Bay, the traditional homeland of the Wiyot Tribe, studded with islands and oyster buoys and nestled into the redwood forest–covered mountains. It is a physically impressive landscape in a green and blue palette, sliced up by the visual effects of attempted human ambition and an industrial history: a half-closed strip mall, aging burger joints, an abandoned paper mill, and motels that double as homeless shelters. There are signs of perpetual renovation projects in the quaint downtown, just a few blocks off of Highway 101, which connects Oregon to San Francisco.

Both the town and the school have become much more racially, ethnically, and linguistically diverse since I grew up there in the 1990s as a result of migration and birth-rate patterns. With a current population of approximately 27,000, Eureka is two-thirds White; roughly 10 percent of the population identify as Hispanic or Latinx; and the remaining minority groups are Native American, Asian American, Pacific Islander, and African American or Black. Native Americans make up 6.4 percent of the total population of Humboldt County, whereas they compose 1.7 percent of California's population, according to 2016 census data (Carpenter IV, 2018: 25).

Eureka holds an unsavory reputation on many fronts. Initially a settler-colonial town that developed as a result of White migration in California's gold rush, its early residents formed White militias to murder the Native Yurok, Hupa, and Karuk communities that had called the area home for millennia in order to steal their land (Norton, 1979). In addition to gold panning and mining, Eureka became the base for a logging economy that spanned the nineteenth and twentieth centuries, ravaging the old-growth redwood forests. When the logging economy collapsed—epitomized by the Pacific Lumber Company's filing for bankruptcy in 2007—the area slid into an economic downturn, mitigated by the region's notorious and only recently legal crop, marijuana.

Migrants from many backgrounds have been attracted to the area for marijuana farming, as well as less contentious industries such as dairy farming, commercial fishing, and flower production. Yurok lands continue to be exploited for marijuana cultivation by settler-descendants, with continuing controversies over land rights, water usage, and pesticide contamination (K. Reed, 2019). Accompanying this assortment of jobs is a concentration of vices that often accompany low-income areas. Methamphetamine, alcohol, and other drug use is high, as are domestic violence rates and homelessness and housing instability across a range of demographics. Humboldt County has the lowest household income and some of the highest trauma scores[1] in California.

EHS was founded in 1896 and is the only comprehensive high school in the Eureka City Schools (ECS) system, with 1,170 students enrolled in 2018 (DataQuest, 2020). While some students live in the town of Eureka itself, others travel significant distances by car or bus to attend school. The demographic composition of EHS students varies from year to year, but it is approximately half White and half students from racial- and ethnic-minority backgrounds. During the period of data collection for this study in 2017–2018, EHS students identified as 53.8 percent White, 19 percent Hispanic or Latino, 12 percent Asian and Filipino, 4.2 percent American Indian, 2.3 percent Black, and 1.6 percent Pacific Islander, with 7.1 percent of students reporting more than one racial or ethnic identity (DataQuest, 2020). Just over half of EHS students are considered economically disadvantaged (EdData, 2020), though this population does not exactly correlate with minority status, as a significant number of White students are included in the low-income group. Students as well as staff and faculty identify as members of various racial and ethnic groups, but the majority of teachers and administrators are White.

Students at EHS come from a broad range of household types in terms of family income, levels of education and employment, and cultural background. While many students report having friends across many categories of fellow students, segregation along racial, ethnic, and class lines appears persistent. Some students struggle with a range of issues that are also problems for the community in general, including having drug-addicted parents and relatives, high burdens of caregiving for younger siblings, food insecurity, homelessness, domestic abuse, and immigration status. Other students appear quite sheltered from these issues and do not display much cross-cultural knowledge or sensitivity to those from different backgrounds.

At EHS I carried out fieldwork in all levels of Yurok language classes and observed and did comparable numbers of interviews, surveys, and focus groups with students in Spanish levels two through four, U.S. History, and Civics classes. I also interviewed teachers, counselors, the school principal, vice principal, and assistant superintendent at the district level. Data totals for EHS include 87 surveys, 56 interviews with students, 2 focus groups with students, 14 interviews with teachers and administrators, and 70 classroom observations. This data is the basis for the analysis below, which looks at school climate, particular issues faced by Native American and other minority students, and the impact of Yurok language access on EHS students and in the district more broadly. I conclude with an assessment of the challenges and strengths of EHS students related to school success, similar to the previous case-study chapters.

Impact of Yurok Language Access at EHS

Mr. Gensaw, one of roughly a dozen Yurok language-keepers, has his subject teaching certification in American Indian Languages and American Indian Culture, and he holds several other community-based positions in addition to this role to make ends meet.[2] Mr. Gensaw serves as a college technician for the Yurok Tribe, helping Yurok youth in the Eureka area understand their academic options and facilitating their application processes. He has worked for the Tribe at the visitor center in Klamath and as a language teacher at youth summer camps; he has also been contracted by the U.S. Park Service to translate signs in Redwood State Park into Yurok for symbolic cultural acknowledgment of the traditional owners of the land. Mr. Gensaw also coaches youth wrestling and is involved with Yurok culture as a dancer and language-keeper. His tattooed biceps, notoriety as an eel fisherman, and general down-to-earth attitude make him a respected and skilled confidant of young people, especially Native kids at EHS.

In the course of my research from 2018 to 2020, I sat in on dozens of Mr. Gensaw's Yurok classes at levels one through four, interviewed his students, spoke with them in focus groups, and analyzed anonymous student survey data from his classes. His commitment to exposing young people to Yurok language and culture, and building awareness of contemporary Native peoples in the region, was overwhelmingly evident in each of the data tools.

Impact on Native Students

Among Native students taking Yurok classes, there is a general sense of pride in Native identity and gratitude for both the language class and Mr. Gensaw, whom they see as working to make Yurok culture visible to all students. Interviews with students across a range of Yurok classes revealed the significance of language access: "The language is dying and I don't want it to ... because, like, it's my own culture and the language dying means that that's a part of our culture, dying. And that's sad ... I guess having our own language, it's ... something to, like, identify with" (Anonymous, 2018ac).

For this student, preventing language death is part of what motivates them to study Yurok. This student also recognizes that Yurok language is connected to Yurok identity, a sentiment shared by another student: "I knew it was a dying language and it wasn't used much. My grandpa uses it all the time so I decided to use it, too ... I can talk to my grandpa more and it makes me feel better knowing it's not going to die with so many people using it. I mean it's not used often but it's used ... I want to become a Yurok teacher and continue on teaching it because I don't want it to die. It's important" (Wonnacott, 2018).

The sense of destiny and intimate connection between the Yurok language and identity is shared by many Yurok students, including those who have taken several years of the language and those just beginning: "I feel like being Yurok, learning the language is something that we've always meant to do. Because I don't know, nobody else in my family besides my grandpa knows Yurok, because of the boarding schools and all that kind of stuff ... I'm a drummer, and I sing and dance in the traditional dances ... and I protest on Indian issues with my family" (Anonymous, 2018e). This student, at fourteen years old, shows an astute ability to connect the historical trauma of his grandfather's residency in the boarding schools to language loss, and therefore to his own motivation to help keep the language alive by learning it. He also shows a high level of cultural connection through his participation as a drummer, singer, and dancer in Yurok ceremonies. Just as ceremonial participation is something he is "meant to do," so is language learning.

The quote from the drumming student is also notable for the way he seamlessly connects his cultural participation through ceremony and language learning to political issues, saying he protests on "Indian issues" (Anonymous, 2018e). He went on to say that he had attended protests about the Klamath River dams, which prevent successful salmon migration, and that his family talked to him about how they used to go to protests against the G-O Road. The G-O Road was a USDA Forest Service project to connect the small towns of Gasquet and Orleans by way of Six Rivers National Forest, which cuts across lands sacred to Yurok, Karuk, and Tolowa people (Buckley, 2002: 170–201).

A concerted Yurok challenge to the legitimacy of the G-O Road went all the way to the Supreme Court, where the Justices appeared to overrule the 1978 Public Law on American Indian Religious Freedom, which allowed for protection of lands sacred to Native Americans, by green-lighting Forest Service road construction (Buckley, 2002: 170–201). The G-O Road had been started on both the Gasquet and Orleans sides but the thirteen-mile connection strip was left unfinished (Maher, 2018). The area was ultimately designated the Siskiyou Wilderness Area under the 1984 California Wilderness Act, prohibiting a range of resource extraction processes and leaving some Native sacred sites untouched (Maher, 2018).

The same student also described participating in protests against notorious Eureka businessman and developer Robert Arkley, who tried to buy Duluwat Island, just off the coast of Eureka in Humboldt Bay. Duluwat—formerly known as Indian Island but restored to its original name in the Wiyot language—is sacred to the Wiyot people and plays a significant role in their cosmology and food cycles. In 1860 Tuluwat village, on Duluwat Island, was the site of a massacre by White settlers of Wiyots, primarily women and children. It was then owned by the City of Eureka until it was officially returned to the Wiyot Tribe in 2019. When Arkley attempted to purchase Duluwat, the student described how "we went in front of his office and just protested all day" (Anonymous, 2018e).

The student astutely described the reasons for the protest and why Duluwat should be returned to the Wiyot Tribe. When I asked how he felt at the protests, he responded, "I enjoyed it. I got to see lots of my family members; it was really good seeing them. But it was fun 'cause there was, like, a lot of people there and there was singing and dancing and drumming and stuff like that. It's enjoyable just protesting and it's just powerful. Just being there helps . . . in small ways" (Anonymous, 2018e). In this case, the protest truly was powerful. It is unclear what made the City of Eureka finally decide to return Duluwat to the Wiyot Tribe—it had made symbolic overtures in the past—but it is likely that the protest helped shape the climate of debate that led to land-back.

A female student I'll call Naomi[3] who identifies as Yurok talked about how language and politics blend together in her own life. Naomi describes why she enrolled in the Yurok language class:

> I wanted to get closer to my culture, 'cause I didn't really grow up, like, fully immersed in it. We didn't really live, like, the traditional life, and I thought it'd be cool to learn more about it. . . . I feel like [Yurok class] gives people, like, a sense of something bigger in the world than just themselves. Learning about different cultures I feel like that's important, 'cause it makes people not so closed-minded all the time . . . like, people don't really know a lot about local culture, and especially, 'cause this is, like, very local culture, Yurok, is right here. But now they know more and they know what's, like, respectful and what's not in that culture, and they can learn to respect [Yurok culture] more. (Anonymous, 2018q)

Naomi has a small but close social group made up of three other girls who are White, Laotian, and Latinx, respectively, and tended to think of EHS as a fairly accepting place that she was hesitant to criticize. But she had concerns about what was happening in the larger community, and her Yurok identity was a vital part of the lens she used to evaluate local politics.

Naomi's grandmother lived up in Weitchpec, a remote part of the Yurok Reservation along the Klamath River, and Naomi shared that her grandma was worried about the dams, salmon, and water levels there. Though Naomi didn't attend the dam protests, she knew about them, and she did go to the Duluwat Island protest where she saw her grandmother also protesting (Anonymous, 2018q). In Naomi's words, she went to the protest because:

> I saw an image being, like, shared around Facebook [of the Duluwat and Arkley protest], and I was like "ooh, we should go," so when my mom got off work, we—me and my brother—went to the Dollar Tree,

we got markers, we made a sign, and then we went . . . I felt, I don't know, happy and sad at the same time. I was happy because you know, everyone gathered to support this, but then also sad because of why we were there and the reasoning behind that. So it, it was, I don't know. When I heard people chanting, it almost made me tear up, you know. But I thought it was so cool. (Anonymous, 2018q)

For Naomi, the ability to act on an issue that was important to her larger Native community—Duluwat Island's return to the Wiyot Tribe—also helped her consider ways she could be involved in issues closer to her own Yurok roots, such as controversy over the Klamath dams (Anonymous, 2018q). While Naomi's ability to take Yurok language classes did not play the sole defining role in her life, it was a major factor in her own self-definition as a Yurok young woman who had a voice and could speak up on a range of issues, from regional politics to racism among EHS students.

Naomi's experience stands in contrast to that of the majority of EHS students, who generally describe being very disconnected from politics, with only a few exceptions. While some students took part in cultural activities such as 4-H or Future Farmers of America, church groups, or ethnically based cultural activities, almost no students besides Yurok-identified students cited any sort of political activity. Only a small group of students mentioned their civic engagement in any way—such as helping out in their communities— and nearly all of these students were Native.

Most EHS students overall demonstrated low levels of political awareness, and there were some moments that showed just how narrow their concept of politics was. When I asked a White male student taking Yurok I if he followed politics at all, he asked, "What do you mean, like, the president?" (Anonymous, 2018x). Students, including this one, were sometimes unable to name the vice president of the United States, and few could name the governor of California or comment on how decisions were made in their communities—all basic indicators of political awareness. Of the students who did say they absorbed the news in some way, most reported getting their news from internet-based sources, some of which were traditional journalistic sources but the vast majority of which were social media feeds. A small group of students said they heard or saw news on the radio or television when their parents had it on, and sometimes they would listen in, or in the case of a few students, they didn't have a choice because it was on in the car when their parents were giving them a ride somewhere.

Almost no EHS students demonstrated the ability to analyze the credibility of their news sources. This was true for students from a range of ages and backgrounds at EHS, including seniors approaching graduation. The Yurok language class itself did not seem to lead to an increase in political participation, but attendance in the class laid the groundwork for a type of critical questioning of the world around them. Such willingness to question the status quo can be foundational to political participation.

Impact on Non-Native Students

The formally sanctioned existence of Yurok language as part of the official EHS curriculum plays a role in dispelling myths about Native people in California. What emerged from a range of interviews with people from many backgrounds at EHS, in ECS, in Eureka, and at the Yurok Education Department, alongside focus groups and participant observation in the classroom, is that education about the contemporary existence of Yurok people is impactful in fostering awareness about Native presence. Such awareness is built through ongoing activities that take place both in and out of the classroom. The existence of the Yurok class in formal curricula at all is an opening that educators like Mr. Gensaw utilize to demonstrate how Yurok culture is contemporary, not only a thing of the past.

Many White students—settler-descendants in the eyes of many Native residents—do not perceive Native culture in Northern California as part of contemporary reality. Some of these students think of Indigenous peoples in California as folkloric myth, relics of the past that do not play a role in today's world. In California, this is a predictable result of careful, racist curricular planning. For example, until 2017, a California mission unit was recommended for all fourth-grade teachers in the state. This unit erased the reality of enslavement, sexual abuse, and culturecide that the missions embodied, focusing instead on the "generosity" of Spanish colonizers through arts and crafts. While the creation of the California Indian History Curriculum Commission in 2014 set out to reshape the state's curriculum into something grounded in fact and awareness of human rights violations, many California mission kits[4] continue to be sold, reflecting the ongoing inclusion of the unit in public schools (Imbler, 2019).

Some spaces for protest against the California mission unit have gone public. For example, in 2017, Hoopa Valley Tribal member Cutcha Risling

Baldy, a professor of Native American Studies at Humboldt State University, worked with her daughter on the required fourth grade San Diego Mission model (Baldy 2017). Their rendition included representation of the Kumeyaay people's torching of the mission as part of a staged revolt in 1775 (Imbler, 2019). But this representation of dissent is an anomaly within the system, which is set up so that students finish the unit feeling proud of their arts and crafts and of the role of the Spanish missions in shaping California. The assignment is not critical of the regional history of culturecide but rather promotes it as a founding narrative.

With this state-level context in mind, it should therefore be less surprising that many White students at EHS had never learned about the real history of White-Native relations in the area. In my interview with Nathan, a White male student who was taking Yurok III, he described his impressions of Native people before enrolling in Yurok classes and his own reckoning with his history education to date: "I knew [Native Americans] were in the reservations and I knew they were really poor, but that's all I know about them. I grew up in a really poor neighborhood next to Alice Birney [Elementary School][5] so I felt like lots of poor people were mean and cruel and all that. So that's why—Native Americans, too [were poor and mean and cruel] and that's why I thought they were massacred—until I had the Yurok class and I was like whoa, that's definitely not what happened" (Payton, 2018).

Nathan's ascription to his previous understanding of why Native people were killed—because they were poor, and poor people (from his experience of growing up in a tough, low-income area in Eureka) are "mean and cruel"—illuminates how White people from working-class backgrounds can develop causal analysis of genocide that justifies violence against "others." In this case, Nathan's encounter with the narrative of events in Mr. Gensaw's Yurok classes that recognizes the role of White people in genocide, culturecide, and displacement has helped reshape his conceptions about Native people:

> I feel like the [White] American people, they were really bad to [Native Americans]. I feel really bad for the first Americans, the Native Americans. Why would [White people] go kill millions and millions of people? The second biggest holocaust in the world is the killings of Native Americans, you know, so it's like [White people] lied to us about their reasonings! I should have listened to the Native American's point of view [when I was] younger . . . but there

are also those stubborn people that are like "this is the way it's
supposed to be. We're not doing it any other way." (Payton, 2018)

When I asked Nathan how some of the stories he had heard and ideas he
previously held about Native people came to him, he immediately said the
following: "It was definitely history classes and just watching the poor
community where I grew up at. 'Cause, like, they teach you that the Native
Americans were poor people so then it's like, does that mean they behave
the same way as the other poor community groups, where they're smoking
and there's all this rape happening, and they're killing people left and right
because that's just how they are? Where in reality they're actually not like
that" (Payton, 2018).

Nathan's description of his own stereotype origins, from growing up in
a poor community, coupled with his history education sends a warning sig-
nal that extends far beyond the specific case of EHS. In this way, Nathan's
story of learning to categorize "others" is reflected in the views held by many
White people in the United States. A public education that only presents a
White settler-descendant majority narrative, in tandem with experiences of
poverty, can lead to negative stereotypes about others that feed into the jus-
tification for how those others are treated. This example raises real questions
about the obligation of public school curricula to promote diversity through
accurate historical truths—versus relaying victors' myths—and is highly
contested terrain in many countries (Ceylan & Irzik, 2004; Gellman, 2015,
2019; Gellman & Bellino, 2019).

In terms of giving young people accurate information about the past, parents and school boards routinely avoid the matter, saying that children are
too young to hear about violence (Imbler, 2019). Eureka is not yet at the point
of approving curricula that depicts how settlers and their descendants conducted campaigns of genocide. The school and district is not yet willing to
grapple with its logger mascot, let alone the intentional massacres designed
to steal Native land or campaigns of culturecide through forced removal of
Native children from their families and internment in boarding schools.
This information is only making its way to students in small doses, as
language-keepers like Mr. Gensaw assert their space in the formal education
curricula.

Yet Native students grow up with these stories of past violence because
they explain the hardships their families have experienced and continue to
live with. Language is lost because of the boarding schools; grandparents are

addicts as a response to depression and trauma from being separated from their families when forced to attend the schools; the land available for Tribal members is small because it was stolen by settlers and broken treaties (Anonymous, 2018o; J. Gensaw, 2017; Lowry, 2014; Norton, 1979; Wonnacott, 2018). As is the case for many minorities in the United States, Native children do not have the luxury of ignorance about historical treatment of their people because it directly affects them in the present (M. Gensaw, 2017). White children, on the other hand, continue to be seen as in need of protection from these historical facts.

With this context, it is unsurprising that several White students commented in various interviews and informal conversations that before taking Yurok, they did not know anything about contemporary Native Americans (Anonymous, 2018n; Payton, 2018). One student said, off the record, they had thought Native people were "extinct"—only Mr. Gensaw's lessons had taught them otherwise. A few Native students also mentioned that they had had conversations with White counterparts in the Yurok classes conveying this same idea, that the Yurok classes had opened their eyes to so much they didn't know (Anonymous, 2018a; Wonnacott, 2018). In fact, it is clear that as an intercultural competency tool, the Yurok language classes do much more than impart language and cultural knowledge. The classes also serve to disrupt myths of Native disappearance.

The learning curve for White students as shown above, coupled with the positive role of Yurok classes for heritage-speakers, confirmed the first two hypotheses set out in Chapter 1. That is, heritage-speaking students articulated an increased sense of ethnic pride and well-being (hypotheses one and two), and White students demonstrated increased intercultural competency and allyship (hypothesis three) as a result of taking Yurok language classes. It was harder to address the fourth hypothesis—that Yurok language access would also facilitate ethnically based pride, interest, and participation for ethnic minorities of non-heritage-speaking backgrounds. Mostly this was because few non-heritage-speaking minority students returned study permission forms, which was somewhat unsurprising given the generally low return rates for the forms and the low representation of this student type in Yurok classes.

Nevertheless, the lack of formal data does not undermine the hypothesis altogether. First, several Native students of multiethnic backgrounds, not necessarily Yurok, identified strongly with the positive impact of the Yurok classes, but it was not always clear (and also uncomfortable to figure out) which ethnic box to place these students in. Second, students from different Asian American backgrounds enrolled in Spanish classes at various levels talked about the positive identity role Spanish classes played in terms of expanding their cultural horizons and also helping them recognize the virtues of their own heritage languages (Huang, 2018; Phanhsavang, 2018).

These findings indicate that it may not necessarily be the Yurok class alone that serves as a mechanism of identity validation for minorities but rather any class that is deliberately intercultural and affirming of non-majority cultures (Banks, 2004; Bénéï, 2008; Lara-Cooper, 2017: 1–10). Such a finding might encourage schools and districts to think more expansively about their "foreign" language curricula and links to broader questions of citizenship formation. Beyond the important expansion of minority language offerings, the mainstreaming of minority cultural content in existing classes could also potentially play this positive role for young people from a range of backgrounds.

Language, Racism, and Protest

The call for more curricula that will expand awareness of and sensitivity toward minorities is not theoretical but rooted in a tangible need to intervene in the culture of racism and discrimination that has pervaded EHS and many other schools in Northern California. School climate, among numerous other factors, was named as perpetuating racist and discriminatory behavior in a damning report by ACLU NorCal that chronicles the ways that Humboldt County schools are not supporting Native student success (Simon et al., 2020). In the 2018–2020 period, Native students as well as Mr. Gensaw reported a wide range of denigrating behaviors exhibited toward them by students, faculty, and staff alike. Student-to-student microaggressions that were commonly reported included White students making stereotypical gestures like the tomahawk chop or ululating war cries toward Native students, calling them "chief," or greeting them with "how" or other Tonto-like broken English. In one extreme example, a White student brought a knife to EHS and threatened to "scalp" a Yurok student, calling him a "redskin" (Anonymous, 2018a). Though the Yurok student immediately reported the incident to the school office, he eventually had to go to the police himself to get a restraining order against the student because the school chose not to pursue the incident (Anonymous, 2018a).

Mr. Gensaw has experienced racist behavior from students, and fellow faculty members have also engaged in subtle, but problematic, behavior. For example, in his first year of teaching, a fellow teacher left a feather in his school mailbox, ostensibly meant as a welcoming gesture. The feather, however, was a random one that does not hold cultural significance for Mr. Gensaw, thus stereotyping Mr. Gensaw as an Indian who wears feathers.

There are bigger systemic issues with regard to recognition of Native culture at EHS as well. Since Mr. Gensaw began teaching at EHS in 2012, he has worked with the Native American Club, which is another gathering place for Native students from all backgrounds on campus. Despite other similar clubs being invited into a variety of assemblies or formal spaces, Mr. Gensaw remarks that:

> The only day we are invited to do something [at EHS] is on California Indian Day, when they ask us to do a dance at lunchtime on the quad, when all the kids are walking by, hollering and saying rude things. The school calls in Channel Three News to film us and they say, "look at our diversity." But the kids walking by are disrespectful, maybe a few will sit and watch but others flap their hands over their mouths whooping and making fun. There is no Native American History Month celebrated at EHS. There is Black History Month, where there is a required assembly for two periods. Classes sign up and go into the auditorium. But for us, we dance for twenty-five minutes during lunch, and its, "call the news." But people aren't paying attention, they're walking around. Why can't we have an assembly where people have to sit and be respectful?
> (J. Gensaw, 2019)

For years the Native American Club was only invited to dance during lunchtime in the open school campus on what California has named Native American Day, celebrated as an alternative to Columbus Day. Ironically, it seems because of the Thanksgiving holiday break, teachers in ECS have resisted having extra cultural curricula during the month of November, which is Native American History Month, because the break already shortens the teaching month (J. Gensaw, 2019). Therefore, Native American Day was the only day the Native American Club was invited to participate in a visible way for the student body.

One heritage-speaker and Yurok III student brought this issue up on her own when I asked her about feeling included at EHS: "Yes, we have a Native American Day where we show you what the Brush dance is, but I feel like there should be more shown. Because Day of the Dead gets more than one day. Everybody else gets more than one day. But we get one day to show who we are. One day to give our strength to you, to show the power we have. And I just feel like it should be shown more, not hidden more. Because it's truly hidden. It's not talked about. It's not shown" (Wonnacott, 2018). The invisibility of Native students and culture at EHS is worsened by the spectacle made of them when the Native American Club is invited to dance on the quad and not in a formal assembly space.

Mr. Gensaw and I spoke about the Native American Day spectacle several years in a row, and when we talked in person in his classroom in November 2019, he told me that when he was asked to have the club perform on the quad for yet another media-filmed public dance, for the first time he declined and instead asked for a special assembly to showcase the students' dance (J. Gensaw, 2019). His request was granted, and in November 2019 the first sit-down assembly for the Native American Club took place (J. Gensaw, 2019). Though small, this example shows that collaborative researchers can also act as sounding boards for stakeholder ideas that have the potential to catalyze change. Relocating and reframing the performance of the Native American Club might appear to be a very small thing, but it is part of a larger process of asserting the legitimacy of Native culture at EHS.

The Culture of Racism at EHS

Despite an ACLU NorCal lawsuit and settlement (2013–2015) over discrimination toward BIPOC students in Eureka City Schools, a culture of racism continues at EHS, and it is not only directed toward Native students. This section documents the wider context of racist behaviors toward a range of minority students and faculty at EHS to put in perspective the challenges that exist for addressing Native silencing in school. By highlighting the fact that all non-White groups are targeted, this section makes a case for increased intervention regarding intercultural competency at every level. From curricula to school assemblies and training for faculty and staff, EHS has much room for improvement in terms of the promotion of intercultural competency and reduction of micro- and macroaggressions. Though intercultural competency may be seen as insufficient when the larger goal is decolonization, the data below shows an urgent need for reducing hostility toward minority students as a baseline for coexistence.

The information that follows came from interviews and focus groups with students from a range of ethnic and racial backgrounds, and from a range of courses in 2018, including Yurok and Spanish at different levels, U.S. History, and Civics. Many White male and female students from several classes described the general school climate as "fine." In general, White students did not express any concern about racism or discrimination, citing the fact that they have friends across races as proof and stating that everyone generally gets along. A small sample of ethnic-minority students echoed these sentiments, while others shared intense depictions of a hostile environment.

A Black female student, in talking about what EHS was like for non-White students, disclosed the following: "During lunchtimes around the quad, the White male sports players taunt the Black sports players with phrases like 'go back to Africa' and 'have a banana, monkey'" (Anonymous, 2018l). In turn, the Black male sports players say these and other discriminatory statements to Black female students who are nearby, including to the interviewee (Anonymous, 2018l). This transference of shame—from shamed to shamer—is a clear behavior pattern: people who are victimized in turn victimize those they perceive as weaker. The Black male sports players did not feel powerful enough to confront the White male sports players directly, so they redirected their discomfort to Black female students.

Another Black-identifying female student noted the following: "A lot of times, just walking around, I hear, like, racial slurs and stuff on campus . . . yeah, people say, like, racial things but as a joke, but it's not that funny, like, they're being ignorant. They . . . like, they say it when they get mad, like, I don't know . . . when I tell them not to say that, they say 'oh, it's just a joke, chill.' Yeah, but they tell me to go back to Africa, and, like, call me monkey and stuff. And the N-word sometimes [from students who are] . . . White, Black, and . . . some Islanders, it's mixed" (Young, 2018). When I asked this student if she had ever talked to teachers, counselors, or administrators at EHS about the fact that these things are being said to her and her other Black friends, she said no, that adults at the school don't usually observe it happen because it occurs at lunch or after school (Young, 2018). She also said that she had never heard teachers or administrators talking about what language is appropriate for students to use, but she thought it would be good for them to address language use (Young, 2018).

A female student who identifies as Laotian and Filipina says she regularly encounters people in Eureka, in town and at school, who use stereotypes when they talk to her: "'Are you Chinese?' Or . . . trying to make fun of the language . . . or, like, 'do you eat this thing?' Or, 'oh my gosh, do you eat dogs?'" (Phanhsavang, 2018). A Chinese student talked about the stereotypes of Hong Kong and China she saw in class projects and how teachers were unable or unwilling to correct students or redirect them (Huang, 2018). In one focus group, a Hmong American male sports player acknowledged the culture of racist joking and that he also had things said to him, such as "dog-eater," but that it was just "guys messing around" and that "I can take it" (Focus Group, 2018a). While he described this, the several other male students in the focus group, who were White and Latinx-identifying, squirmed uncomfortably and tried to avoid eye contact with me. It felt as if the speaking student was sharing something that all the students recognized as unacceptable when held up to the light of adult eyes, but no one was sure how to respond.

Several Latinx EHS students described being told to "go back to where you came from" in various scenarios, including by a man from the community who shouted at them from a truck while driving by the students on school property (Fregoso, 2018; Montero, 2018). Other Latinx interviewees described being followed in Eureka stores as though they were potential shoplifters, or watching their family members be given incorrect change in shops because they were speaking in Spanish (Montero, 2018). Others also described generally feeling accepted at school (Valadez, 2018).

Derogatory comments came from classmates, even if they were not always described as such by Latinx interviewees, who tended to normalize or rationalize the behaviors. Some Latinx students described statements that would clearly be labeled racist or discriminatory if said by students in my home institution, but Latinx students often downplayed these remarks, believing that the comments were accepted by others at school (Valadez, 2018). This was less common with male Latinx students who would name behaviors as abusive.

One student, who identifies as bilingual in Spanish and English and is Mexican American, talked about the outpouring of racism at EHS in the weeks following the 2016 presidential election of Donald Trump:

> I was just hearing constant verbal abuse and just kind of, like, really
> nasty comments about other races, not just my own. And I don't
> kind of want to throw anybody under the bus, but it was mostly

hicks, or I could say White people, that were doing it. And it kind of hurt me because prior to that, they were so close to everybody else, and now they're kind of, like, pointing the finger, like "okay, you need to go back to where you came from. The United States isn't for you," and it really kind of hurt me as a person 'cause I'm like, before all of this, we were all brothers and sisters, and . . . it made me go puzzled because in elementary school and middle school, they were never like that. It was like, they were all still accepting of each other and you know, all of a sudden, I guess they showed their true colors—they just needed that platform [the president saying racist things] to show what they truly felt. And for all I know, they could have been feeling that the whole time, they just never spoke up about it. (Lopez, 2018)

Yet students from other backgrounds described letting barbed statements roll off them regularly.

When asked about his experience at EHS, Greg—who identifies as Black from a mixed background, including possibly some Native American heritage—related the following: "I've always been a person to make friends with any type of person. I'm just that type of person. I've never been offended by anything that people say, like, if it was, if it's racial, I really don't mind it, like, I just don't get angry about it 'cause I know the meanings of the words, if they use the [N-]word to me, and I know its background so I know not to get offended about something like that, or get very angry and put actions into it" (Daniels, 2018). Greg's ability to not get angry or take action when fellow students use racist language toward him exemplifies a coping strategy—and also flags major issues of coexistence at EHS.

On the one hand, students' resiliency in the face of such language—and to take it both in historical context, as Greg does, and as "just joking" like many other students of color noted—is a survival strategy. On the other hand, educators, administrators, and policymakers alike should reflect on what we are asking minority students to withstand and where intervention might help change the cultural norms at play in schools and within youth socialization patterns.

Also, at EHS and within many societies, while the majority of the micro- and macroaggressions are directed at ethnic and racial minorities by ethnic majorities, there is also significant discrimination both within and across racial and ethnic-minority groups. Latinx and Asian American students described trading barbs with each other, and within the Latinx student body there is also tension across different groups: for example U.S.-born Latinxers taunt Mexico-born students about their migration status, whether or not they are documented. This is mirrored in HVHS and in the Mexican schools, where minority students also participate in disparaging minorities who are disassociated from themselves in some way. Students of color across a range of backgrounds describe the color hierarchies that inform social status, with light skin being the most prized and therefore increasing someone's popularity.

Of the 120 students I spoke to across all case-study schools, only a few at each school—and always members of the racial, ethnic, or sexual minority being made fun of—articulated that the culture of joking was a problematic and offensive behavior. The rest wrote it off as rowdy teenage behavior or as something they expected to have to endure because of who they were. This may be a survival strategy, but it also indicates the social acceptance of discriminatory speech as a normal part of adolescent interaction. This normalization of assimilation of discrimination has repercussions, ones that institutions should take seriously.

Of most concern is the fact that there is little institutional awareness of racism and discrimination in any measurable way because such behaviors are not reported. Numerous students commented that they never put anything in the anonymous "report a problem/make suggestion" boxes near the main entrance of EHS, claiming it would still feel like tattling even though they recognized the boxes were there to report problems like racism. Each of these students stated that they preferred to just tough it out—a resounding theme from all minority students at EHS. When I pressed these students about how the school could address problematic behavior if they didn't know it was happening, they generally responded, "I don't know," and waited for me to move on. It is worth noting that while EHS students had a complaint box and didn't use it, no such mechanisms for filing anonymous complaints or suggestions existed at either of the Oaxaca schools or at HVHS.

Quantitative Data on Inclusion and Discrimination

The survey data provides another way to assess student perceptions of their own inclusion in school and their communities. As this is the final empirical chapter, I provide a small amount of cross-case analysis here to show some of the ways these perceptions were assessed. Questions 24 to 33 of the survey asked students to reflect on their feelings of inclusion in both their schools and surrounding communities. The students responded (using a five-point scale) to statements such as "I feel included in my school," "I feel included in my local community," "I regularly spend time with people from backgrounds or cultures that are different from my own," "I enjoy spending time with people from cultures different than my own," "I would like to become more comfortable engaging with people from different cultural and language backgrounds," and "My school encourages knowledge of diverse communities and cultures."

The survey data from this section on diversity and inclusion is mixed. The majority of students in all schools responded affirmatively to most statements, with 50 to 60 percent strongly agreeing that they felt included in their schools or communities, and another 20 to 30 percent slightly agreeing that they felt included in both realms. In response to Question 27, 65 percent of all respondents said that they regularly spent time with people from backgrounds or cultures different from their own. On the one hand, this data shows general positive trends in diversity and inclusion at the schools. On the other hand, one or more students at each school strongly or slightly disagreed that they felt included or wanted to feel more comfortable in intercultural contexts. Seven percent of students in both Oaxaca and California felt excluded at school, while 17 percent felt neutral about whether or not they were included. Thirteen percent felt excluded in their communities and 29 percent felt neutral about the statement "I feel included in my local community." Across all schools, 8 percent strongly or slightly disagreed with the statement "I regularly spend time with people from backgrounds or cultures that are different from my own," while 20 percent answered neutrally.

Question 27, below in graph form, presents data showing that many but not all students do spend time with people different than themselves. However, at each school, at least a few students disagreed or were neutral on this question. Survey Question 28 states: "I enjoy spending time with people from cultures different than my own." Nobody strongly disagreed with this statement, 2 percent slightly disagreed, 11 percent were neutral, 22 percent slightly agreed, and 65 percent strongly agreed. These percentages were very similar for Question 30, "I would like to become more comfortable engaging with people from different cultural and language backgrounds." While at least 20 percent of students felt either neutral about these statements or disagreed, the majority of the people surveyed indicated some type of openness to having diverse social groups, with many explicitly saying they would like to have more diverse groups than they do.

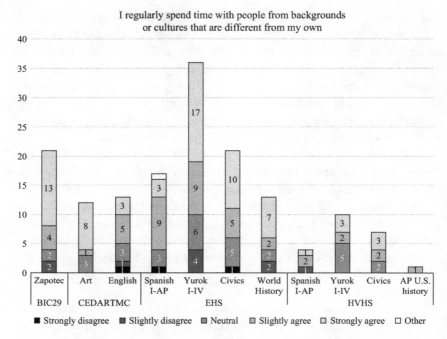

Figure 2. Question 27 Tableau: Cross-tabulated responses showing diversity and inclusion indicator.

District Responses to School Climate

Addressing school climate is a complex issue. Eureka City Schools Assistant Superintendent for Educational Services Michael Davies-Hughes,[6] who coordinates the Indian Education Program,[7] takes it seriously and also acknowledges the long-term challenge of such deep culture change. He reflects:

> We have a professional and social responsibility to make sure that we're not leading our students through our own implicit bias lens. So I think that that's an obstacle because, you know, as much as I'd like to say that doesn't happen here, that we're all culturally responsible and respectful it's just—that's not realistic to say, or accurate. So professional development around cultural responsiveness is something that, you know, it's been an obstacle because we've

got to build that professional development in for our staff along with all the other things that we're doing. (Davies-Hughes, 2017)

Addressing bias and developing intercultural competency can take place in many ways, including expanding curricular offerings in direct culturally relevant content such as Indigenous languages or mainstreaming diverse content into other courses. But Davies-Hughes notes: "I think the language classes, that's not the only way. There are other opportunities within our community. There's obviously the responsibility of parents and guardians to be active participants in ensuring that their children grow up to be culturally responsive and respectful. There's teachable moments everywhere at all times. It's just a matter of who's there to guide our students through that, help them navigate through that. That's a tough one" (Davies-Hughes, 2017). Fostering positive youth development, in other words, is a community project, not just a school objective.

Davies-Hughes stresses that even if schools encompass best practices around diversity and inclusion, other variables such as family influence may undercut efforts: "For students, you know, we have them for six-and-a-half hours a day and then they go home. They go home to families that may have a different outlook on life and who may see cultural differences as not being something positive, so we encounter that as well. . . . The values that we're teaching at school might not be congruent with the values being taught at home—I think that that's definitely an obstacle" (Davies-Hughes, 2017). Davies-Hughes is right that schools can only do so much and that many other spheres of influence, especially families, play central roles in youth identity development. Yet such incongruency of values should not be a deterrent. Instead, the district's role is one of reeducating students who may have been indoctrinated with racist rhetoric at home but who are capable of doing intercultural work when provided with appropriate opportunities. As school districts balance many competing priorities, both their own and those of their state regulators, there will be roadblocks as old-timers might not want to change their approaches and districts and schools might not want to modify curricula. But without high-level leadership, it will be hard for individual teachers to take up the burden of this work.

Jim McQuillen, director of the Yurok Tribe's Education Department, writes about the interconnectedness of cultural competency and curricular reform:

The Native language revitalization movement is vital to the cultural education in the schools. It is also vital to helping public educational institutions be more welcoming and culturally competent places so Native students feel accepted there and in society as a whole. Cultural inclusiveness and cultural awareness is so much more than a one or two day professional development teacher in-service training with panels and speakers. It is realized by system-wide reform, by a paradigm shift in the curriculum and course selection where tribal culture, language, and the staff are reflective of the students served by the school system. We need courses in Native American studies in grades 8–12, Native language courses at the K–8 grades, and accurate curriculum which reflects the local culture, history, and identity. (J. McQuillen, 2019: 286)

McQuillen challenges all of us to see cultural validation as a true shift in paradigm, something closer to decolonization than an institutional diversity and inclusion mandate. Such work is necessary to make a safe environment for students from all backgrounds, and to prepare them for democratic coexistence.

EHS is ripe for intervention and innovation, but given the rampant racism among students and within the larger community, decolonization there is no easy task. I have offered a first look at how Yurok language, in its early days within the EHS curriculum, can be part of the "paradigm shift" (J. McQuillen 2019: 286). Visibility, as a form of survivance, is part of decolonization.

Participation for EHS Students

Most of the adults I know would not consider high school as the best time in their lives, or even a time they would willingly return to. In part, this is because the hormone-fueled immaturity of the fourteen- to eighteen-year-old experience is one frequently tormented by self-doubt and vulnerable to the cruelty of peer perception and remarks (Koomler et al., 2017; Sadowski, 2008). The large increase in mental illness and disability diagnoses of college students across the United States reveals that the years directly after high school are also difficult (Auerbach et al., 2018: 624; Liu et al., 2019: 8–10; Tutsch et al., 2019: 438). Yet the challenges of high school are unique in that many students are still within the nest of family, or at least are not yet legally adults, while also trying to define their own identities in relation to the world around them.

Youth political participation is linked to individuation (Earl et al., 2017: 3), meaning the process by which people establish identities separate from others. Though individuation may be a lifelong process, it typically surges during adolescence and young adulthood in the United States (Qu et al., 2016: 1512), when young people come into greater contact with people beyond their microcommunities and develop the tools to engage in the world. Much of this happens in person in schools and community spaces, but it also happens online, through Zoom schooling, on social media, and so forth. Though not the focus of this book, today's young people are dramatically shaped by and in turn shape online content like never before (Loader et al., 2014: 143). Such impacts are being researched at this very moment, especially since the Covid-19 pandemic has increased the amount of time people are spending online.

Participation as a Local and Culturally Situated Phenomenon,
Quantitatively Assessed

This brief section addresses participation across the four case-study schools as documented in the survey. Some questions focused on different ways students participate (or not) in their families, local communities, and communities more broadly defined.[8] Students responded to statements (using a five-point scale) such as "I volunteer in my community," "I attend political gatherings in my community," "I attend club meetings either in or out of school," "I help elders in my community," "I participate in cultural projects in my community," "I learn and make traditional artistry," and "I do childcare, cook, or other domestic chores to support my community." This section of the survey addressed a range of types of participation, from typical family participation such as doing household-based chores, to civic participation by helping elders, to cultural participation through clubs or artisan production, to political participation through youth committee membership or protest attendance.

The participation section of the survey shows overall that students at BIC 29, CEDARTMC, and HVHS all participate more in a variety of ways than do students at EHS. In general, students at EHS showed consistently lower levels of participation in comparison to the students at the other schools across all participation questions. This phenomenon shifts slightly when broken

down by race, as White students at EHS participate the least in most categories, while students from a range of minority backgrounds in general participate more. In this way, participation is not specifically an Indigenous
behavior but rather is connected to any ethnic-minority identity where
cultural expectations for youth dictate what they do with their time outside
of school.

For example, more HVHS students overall, and more Native students at
EHS, gather and give food or other resources to people who need help in their
communities, which is in line with Yurok, Hupa, and other Indigenous
peoples' expectations of young people. In both BIC 29 and CEDARTMC, and
among minority respondents in HVHS and EHS, many more students
strongly or slightly agreed that they helped with childcare or other household
chores than White EHS or HVHS counterparts did. Again, the communitarian cultural norm within Indigenous and other minority communities of
valuing the family well-being over individual priorities is evident. This was
strongly affirmed by interview data, where many non-White students talked
about heavy at-home responsibilities. For example, one Asian American student at EHS was tasked with complete responsibility for younger siblings at
home while the parents were at work. In addition, numerous BIC 29 students
reported spending several hours each day preparing food, washing, and
cleaning.

According to their responses to the survey, across all four schools, White
students had the lowest total participation rates. For example, in response to
Question 17 ("I attend political gatherings in my community"), twenty-nine
White students at EHS responded "strongly disagree," "slightly disagree," or
"neutral," while eleven agreed slightly or strongly. In comparison, seven Native American students responded that they slightly or strongly agreed with
the statement, while nine responded strongly or slightly disagree, or neutral, showing a more even split. White students also talked in interviews
about spending more time online playing games or listening to music and
not having high family expectations of participation. This data thus provides information about one cultural resource that Indigenous and minority students have in abundance: a cultural expectation of family and
community-based participation that White students in California lack.
While clearly there are exceptions to these generalizations, the survey and
interview data together show that many Indigenous and minority students see themselves as active members of communities that expect them to
participate.

While Indigenous and minority students may not be politically active in terms of joining protests or engaging at the national level, in many ways their work ethic and sense of identity as belonging to a specific type of community with strong communitarian values can translate later in life into different kinds of participation depending on the issues at hand. This is an extrapolation from the survey, but taken together with ethnographic and qualitative data, it captures important differences in the relationship between identity and participation.

In contrast, many White students, particularly at EHS, appeared culturally isolated. While most had cliques they readily identified with, including student-labeled categories of jocks, hicks, and artists, their pursuits out of school or during lunchtimes tended toward solitary activities that did not demonstrate broader solidarity with other people. How White youth identity formation experiences might translate into participation later remains unanswered. Question 17 is an imperfect measurement because many high schoolers may think about politics but have not yet had the opportunity to participate. For this question in particular, I was grateful for the mixed methods of the study, which allowed me to better understand youth participation patterns in interview and focus group conversations shared above, rather than solely through their survey answers, which reveal mixed political behavior.

Obstacles and Support for Student Educational Success at EHS

The most significant obstacle for EHS students in completing their high school education is their own mental health. In surveys and interviews, students mentioned depression and anxiety as two factors that impacted their choices and behaviors around schoolwork as well as whether or not they participated in social and extracurricular activities. In one student's words: "The way that I interact with my classmates and fellow students is a little odd because they're just really stressful and the way that they live just really stresses me out and we'll just say it does not do wonders for my mental health" (Gillespie, 2018). There are two psychologists on staff at EHS, but no student—even those who openly disclosed their own mental health struggles—ever approached either of them for help.

As at HVHS, EHS teachers are involved in helping students daily with their mental health struggles. Teachers informally talk with students and help them through whatever obstacles they are facing at the moment. These conversations often occur before and after classes, or at lunchtime when teachers who are more willing to play this role tend to leave their classroom doors open, creating a safe haven for students who may not feel socially comfortable elsewhere in the school or who are struggling with a particularly difficult issue.

The second most frequently mentioned obstacle students mention is personal motivation and academic focus. Frequently this lack of motivation derives from individual behavior and personality, but it is also connected to the drug economy and culture of Humboldt County. Lack of motivation was often mentioned in interviews when students disclosed a preference to "party" or "mess around," and students who talked about this also tended to have vague personal goals for the future. In contrast, students who articulated clear professional goals for themselves did not cite lack of motivation as a factor in their educational pathways. In Humboldt County, some young people have been able to channel their preference for drug use into lucrative jobs as marijuana trimmers, dispensary operators, or cultivators. Though outside the scope of this book, Humboldt County's long-time black market marijuana economy, though dramatically impacted by recreational marijuana legalization in 2016, is still a major source of informal employment for people in the region. Many young people know this and invent their identities accordingly.

The third most mentioned obstacle to educational success is a lack of financial resources. While this is less of an obstacle than at HVHS, EHS teachers constantly address the acute economic needs of their students. For example, teachers provide food for those in need at their own expense. Jamie Bush, a member of the social studies faculty who teaches sophomores, described how "we have a very large population in all of our schools in Eureka on free and reduced lunch. So I keep granola bars in here [indicates a drawer in her desk in her classroom] and I have some students who know that they're here, and they can just quietly come in and grab one, whether they're still my students or not. Some of them, I have coming back even as juniors or seniors, 'cause they'll know I'll have things here, and ask, like 'can I have a granola bar?' I say, 'Sure!'" (Bush, 2018). While EHS offers free breakfast and lunch to income-qualifying students, families have to apply for the assistance,[9] and there is no dinner or weekend food service. Instead, faculty fill in the gaps, as Ms. Bush describes above. A local Eureka-based nonprofit, Food for People, coordinates extra food assistance with many schools in Eureka but not at EHS.

Effects of Physical Insecurity

Student trauma from past violence, fear of future violence, and resource scarcity significantly shapes student behavior. While EHS has more resources and a smaller high-trauma caseload than HVHS, there are still many students who experience homelessness, food insecurity, and domestic violence. Witnessing family violence, particularly by fathers or a mother's male partner against mothers, is a major trauma factor in the Eureka population.

EHS, like many other high schools, strives to make the school a safe haven that can meet as many student needs as possible. Though school officials may sometimes call on government agencies to get involved if the student's situation warrants it, in general, students feel immense shame about the conditions of their own physical insecurity and try to keep it as little known as possible. Given this context, schools like EHS can continue to improve in terms of providing food, clothing, school supplies, and other resources to address economic insecurity. They also need to find ways to include discussions in the curricula about power-based violence and healthy relationships.

Teachers can surmise what their students are dealing with at home based on how they relate to teachers and fellow students, as well as how they interact with the curriculum, current events, and material realities of schooling. For example, teachers hear students parroting political ideologies handed down from parents; they see telltale signs of homelessness in unwashed clothes or bodies; or they observe a student who becomes upset and leaves the classroom during a film on undocumented immigration. There are both undocumented students and students who live in mixed-status families at EHS, meaning some members are documented and others are not. The constant state of fear and paranoia that accompanies undocumented status wears on students in subtle ways. Studies find that undocumented students try to avoid any transgression that would bring attention to their families (Combs et al., 2014: 191–193). This also means undocumented students are less likely to intervene if they see other students subjected to racist treatment, as doing so opens themselves up to targeting.

Sources of Support for Students

As in many other high schools, students at EHS cite their family members, administrators, teachers, and friends as sources of support. Many students spend significant time talking to teachers outside of class. Mr. Gensaw's door is generally open at lunchtime and break time, and Native students usually gravitate to his room during those intervals; it is a place where they feel comfortable and recognized for who they are. They also sign up for his class, knowing it is a place they will be better understood:

> Working with Indigenous populations in the school systems, there always seems to be other teachers say[ing], "well this kid is just a horrible student, this person's disrespectful, this person's this way," you know. And there's, I don't know why, but there's a lot of these Native kids that seem like they get pushed through or kind of get excluded from other classes, and they may even seem like they're failures. But to have those kids come into my classroom and actually succeed and actually feel connected to the language, and feel part of a family almost, I think that's one of the major successes I see as a teacher. It's kind of neat. Like last year, I had all these kids—I had five or four IEPs,[10] behavioral issues, and kids that were acting out in other classrooms. And I never knew that because in my classroom they're paying attention, they're doing their work and they're engaged, and always raising their hand and volunteering. (J. Gensaw, 2017)

While many other teachers play non-curricular supporting roles for students at EHS, it is important to highlight the role that the mere existence of Yurok language at EHS plays. Beyond Mr. Gensaw's role as a language teacher, his presence as a Yurok person at EHS provides a safe space and recognition for Yurok students and those from other Native backgrounds. His classroom is a place where Native students can retreat with the knowledge that they will not be harassed for their Native-ness but encouraged to appreciate their identity as a shared strength. Mr. Gensaw also understands the microcultures in which they and their families may be operating and gains student respect in a way that White or other non-Native teachers may not be able to.

Teachers across disciplines talked about the importance of the open-door policy for students, but it is not at all universal across the faculty (Bush, 2018; Haun, 2018). Some teachers play more of a supportive role than others, with some locking their doors at lunch or otherwise maintaining distance from students outside of classtime. Mr. Olson, who is White, teaches Spanish classes at EHS and runs an annual class trip to Oaxaca, Mexico, for advanced Spanish students, has an always-open door. Spanish-heritage kids and others know that his warm and joking style will make them feel welcome, and his ease in Spanish, and in his own positionality, crafts a dynamic and welcoming atmosphere. As a veteran teacher and a non-Native speaker who himself worked hard to learn the language, Mr. Olson's keen attention to issues of migration faced by many of his students sets him up to be an ally, something I observed during numerous hours sitting in on his classes in 2018, 2019, and 2020.

Students at EHS have a range of goals and dreams for their futures. In interviews, students mentioned a wide range of potential professional paths for themselves, from being doctors and scientists to construction workers. Students also articulated a variety of college plans, including attending College of the Redwoods (the local community college), completing professional certificates, attending Humboldt State University (California State Polytechnic Institute, Humboldt in 2022), going to a University of California school, or going to a private college out of state.

The majority of student goals appeared both modest and pragmatic. For example, one student had already researched the mortuary science program she wished to enroll in and said that she thought there would be good job security in such a field (Anonymous, 2018l). Others clearly held their parents' goals for them in tension with their own; one student said her family wanted her to go into the medical field but she was more interested in working in Hollywood (Phanhsavang, 2018). Given this backdrop of challenges and opportunities for student success at EHS, it is evident that language access happens in a politically and socially complex place. Adding Yurok to the curriculum is one of many interventions needed to shift the culture in Eureka to one more invested in pluriethnic and multicultural coexistence.

Conclusion: A Less Racist Eureka Is Possible

The case study of EHS does not show a universal link between Yurok language access and civic, cultural, and political participation via the mechanism of positive identity consolidation. But, broken down into several strata of both student and participation types, there are significant findings that reveal the importance of Yurok in positive youth development. First, for Yurok heritage-speakers, the availability of Yurok in the formal EHS curriculum is an unqualified good; it boosts self-esteem and pride in heritage, which in turn helps young people feel more culturally connected to the Yurok community and leads to increased civic and cultural participation. Political participation is variable, and while it appears to correlate, it cannot be considered causal because of the range of other factors that appear to contribute to this participation form, including family political involvement and the relation of a given family to the Tribal political landscape.

For White students, there is clear evidence that Yurok classes serve as disruptors of negative myths and stereotypes about Native Americans. The data overwhelmingly showed that Mr. Gensaw's teachings help undo problematic previous lessons such as the California mission unit and the underlying sentiment of Manifest Destiny as part of the United States' foundational narrative. While no real increase in participation was noted for White students, the critical analytic skills to question the information they are given, in particular in relation to stories about minorities, were very evident. In this way, Yurok language access at EHS serves an even larger educational goal than previously predicted—it teaches students to seek out multiple perspectives and adjudicate between them before deciding what they believe. Such a skill is a fundamental quality of an engaged citizenry capable of peaceful coexistence with others from different backgrounds.

While there was limited data from non-heritage-speaking minority students in Yurok classes, data from Asian American students enrolled in Spanish classes shows that space for minority language affirmation can promote positive identity consolidation regardless of the language. Further research could explore the potential for this identity consolidation in other curricular spaces. History classes are prime sites to explore the availability of alternative narratives, for example. Yet there are so many intervening variables in youth identity formation; the influence of family and community norms, gender patterns, migration experiences, and economic status all compete with curricular offerings in shaping young people's sense of self and ability to participate.

One way in which variables such as family and community values are visible is that the high levels of racism in majority-White towns around EHS appear to serve as a disincentive for some students to enact their cultural practices more fully. Adding Yurok to the curriculum is not an instant panacea at EHS. It may take years of Yurok classes and other culturally relevant curricular access for Native students to gain pride in their heritage and claim their language and cultural skills more fully.

While the Yurok I class may plant seeds of relating to the world in multiple ways, students in Yurok III were far better able to articulate how the class related to their worldviews. This demonstrates both the process of human development from fourteen-year-olds to seventeen- or eighteen-year-olds and possibly the effect of ongoing exposure to curricular content as well as time to reorganize how one operates in the world. Regardless, Yurok language classes provide a venue to legitimize Native youth identities in educational and social spaces at EHS. While some students may already claim these identities in a more public and socially grounded way within Native communities and families, others benefit from the space created by the class to begin such self-exploration.

Language classes alone cannot carry the burden of building Indigenous visibility. Rather, there are many spaces—U.S. and World History classes, Civics classes, and discussions about different heritages throughout the year—that present learning opportunities for students, faculty, and staff alike. Conscientious school attention to diversity will benefit all students and families.

Nearly a quarter of EHS students are either migrants or the children or grandchildren of migrants who hear a language other than English at home. Increased efforts to facilitate more intercultural learning for students, staff, and teachers will convey the importance of diversity in Eureka's changing demographics. Without such attention, the potential for xenophobic and racist thinking and actions to perpetuate in communities like Eureka is very real. Offering Yurok language classes at EHS is one good step forward.

CONCLUSION

Advocating for Multilingual, Pluricultural Democracy

> When a language dies, so much more than words are
> lost. Language is the dwelling place of ideas that do not
> exist anywhere else. It is a prism through which to see
> the world.
>
> —Kimmerer, 2013: 258

Showing Up as Resistance

Every school day in Oaxaca, Mexico, Noemi[1] greets her grandmother in Zapotec before taking a motorcycle taxi from the center of her village to school. She is welcomed through the school gate by a sign in Zapotec, and several times a week she studies the Zapotec language in a class period specifically dedicated to the topic. Her grandmother is glad that Noemi is more interested in speaking Zapotec with her since she started taking it at school and that Noemi is encouraged to speak it, rather than being hit for using it, as the grandmother remembers from her own childhood.

In Hoopa, California, Lena[2] gets a ride from her grandmother to school, which sits on the opposite side of the reservation from where they live. As they drive by the rushing Trinity River, Lena tells her grandmother one of the nearly one hundred Yurok words for fish, *nuenepuy*, that she learned in her language class. Her grandmother nods with interest. Lena knows her grandmother feels sad that their family lost the language after her great-grandmother never recovered from the trauma of her boarding school experience, which took place in nearly the same spot Lena's high school now sits.

Noemi and Lena are part of a new generation of Indigenous students who, for the first time, have access to heritage languages in their public high schools. Both navigate family poverty and historical trauma in their daily life, and both are determined to be the first in their families to go to college. By showing up to their respective Zapotec and Yurok classes each day and engaging with interest in their heritage languages, Noemi and Lena are participating in acts of resistance to culturecide that have pervaded their family legacies. They are, in the spirit of Ngũgĩ wa Thiong'o, decolonizing their minds (1986).

Within both Noemi's and Lena's language classrooms, Zapotec and Yurok language ability is a source of pride. Outside of schools, Indigenous language skills were historically more often a liability than a benefit. In both Mexico and the United States, Indigenous language use was directly connected to punishment in school systems for generations, so convincing parents or elders that Indigenous language learning is a good use of school time remains difficult.

Robin Wall Kimmerer captures the essence of why language is such a critical bridge into cultural survival: "Despite Carlisle, despite exile, despite a siege four hundred years long, there is something, some heart of living stone, that will not surrender. I don't know just what sustained the people, but I believe it was carried in words" (2013: 256). The language-keepers are those who carry words forward, planting them in the next generation. Schools are one potent arena where the creation of youth identity plays out. Indigenous language access provides a path to resisting culturecide as a part of identity formation.

Culturecide, Decolonization, and Education

In the remainder of this conclusion, I reflect on language access as part of decolonization and democratization processes, situated in a human rights framework. Resisting culturecide is part of decolonization, which entails the undoing of dominating relationships between rulers and the ruled. In formerly colonized communities, alongside allies or "coconspirators" (Love, 2019: 117), remaking the world in more just and equitable ways is the project at hand. Decolonization is not a reversion to a mythical or primordial notion of the past. It frequently includes reclaiming cultural knowledge while also living each day in the web of cultural, political, and economic globalization that colonialism and neocolonialism have wrought (Jacob, 2013: 6). As an outsider, I do not weigh in on what decolonization should look like in any of my research sites. But the collaborative methodological framework has prepared me to listen to what community partners have identified as their goals.

For deep change, decolonization cannot only happen within Indigenous communities but must be reflected in settler-colonial and ethnic-majority communities and institutions as well. Such decolonization might look like many different things. In Mexico, it could include eradicating the stigma of Indigenous people as less than mestizo counterparts by valuing languages, foods, dress, and other cultural practices equally. In the United States, it may be advocating for dam removal from rivers (Wear, 2021) or land return by White people to traditional Native owners (Greenson, 2021). The collaborative methodology framework is one way that researchers can attempt to decolonize their own profession by listening to what community partners have identified as their goals, and working with them to craft a mutually beneficial process, as I have tried to do.

Decolonization can also take place in the redrafting of what public education communicates to young people through curricula about the values of Indigenous cultures. Yet while decolonizing schools and curricula has become a popular idea in the progressive education field as of late, it should not be used lightly as a concept. Eve Tuck and Wayne Yang argue that "decolonization is not a metaphor. When metaphor invades decolonization, it kills the very possibility of decolonization; it recenters whiteness, it resettles theory, it extends innocence to the settler, it entertains a settler future. Decolonize (a verb) and decolonization (a noun) cannot easily be grafted onto pre-existing discourses/frameworks, even if they are critical, even if they are anti-racist, even if they are justice frameworks. The easy absorption, adoption, and transposing of decolonization is yet another form of settler appropriation" (2012: 3). Tuck and Yang's article serves as a warning to not transpose decolonization onto existing settler-colonial frameworks and call it change. This is an important point to keep in mind given that the Indigenous language classes documented here operate in mestizo- (Mexico) and settler- (U.S.) dominated public education sectors, which are certainly preexisting discourses.

Expanding Indigenous language access is a mechanism by which mestizo- and White-dominated educational institutions can link their agendas to that of decolonization. Such linking may or may not constitute decolonization itself, in the way Tuck and Yang call for, but the link is a starting point. Indigenous language access for youth unsettles mestizaje and Whiteness in Mexico and the United States, respectively, even as it takes place within historically dominating institutional spaces. In this way, schools can be "decolonized landscapes" (Middleton-Manning et al., 2018: 175), at least within the special spaces of the Indigenous language classroom.

Such microspaces do not by themselves rectify the impact of historical and contemporary colonization and genocide. They are not the same as an apology, reparations, or giving land back. But Indigenous language classes are spheres where young people can resist ongoing culturecide by expressing pride and curiosity in their Indigenous identities and push back against narratives of disappearance or inferiority. Such resistance is one expression of decolonization even as it takes place within institutions that may continue as neocolonial operatives.

Participation as Decolonization

I have argued in this book that building solid identities is key to building potentially engaged civic, cultural, and political youth capable of resisting culturecide. A seventeen-year-old HVHS student describes that "my whole life had been in training for my voice to be heard. Standing Rock created a unique space to speak up. . . . There was a time when I stood up and talked at a water board meeting, and I remember asking them, 'Does it make you feel good knowing that you are slowly killing my culture?'" (Joseph, 2019: 308). When equipped with the tools to develop positive self-identity and use their voices in a range of participation types, Indigenous youth and their non-Indigenous allies resist culturecide through survivance, or what Cherokee scholar Jeff Corntassel calls "Indigenous resurgence," which he describes as "struggling to reclaim and regenerate one's relational, place-based existence by challenging the ongoing, destructive forces of colonization" (Corntassel, 2012: 88). Such resurgence is taking place in Oaxaca and California all the time.

Young people are resurgent in large and small ways in their communities. In Oaxaca, helping with childcare, taking care of elders, or learning the craft of artisan production of wool or weaving may not appear as a political struggle. But choosing to continue Indigenous customs and cultural practices is an assertion of Indigenous presence in the face of culturecidal state policies. Such practices are not always easy. Young people may be teased by those who have assimilated more into dominant cultural frameworks. Indigenous youth resurgence may also take place in the face of profound obstacles, including mental health issues, family members in crisis, economic hardship, migration situations, or lack of transportation to events where they could speak up, among many others.

Yet many young people still find ways to make their voices heard, albeit in ways that may not immediately appear to be standard indicators of participation. For example, survey data from Mexico showed that while students from both Indigenous and mestizo backgrounds identify as being culturally connected to a larger communal identity, Indigenous students in Oaxaca demonstrate communal identity through active labor in ways that mestizo students generally do not. In a parallel manner, Indigenous students in California engage in much more communal participatory work than their White counterparts do. Helping elders or doing childcare may not translate directly into political engagement as defined by classic political science, such as participating through voting. But when taken together with the qualitative data, the study results show that this participatory behavior helps Indigenous youth define their responsibilities as connected to something larger than themselves.

As the previous chapters have shown, Indigenous language classrooms equip young people to resist culturecide for multiple reasons. First, Indigenous language classrooms are spaces for pride in minority identity. These classes are perceived as safer and more accepting of ethnic and racial diversity than the schools or communities at large. They are also places where heritage and non-heritage-speaker students voice thoughts about identity and culture that they might not be able to say elsewhere. This was reinforced by students and teachers alike during interviews and also through ethnographic observations.

Second, the impact of Indigenous teachers in schools is significant. The level of community accountability that occurs by having an Indigenous person working among Indigenous students and then having the adult see the student outside of class in the community should not be underestimated. In the Yurok community this was particularly true. Native American teachers were connected to adult family members of their students in a variety of ways that signaled accountability and the need for mutual respect. Teachers knew the parents or guardians of students through close community ties, and in some cases were relatives of the students. Students were not, therefore, taking classes with anonymous adults, but with an auntie or an elder to whom they were accountable through kinship or community ties, not only through school accountability.

Indigenous language classes provide a means for Indigenous teachers to be part of high school communities, serving as role models for students who otherwise have non-Indigenous teachers. For example, during this study period, without the Yurok or Tolowa language teachers, the other three high schools in California where Yurok is offered (excepting HVHS) would have had no other Yurok or Native person of any tribe on staff. This is somewhat comparable in Mexico, where in the BIC system the Indigenous language teacher is looked to as a role model by Indigenous students. However, more teachers and staff in Oaxaca's BIC system overall identify as Indigenous, although still not the majority; the issue of representation is not quite as extreme as in California. Yet Indigenous stigma is hugely pervasive in Oaxaca overall. Outside the BIC and other specifically Indigenous-focused education programs, Indigenous teachers in Oaxaca tend not to advertise their Indigenous identities, knowing that it can bring discrimination. In Oaxaca as well as California, Indigenous language programming plays an important role in positive Indigenous visibility.

Of course, the schools in which Indigenous language classes are available are not necessarily universally good for students. In the course of this research, I identified numerous problems that schools, districts, and states are in a position to address, including: negative school climate; a lack of training for faculty, staff, and students on fostering inclusive environments (especially in working with minority and migrant students); insufficient mental health services; and economic instability for students, who struggle with food insecurity, inaccessible transportation, and, in Mexico, the inability to afford uniforms and educational materials. Resource-lacking schools, districts, and states may struggle to meet these challenges, but this is part of addressing the larger school ecosystem in which Indigenous language classes are situated. Confronting these problems, and finding solutions to them, are part of social and educational justice.

Conclusion: Learning to Live Together Well

My focus in these final pages is on how sustainable advocacy for a more multilingual, pluricultural democracy can be viable in the context of ongoing structural violence and marginalization. Public schools around the world have mandates from ministries or departments of education to use the formal education sector as a means to inculcate certain values across the citizenry. Those values frequently include the development of nationalistic pride, identity with the state, and the founding myths of racial, ethnic, or religious majorities. Many who write books like the one you hold in your hands, and many of us who read them as well, may be products of school systems that whitewashed the history of genocides.

I certainly experienced one such public school narrative and have spent much of my adult life learning the real stories of violence that took place in my communities, country, and the world. We now have the tools to model best practices in inclusive and anti-racist teaching, from curricula to materials to teaching techniques. And yet, classrooms continue to be sites of struggle that reflect culturecide (Foxworth et al., 2015; Jacob & RunningHawk Johnson, 2020; Lindsay, 2015: 346). Homogenizing politics and history are part of culturecidal practices that repress minority truths.

A one-size-fits-all approach to educational material, as with centralized political arrangements in institutional design, has done democracies no favors. Monoperspective education does great harm with politicized content when, for example, history is told only from one perspective (the victors') or when one language or set of cultural practices is elevated over other, minority practices. The issue of cultural relevancy in education has garnered some attention in the last decades (Gay, 2010; Hammond, 2015). But accommodation of minorities in the formal education system continues to confront a neocolonial idea of education made by racial and ethnic majorities who frequently occupy power positions in key institutions. For minorities to survive socially and economically, it is assumed they must acquiesce to certain standards of the majority, including in formal education.

How, then, can coexistence take place where the uniqueness of each minority is respected and upheld? How might states move away from the melting pot notion of diversity and toward a framework, mosaic-like in Canadian parlance, or in Latin American terms, toward *el buen vivir* (living well), of harmony, abundance, and self-determination for Indigenous peoples (Chassagne, 2019; Merino 2021)? Questions about educating for coexistence have implications not only for academics but for educators and policymakers working on the front lines of citizen formation (Goering, 2013). In long-range terms, fostering intercultural exchange in classrooms strengthens democratic culture, when democracy is taken to mean inclusive and equitable participation in a polity. In the face of Castilianization in Mexico and Englishization in the United States, Indigenous language learning contributes to educational practices that support multilingualism and pluriculturalism in both countries. Institutions form and are formed by everyday practices of citizenship. This book has exemplified how and under what conditions of schooling young people take up their rights and responsibilities as citizens.

In examining language regimes in Oaxacan and Californian schooling, I have shown the insidious ways that norms and values of dominant cultures are embedded in and play out through the lives of young people. Messages of mestizo and White cultural values are communicated through language regimes, curricula, and daily practices within schools and the wider communities. As young people form their independent identities and struggle to determine not just who they are in the world but how they will participate in it, the role of public sector education should not be seen as a benign universal good. Access to education as a right as articulated in Article 26 of the Universal Declaration of Human Rights is good for everyone in theory. All people should be able to learn in ways that facilitate self-actualization. In its implementation, however, education can be a mechanism of acculturation that, while imparting many valuable skills, furthers culturecide.

Five Takeaways

This book has grappled with how access to Indigenous language learning in formal educational spaces shapes youth identity and facilitates participation in political, cultural, and civic arenas. I have argued that when young people take Indigenous language classes in high school, such language access opens up space to resist various forms of culturecide. Overall, my research offers five core conclusions, the first two methodological and the remaining three substantive in relation to the book's argument.

First, collaborative methodology is a must for decolonizing research. When working with Indigenous communities and other historically marginalized peoples, such an approach is imperative to be able to center stakeholder voices. Doing so is part of decolonizing the social sciences and making sure that research is useful in real life.

Second, the comparative mixed-methods approach is useful for working with young people as an outside researcher. Even if the majority of students say things are going well in their lives, parsing data on specific indicators may tell another story. The reality of exclusion and seclusion in in-group-only enclaves is captured across both qualitative and quantitative data. Classroom observations, interviews, focus groups, and surveys, along with many informal interactions on school campuses, informed the multifaceted perspectives on youth identity and participation documented here. Overall, triangulating data across multiple methods and case studies allowed assessment of patterns and outliers more readily than with only one type of method or in one deep case, or many shallow ones.

Third, Indigenous language access in public high schools does not repair the history of genocide and culturecide against Indigenous peoples. But such access does provide vital spaces for language survival while also affirming positive identity formation for Native American youth and increased intercultural competency for their White counterparts. Such results may be generalizable, in that not only do Zapotec and Yurok language classes serve as useful to heritage-speaking students, but Indigenous language classes writ large also hold space where young people may develop their understandings of diversity as they form and consolidate their own identities. These are clearly not only Zapotec or Yurok realities. Identifying the more universal elements of the puzzle allows for generalizability to other schools, districts, states, and communities.

Fourth, one of the many ways Indigenous young people learn to express their identities is by resisting culturecide through Indigenous language study. Resistance to culturecide goes hand in hand with reducing stigma and stereotypes about Indigenous peoples, while also addressing historical and contemporary traumas that have impacted the trajectory of Indigenous communities. Though it is not solely sufficient for decolonization, resistance to culturecide is part of the process, and one that is available to young people in a range of circumstances.

Fifth, creating engaged youth capable of participating in a range of ways with people both similar to and different from themselves strengthens pluriethnic, multicultural democracy. Education policymakers who weigh the long list of factors necessary in producing the next generation of citizens should take note. Indigenous identity affirmation in the classroom is related to engagement in the larger world.

Democratic coexistence requires supporting the rights of Indigenous peoples to cultural survival. Assimilationist educational paradigms, effectively relics of settler-colonial state-building, further neocolonialism in the present and impede this survival through culturecide. Indigenous language access is not a panacea to the democracy problem as it stands today. Nor is it the sole solution to culturecide. Rather, such access is one of many elements that can, and indeed should, be part of education policy to reverse systematic culturecide and strengthen the space for pluriethnic coexistence.

Indigenous language access spurs youth resistance to culturecide and leads logically to demands for more culturally relevant and locally resonant curricula, improved social and academic climates, and increased public discourse on Indigenous rights. This is part of a long and arduous process to examine the potential for decolonizing the formal education system and, relatedly, the research process itself. Both are ethical imperatives and will strengthen our ability to live together well.

===

Informational Letter for Students, Parents, Guardians, and Community Members

Project Title: Education, Citizen Formation, and Cultural Resilience: Indigenous and Spanish Language Politics in California and Mexico
Researcher: Dr. Mneesha Gellman
Assistant Professor of Political Science, Emerson College

Introduction and Purpose

My name is Mneesha Gellman and I am an Assistant Professor of Political Science at Emerson College, Boston, USA. I research how individuals and communities participate in their communities in civic, cultural, and political ways, as well as how people develop skills in and across cultures. Information from this study will be used to develop academic materials such as articles, conference presentations, and books. I may survey, interview, and do focus groups with approximately 200 people for this project.

Your Potential Role and Procedures

You are being invited to participate because your child is enrolled at a secondary or high school in California or Mexico, or because you are connected to the study themes through your own work or interests. Active participation can take three forms: surveys, focus groups, and interviews. Surveys are anonymous and may take ten to fifteen minutes to complete. Focus groups will be anonymously coded, but with audio-recording, and entail loss of privacy given that one is conversing with one's peers, and generally will take 60–90 minutes. Interviews can be anonymous or with name, audio-recorded or not, depending on the preferences indicated on the consent forms. Interviews will take approximately 60–90 minutes and will be one-on-one conversations between the interviewee and the researcher. Interviews and focus groups begin with me posing some initial questions and then making space for people to respond or not as desired. After the interview, I may contact you by email to follow up on points of clarification, but you are not obligated to respond.

If you choose to participate anonymously, I will not ask you for your last name at any point, and your contributions to focus groups and interviews will be recorded anonymously. I will assign to you a unique code that will allow me to match your answers in my notes, but any identifying information will be stored in a separate cabinet or electronic cloud from notes on your opinions.

In the surveys, focus groups, and interviews, depending on your own expertise, I may ask questions about civic, political, and cultural involvement in local, national, or international settings, as well as questions about language, identity, and education. You are invited to participate in all aspects of the study, but you can mix and match your preferences for participation on the informed consent form, for example, participating in one type but not the other, or not participating at all. These ways of participating will conclude your role in the study at this time.

Your Rights

To be able to participate in this project, it is indispensable to have both student and parent/guardian consent. You can give your consent, withhold it, or take it back at any time. Please read this entire form before you decide if you want to participate. Even if you initially agree to the survey, focus group, or interview, you can end these processes at any time you wish. I will take notes in focus groups and interviews, but I can destroy the notes pertaining to you if you change your mind about participating.

All focus groups will be anonymously coded. Interviews will be either with your name or anonymously coded, depending on your preference indicated on the consent form. Anonymity will be handled by writing a number or pseudonym in my notebook that corresponds to our interview or focus group and referring to our exchange only by the code or pseudonym. Interviewee names and corresponding numbers or pseudonyms will be kept in a separate notebook from the interview notes. Any identifying information, including signed informed consent forms, will be kept in a binder that will be placed in a locked filing cabinet at Emerson College, and will be shredded three years after the completion of this study. Any notes that I type, or audio recordings, will be kept in a password protected cloud that only I and my Research Assistants have access to and will be deleted three years after the completion of this study.

I will only do interviews, focus groups, or surveys with people who have signed an informed consent form, and for minors, who have also returned signed consent forms from a parent or guardian.

Risks and Benefits

Your participation does not involve any risks other than what you would encounter in daily life in school or your community. In relation to the researcher, your opinions and feelings will remain confidential once our discussion ends. However, in focus groups, one potential risk you may encounter is that your identity will be known in association with your comments by the other participants. Though I ask that all participants maintain confidentiality about the conversations, I cannot guarantee it.

There may be no direct benefit to you by your participation in this research study, though a potential benefit may include contributing to social science research about the study themes, including culture and democracy. I will use the information that I collect here to write academic articles and/or books in order to contribute to our understanding about multiculturalism and political processes, and thus may be able to bring your ideas and suggestions to a wider audience. There is no monetary compensation for participation.

Confidentiality

Participation in this research study may result in a loss of privacy, since persons other than myself might view the record of your participation. Unless required by law, only myself, the Emerson College Institutional Review Board, and representatives from the Department of Health and Human Services (DHHS) and Office for Human Research Protections (OHRP) will have authority to review your participation records. However, they are required to maintain confidentiality regarding your individual identity. Results from this project may be used for teaching, research, publications, or presentations at professional meetings.

Please indicate on the informed consent forms if you prefer to be cited with your name or anonymously, and audio-recorded or not.

Contacts

If you have questions about your rights as a research participant, you may contact the Emerson College Institutional Review Board (IRB), which is concerned with the protection of volunteers in research projects. You may reach the IRB Chair by e-mailing [redacted]

You can also contact me directly: Mneesha Gellman

Address, Email, Phone: [redacted]

Thank you for considering participating in this research project.

Permission Form

**THIS FORM SHOULD BE FILLED OUT BY STUDENTS AND PARENTS/
GUARDIANS TOGETHER**

Parent/Guardian/Student Permission Form

I have read the attached consent letter for the study, "Education, Citizen Formation, and Cultural Resilience: Indigenous and Spanish Language Politics in California and Mexico." I understand that any publication produced based on this research will not identify individual students unless I give permission for this in section 3 below. All information will be kept in secure files and destroyed three years after the completion of the project.

Indicate preferences below by marking the corresponding lines

1) **Survey participation:**
   _____ I AGREE to allow my child to fill out survey forms (will be anonymous).
   _____ I DO NOT agree to allow my child to fill out survey forms.

2) **Focus groups:**
   _____ I AGREE to allow my child to participate in focus groups, which will be audio-recorded and anonymous.
   _____ I DO NOT agree to allow my child to participate in focus groups.

3) **Individual interviews:**
   _____ I AGREE to allow my child to participate in individual interviews, which may be audio-recorded.

_____ I DO NOT agree to allow my child to participate in individual interviews.

4) **If you agreed to an interview in section 3, please choose from below:**
_____ I agree to my child's NAME TO BE USED with individual comments.
_____I agree for my child to participate in the interview ANONYMOUSLY. I understand that if my child's individual comments are discussed, their identity will be protected by using a code number or pseudonym instead of their name.

5) **Future participation**
If you are open to the possibility of your child participating in this project in future years, please indicate how I may contact you:
Phone:_____
Email:_____
Other:_____

I understand that I may contact the researcher, Dr. Mneesha Gellman, at any point during the study to ask questions or raise concerns, via telephone, email, or mail [redacted details]. I also understand that my child's participation is voluntary and that I can decline, or withdraw my child from the study at any point without penalty.

*BOTH STUDENT AND PARENT/GUARDIAN SIGNATURES ARE REQUIRED FOR PARTICIPATION

_____

Student's Name (print)   Student Signature   Date

_____

Parent or Guardian's Name (print)   Parent or Guardian's Signature   Date

Please return this to the teacher that distributed it. Thank you!

APPENDIX 3

Examples of Qualitative Interview Questions
for Research

*Interviews will use an open-ended qualitative format that allows interviewees to guide the conversation in the direction they choose; therefore, these questions are to be used only as a guide. Not all questions will be asked—it will depend on the profile of the interviewee. Questions may also be drawn from the list of focus group questions.

1) Please tell me about your professional role in this organization/community. What is your position and what are your daily responsibilities?
2) Please tell me about yourself as a student at this school. What year are you in and what language/arts/history/civics classes are you taking?
3) Can you please say a little about your ethnic identity? How do you identify? What terminology do you prefer to refer to yourself or your community?
4) What elements of your culture are important to you?
5) What resources, organizations, or people help you connect with your identity?
6) What kind of words or phrases do you use to describe the kinds of civic, cultural, or political projects you are or would like to be involved in, or to describe things you don't want to be involved in?
7) How do people in your community talk about the role of your mother tongue/heritage language?
8) Please describe for me how you are, have been, or would like to be civically, culturally, or politically active.

9) Please tell me what things have an influence in your decision to participate in the political process in your country. Civic processes? Cultural processes?

10) How do you decide to participate in different kinds of political processes?

11) What does multiculturalism mean to you? Is there a different term or concept you prefer to use to describe this idea?

12) What sorts of changes in your town, region, country, or in the international community do you hope to see in your lifetime? How would these changes affect you and your community?

13) What does democracy mean to you? What does democracy need to work?

14) How do you feel about engaging with people from other cultural or linguistic backgrounds? What would make this kind of cross-cultural engagement easier for you?

15) How often do you talk to people outside your cultural/linguistic/political background?

16) What do you think it takes students to succeed in school?

17) How could you be better support (for teachers)/better supported as a student?

18) Describe an average Yurok/Zapotec/Spanish/History/Civics/Arts class. How do you feel when you study this subject? What makes this subject engaging/disengaging for you? How could you imagine applying this class material to your life outside of this school?

19) If there was a problem on your street or in your neighborhood, how would you imagine it getting fixed? How could you contribute to its resolution?

20) If there was a problem in your town or region, how would you imagine it could be fixed? How could you contribute to its resolution?

21) If there was a problem in your country, how do you think it could be fixed? How could you contribute to its resolution?

22) What skills/attributes do you think you need to be more involved in your family/community/region/state/country?

23) Have you ever felt excluded based on some element of your identity? At school/community events/larger events?

24) How do you experience privilege?

25) How does your identity contribute to you feeling empowered or disempowered?
26) How do you think you can help other people feel more included in the communities you participate in?
27) What does success mean to you?
28) What do you think you need to succeed in life?

Examples of Focus Group Questions

*Depending on the profile of the participants, questions will be drawn from the list below, but not all questions may be asked. The "you" refers to the group of students in the focus group, and they may answer both individually and through conversations with each other.

1) What do you think is the connection between the languages you speak, or are studying, and your identity?
2) Can you give me an example of when you have used your mother tongue/heritage language in a civic, cultural, or political space?
3) When do you hear your mother tongue/heritage language?
4) When do you speak your mother tongue/heritage language?
5) When do you wish you could use your mother tongue/heritage language?
6) What prevents you from using this language more often?
7) What do you see as the benefits or drawbacks of using this language?
8) How does mother tongue/heritage language use relate to civic, cultural, or political participation?
9) What resources, organizations, or people help you connect with your identity?
10) What organizations or actors help or hinder language survival in your community?
11) What kind of words or phrases do you use to describe yourself as a civically engaged person? As a culturally involved person? As a political person?
12) What does cultural competency mean to you?

13) In what specific ways do you engage across cultures that are different from yours? If you don't, why not?

14) What does multiculturalism mean to you? Is there a different term or concept you prefer to use to describe this idea?

15) What role do you think multiculturalism plays in democracy? Discuss the significance of these two concepts in your own life.

16) How could your mother tongue/heritage tongue be better preserved or supported where you live?

17) What do you want people from outside your community to know about the challenges and opportunities for language use in your region?

18) What are things that help you feel successful as a student?

19) What are obstacles to your success as a student?

20) How could your school/family/community/friends/government better support you as a student?

21) What are your goals for yourself after high school, and how will you try to achieve them?

22) What are ways in which you are, or would like to be, involved in your community civically, culturally, or politically? What do you need to achieve this involvement?

Survey, English Version for Use in Language Classes (V1)

<u>Survey Questions</u> (Designed to take 10–15 minutes, anonymous)

Part I. Demographic Questions

Please fill in the circle corresponding with your answer. If you select "other" for any question, please write in your answer in the space provided. Your answers will be used to better expand the range of options for future versions of this survey.

1) What is your predominant ethnic or racial background?
   a. American Indian/Native American
   b. Asian or Asian American
   c. Black or African American
   d. White
   e. Latinx or Hispanic
   f. Middle Eastern or North African
   g. Native Hawaiian or Pacific Islander
   h. More than one predominant background (please write in)

2) What is your gender identity?
   a. female
   b. male
   c. transgender
   d. other (please write in)

3) What is your current level of school?
   a. freshman
   b. sophomore
   c. junior
   d. senior
   e. other (please write in below)

4) What languages do you predominantly speak at home? Mark all that apply.
   a. English
   b. Hmong
   c. Hupa
   d. Khmer
   e. Laotian
   f. Spanish
   g. Yurok
   h. Native Hawaiian or Pacific Island language (please write in)
   i. Other Native American or Indigenous language (please write in)
   j. Other language (please write in)

5) What language do you usually speak in your daily life outside your home? Mark all that apply.
   a. English
   b. Spanish
   c. Zapotec
   d. Other (please write in)

6) What languages do you speak, read, or understand at any level? Mark all that apply.
   k. English
   l. Hmong
   m. Hupa
   n. Karuk
   o. Khmer
   p. Laotian
   q. Spanish
   r. Yurok
   s. Native Hawaiian or Pacific Island language (please write in)

   t. Other Native American or Indigenous language (please write in)
   u. Other language (please write in)

7) If you have lived for a significant time outside the country where you
   currently live, please mark where you lived.
   a. Mexico
   b. United States
   c. El Salvador
   d. Laos
   e. Other (Please write in)

8) The sun rises from which direction?
   a. East
   b. West
   c. North
   d. South
   e. Other

Part II. Language and Identity Questions

Please choose one answer on the scale from 1 to 5 for each of the following
questions. The target language refers to the language elective you are studying in school (Yurok, Spanish, or Zapotec).

9) I hear the target language spoken regularly outside of my language
   class.
   1. Strongly disagree
   2. Slightly disagree
   3. Neither agree nor disagree
   4. Slightly agree
   5. Strongly agree

10) I am comfortable speaking the target language in a basic conversation.
   1. Strongly disagree
   2. Slightly disagree
   3. Neither agree nor disagree

    4. Slightly agree
    5. Strongly agree

11) I am taking this language class because I identify with it personally.
    1. Strongly disagree
    2. Slightly disagree
    3. Neither agree nor disagree
    4. Slightly agree
    5. Strongly agree

12) I am taking this language class because I am interested in languages and cultures outside of my own.
    1. Strongly disagree
    2. Slightly disagree
    3. Neither agree nor disagree
    4. Slightly agree
    5. Strongly agree

13) I am taking this language class to fulfill a requirement.
    1. Strongly disagree
    2. Slightly disagree
    3. Neither agree nor disagree
    4. Slightly agree
    5. Strongly agree

Part III. Participation Questions

14) I volunteer in my community.
    1. Strongly disagree
    2. Slightly disagree
    3. Neither agree nor disagree
    4. Slightly agree
    5. Strongly agree

15) I attend ceremonial gatherings in my community (for example, religious or cultural events like fish runs, dances, demonstrations, fasting, etc.).

1. Strongly disagree
2. Slightly disagree
3. Neither agree nor disagree
4. Slightly agree
5. Strongly agree

16) I attend community language classes (for example, not for credit, open to all).
   1. Strongly disagree
   2. Slightly disagree
   3. Neither agree nor disagree
   4. Slightly agree
   5. Strongly agree
   6. Option: write in frequency of attendance

17) I attend political gatherings in my community (for example, youth council meetings, protests, tribal council meetings, city or county council meetings, etc.).
   1. Strongly disagree
   2. Slightly disagree
   3. Neither agree nor disagree
   4. Slightly agree
   5. Strongly agree
   6. Option: write in which kind of gatherings

18) I attend club meetings either in or out of school (for example, Associated Student Body, multicultural club, Native American club, fishing club, leadership group, etc.).
   1. Strongly disagree
   2. Slightly disagree
   3. Neither agree nor disagree
   4. Slightly agree
   5. Strongly agree
   6. write in any other club you participate in

19) I help elders in my community.
   1. Strongly disagree
   2. Slightly disagree

3. Neither agree nor disagree
4. Slightly agree
5. Strongly agree

20) I participate in cultural projects in my community (for example, regalia preparation, eel or fish donations, canoe or basket-making, community workshops, women's/men's groups, etc.).
   1. Strongly disagree
   2. Slightly disagree
   3. Neither agree nor disagree
   4. Slightly agree
   5. Strongly agree
   6. Option: please describe if you are willing.

21) I do childcare, cook, or other domestic chores to support my community.
   1. Strongly disagree
   2. Slightly disagree
   3. Neither agree nor disagree
   4. Slightly agree
   5. Strongly agree

22) I gather, give, or help others with resources in my community (for example, sharing food, basket materials, acorns, fixing home or car problems, etc.).
   1. Strongly disagree
   2. Slightly disagree
   3. Neither agree nor disagree
   4. Slightly agree
   5. Strongly agree

23) I learn and make traditional artistry (for example, basket-making, drum-making, jewelry, etc.).
   1. Strongly disagree
   2. Slightly disagree
   3. Neither agree nor disagree
   4. Slightly agree
   5. Strongly agree

Part IV. Diversity and Inclusion Questions

24) I feel included in my school.
    1. Strongly disagree
    2. Slightly disagree
    3. Neither agree nor disagree
    4. Slightly agree
    5. Strongly agree
      (please explain if you are willing)

25) I feel included in my local community.
    1. Strongly disagree
    2. Slightly disagree
    3. Neither agree nor disagree
    4. Slightly agree
    5. Strongly agree
      (please explain if you are willing)

26) I feel comfortable being around people that speak a language other than my first language.
    1. Strongly disagree
    2. Slightly disagree
    3. Neither agree nor disagree
    4. Slightly agree
    5. Strongly agree
      (please explain if you are willing)

27) I regularly spend time with people from backgrounds or cultures that are different from my own.
    1. Strongly disagree
    2. Slightly disagree
    3. Neither agree nor disagree
    4. Slightly agree
    5. Strongly agree
      (please explain if you are willing)

28) I enjoy spending time with people from cultures different than my own.

1. Strongly disagree
2. Slightly disagree
3. Neither agree nor disagree
4. Slightly agree
5. Strongly agree
   (please explain if you are willing)

29) I know how to change my language and behavior when spending time with people from different backgrounds.
   1. Strongly disagree
   2. Slightly disagree
   3. Neither agree nor disagree
   4. Slightly agree
   5. Strongly agree
      (please explain if you are willing)

30) I would like to become more comfortable engaging with people from different cultural and language backgrounds.
   1. Strongly disagree
   2. Slightly disagree
   3. Neither agree nor disagree
   4. Slightly agree
   5. Strongly agree
      (please explain if you are willing)

31) My school encourages knowledge of diverse communities and cultures.
   1. Strongly disagree
   2. Slightly disagree
   3. Neither agree nor disagree
   4. Slightly agree
   5. Strongly agree
      (please explain if you are willing)

32) My language class encourages awareness of culture and history.
   1. Strongly disagree
   2. Slightly disagree
   3. Neither agree nor disagree

4. Slightly agree
5. Strongly agree
   (please explain if you are willing)

33) When I feel included in my school and community it makes me want
    to participate more.
    1. Strongly disagree
    2. Slightly disagree
    3. Neither agree nor disagree
    4. Slightly agree
    5. Strongly agree
       (please explain if you are willing)

34) I am taking this survey in the following class:
    1. Yurok I
    2. Yurok II
    3. Yurok III/IV
    4. AP Spanish
    5. Spanish III
    6. Civics
    7. AP Government
    8. World History
    9. Art
    10. Other (please write in)

Discussion of Survey Data in Relation to Language and Identity

Surveys were one of several data collection tools used to ascertain student relationships to language, practices of participation, and senses of inclusion or exclusion in schools and communities. Questions about language mostly centered on students' level of comfort speaking a language other than the socially dominant or ethnic-majority language, meaning a language other than Spanish in Oaxaca or other than English in California. For language students, the V1 survey version asks questions about whether they hear the target language, meaning the language they are taking as a class (Zapotec and English in Oaxaca and Yurok and Spanish in California), outside the language class, or outside their homes; whether they identify personally with the target language; whether they are taking the target language class primarily because it is a requirement; whether they are interested in languages and cultures outside of their own; and whether they are comfortable speaking the target language in basic conversation. The control group survey asks these same questions but refers to "more than one language" rather than a target language.

V1 and V2 surveys differ slightly, and Question 10 is a good example of how. In V1, the survey statement is "I am comfortable speaking the target language in a basic conversation," and overall, at EHS and HVHS, Yurok I and II students responded that they were not very comfortable speaking Yurok—the target language of the class where they were taking the survey—in a basic conversation. For Question 10 with V2 modification, the question reads, "I am comfortable speaking more than one language in a basic conversation." Civics students at HVHS and EHS felt less comfortable speaking more than one language in a basic conversation than did their Yurok and Spanish classmates in V1. EHS's World History students also showed less agreement with the statement than they are comfortable speaking more than one language in a basic conversation.

The responses from V1 and V2 show that students in language classes at the moment of the survey were slightly more comfortable speaking more than one language, which is not surprising given that they are expected to regularly practice speaking another language. In fact, this and the following question, presented in the graph below, are more revealing when compared across schools than across target and control groups. Students were asked to rank their response to "I hear the target language spoken regularly outside of my language class."[1]

Figure 3 shows that HVHS students are less likely to have heard more than one language spoken regularly, compared with students at other schools, particularly BIC 29, where the highest portion of students report hearing more than one language regularly. This data is unsurprising. HVHS, based on the history of colonization and the English language regime in California, is a majority monolingual English environment albeit with dedicated language-keepers working to sustain and pass down Yurok, Hoopa, and Karuk to young people. BIC 29, situated in a Zapotec community where the majority of adults over the age of thirty are usually native Zapotec speakers, provides the most robust mixing of Zapotec and Spanish for students in daily life. In Mexico, the majority of Zapotec students at BIC 29 and the majority of English students at CEDARTMC report hearing the target language outside of

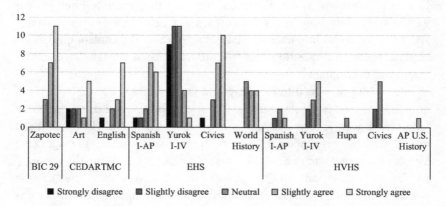

Figure 3. Question 9: Cross-tabulated responses by class taken in each school: "I hear the target language spoken regularly outside of my language class."

school. This means that students have social context and relevancy for language curricula, which arguably help reinforce language acquisition and provide motivation for why language study matters.

BIC 29 and HVHS had the highest proportion of students in Zapotec and Yurok classes responding affirmatively to Question 11, "I am taking this class because I identify with it personally." This was also expected given the density of Indigenous residents in the two communities surrounding these schools. However, it is notable that self-identity with the language was not the only factor in students' enthusiasm for it. Some students who did not identify personally with the language affirmed with their responses to Question 12 that they were taking the class because they were interested in languages and cultures outside their own. Also, they were comfortable speaking the target language in basic conversation.

For discourse about the role of non-heritage-speakers as part of language survival processes, non-heritage students' interest in Zapotec and Yurok classes is particularly relevant. The survey does not show stark identity differences between students enrolled in language classes and those not in language classes. However, there is a strong difference between heritage-speakers, who tend to be much more culturally connected, and non-heritage-speakers, especially White students at EHS, who are less culturally connected or interculturally engaged. Even though they are part of the cultural majority in Oaxaca, Latinx/Hispanic students, a category that includes mestizo students, generally show more cultural connectedness than do their White counterparts in California, likely owing to high participation in particular Catholic and folkloric traditions in Oaxaca such as Dia de los Muertos[2] and Dia de la Samaritana.[3] Overall, the survey data proved to be a complementary information source that worked with the qualitative methods to provide a look at youth identity and participation in relation to Indigenous language access.

NOTES

Introduction

1. A pseudonym. See Chapter 2 for in-depth discussion of the permissions process for student consent, including decision making on using pseudonyms versus real names.

2. In Spanish in Oaxaca, the expression "you are a weirdo" is expressed as "que bicho mas raro," literally, "what a rare insect."

3. In Spanish, "Que Indio!"

4. Not a pseudonym. Students and their guardians were given the option on informed consent forms of having students participate in a deidentified way or with their real names, and I follow their preferences here. Occasionally I decided that students who gave permission to be named should be referred to anonymously because of the sensitive nature of their comments. I note all pseudonyms at their first mention and use real names or refer to them anonymously throughout the book.

5. For example, terms like *lawfare* compress warfare and law to complicate how governance happens (Kittrie, 2016), and *crimilegality* joins criminality with legality to describe a particular kind of regime (Schultze-Kraft, 2018).

6. This example is explained and explored in Chapter 6 on HVHS.

7. In Spanish, Mixteco.

8. *Mestizo* means "mixed" in Spanish; in Mexico it typically refers to people with both Indigenous and European White ancestry, as juxtaposed to people who identify as Indigenous. There is not consensus on whether or not mestizo should be capitalized. I leave it uncapitalized here, but suspect this approach will soon change.

9. See Gellman, 2021b for more on academic support services in Oaxaca.

10. By "far Northern," I refer to the part of the state that lies north of San Francisco and south of the Oregon border, with a microfocus on the language politics of Humboldt, Trinity, and Del Norte Counties.

Chapter 2

1. While there are 48 BIC schools in Oaxaca, since I only include BIC 29 in this book, I alternate between referring to it as BIC and BIC 29, depending on the context. In the community, it is just known as the BIC.

2. See Tripp, 2018: 730 for more on why this type of transparency is of limited benefit for qualitative research.

3. Generation Z refers to anyone born after 1996.

Chapter 3

1. Some teachers in Oaxaca are fluidly bilingual and able to teach complex grammar, while others are barely able to communicate in the target language themselves. Ensuring that instructors are qualified to teach is thus an ongoing issue.

2. This was part of the Committee on Labor and Public Welfare.

3. Del Norte High School is one of the two other California high schools where Yurok is taught (the other is McKinleyville High School) that were not officially included in this phase of the study.

4. Duluwat, previously named Indian Island, was the subject of a protracted legal battle for decades as the City of Eureka fought off Wiyot Tribal claims for the island to be returned to them as the traditional owners of the land. In 2019, the City of Eureka finally returned the land to the Tribe, which includes the historic village of Tuluwat, the site of the massacre.

5. For a literature review on No Child Left Behind and California's Proposition 227, see Hornberger & Cassels Johnson, 2014: 273–289.

6. *Mestizaje* means "mixing" in Spanish and, because of its contrast to indigeneity in Mexico, is used to signify a discourse of whitening there, but the term itself is connected to a history of colonization and Indigenous subjugation (Pérez-Torres, 2006).

7. Translation: fucker. Much has been written about the degree to which Malinche was a willing versus coerced or forced participant in the relationship with Cortés. The notion of *mestizaje*, regardless, is tied to her womb.

8. Jacob's work provides many examples of this. For example, Patsy, a former president of the National Indian Education Association, "knows that being strongly rooted in one's Indigenous culture (language, tradition, and culture—as she states) helps serve as a protective factor for youth. Thus, language revitalization work is inherently decolonizing, as it allows greater access to language knowledge and use for future generations, and provides the opportunity for young Indigenous people to develop healthy identities" (Jacob, 2013: 50).

Chapter 4

1. Chemical dyes are much cheaper and less laborious to make than natural dyes, which require sourcing the plants, extracting the color, and dyeing the wool, rather than the dyeing-only process needed with chemical dyes. Chemical colors are much brighter and eye-catching for many buyers, but buyers have also exhibited an increased interest in sustainable and traditional practices of natural dye-making, in line with the rise of interest in organic and local food production in Oaxaca and the wider world. This market for natural and sustainable products has helped economically incentivize the continuation and intergenerational transfer of artisan skills like natural dyeing.

2. Mexico's population as of this writing in 2022 is just over 130 million.

3. The Education Councillor who first granted me permission to carry out research in 2018, described in Chapter 2, was in the middle of a three-year cargo. When I returned in 2020, I again made a formal request to both the new Education Councillor and the municipal president, as both of them were new cargo-holders.

4. In addition to the BIC system, Oaxaca includes three main public high school systems: *El Colegio de Bachilleres de Oaxaca* (COBAO), *El Centro de Bachillerato Tecnológico Industrial y de Servicios* (CBTIS), and *El Colegio de Estudios Científicos y Tecnológicos del Estado de Oaxaca* (CECyTEO).

5. Pseudonym.

6. Pseudonym.

7. Two of the original quotes were *"No sé, falta buena palabra"* and *"ningún idea como nombrarme."*

8. This is the case at BIC 1, in San Pablo Guelatao, where there is one Indigenous language class for a widely diverse group of heritage-speakers. Northern Zapotec heritage-speakers are from the region of the school, while the high number of internal migrant students from the Sierra Sur region of Oaxaca are heritage-speakers of Mixtec. In 2020, there was one student from Chiapas who spoke Tzeltal, as well as speakers of Mixe, Chinanteco, and Nahuatl.

9. Unique Population Registry Code (Clave Única de Registro de Población, CURP) cards operate somewhat like Social Security cards in the United States, enabling Mexican citizens to do everything from registering for school, to voting, to opening a bank account.

10. See Gellman, 2017: chap. 4 for more on the Triqui encampment.

11. Traditional woven Indigenous cloth shirts.

12. Both in 2018 and 2020, however, there were still a few students who did not have cell phones and a few more who did not have data plans and therefore only had telephone capacity.

Chapter 5

1. This student identified with plural pronouns.

Chapter 6

1. The spelling Hoopa, designated by White people, refers to the place and the reservation, while Hupa is the spelling more commonly used for the people and the language. See Risling Baldy & Begay, 2019: 57n2.

2. A to G requirements include fifteen specific high school courses that must be completed with the grade C or higher, from the following categories: History, English, Math, Science, Language Other than English, and Visual and Performing Arts

3. Hoopa Elementary School, the largest of five feeder schools into HVHS, is described as being 90–95 percent Native American (KTJUSD, 2020). It is also one of the lowest-performing schools in the state (TEDNA, 2010: 32).

4. Though it is outside the scope of this book, the political governance of Indigenous people in the United States is brilliantly critiqued by Kessler-Mata in her book on contemporary Indian sovereignty and citizenship (2017).

5. "The Rez" is how the majority of students I spoke with identify where they live and go to school.

6. Happy Camp, with a population of just over 1,000, is a town on the edge of the Marble Mountains ninety minutes from the Hoopa Valley and has a high school serving sixty students. It is even smaller and more remote than HVHS and does not offer all the courses needed to meet California's A to G requirements.

7. Numerous Yurok and Hupa people I interviewed referred to speaking a heritage tongue like Yurok or Hupa as "speaking Indian."

8. Dr. Andrew Garrett, a White UC Berkeley linguist, is the founder of the Yurok Language Project. He wrote the main Yurok grammar book that is used in the high schools where Yurok is offered, and he participates in regular language workshops with Yurok language-keepers and learners.

9. Tribes in the United States generally allow people to be enrolled in only one tribe, even if their ancestry is from multiple tribes. This is because there are economic benefits to tribal enrollment, including "eighteen money," health care, and other social services.

10. Margo Robbins, the sister of Carole Lewis, the HVHS Yurok teacher, served as the Indian Education Coordinator for KTJUSD during the time of this writing and has been a key champion of implementing the Indian Land Tenure Curriculum in the district.

11. The Standardized Testing and Reporting (STAR) program, which included STAR testing every spring, was mandated by the California Public Schools Accountability Act of 1999. The STAR program ended in 2013 and was replaced by the California Assessment of Student Performance and Progress (CAASPP) System.

12. The Johnson-O'Malley Program is named after Senator Hiram Johnson of California and Congressman Thomas O'Malley of Wisconsin, who sponsored the congressional act passed on April 16, 1934, that designated supplemental funding for Native American education.

Chapter 7

1. Trauma scores are calculated from the ACES tests, which are administered in schools. See https://www.cdph.ca.gov/Programs/CCDPHP/DCDIC/SACB/CDPH%20Document%20 Library/Essentials%20for%20Childhood%20Initiative/Update%20on%20CA%20Adverse%20Childhood%20Experiences%20(ACEs)%207-28-16%20Final.pdf.

2. Mr. Gensaw is in the economically precarious situation that the Yurok Tribe Teacher Training program described in Chapter 6 hopes to mitigate for future teachers by allowing future Yurok language teachers to be fully employed at one school. In fall 2021, Mr. Gensaw also became the Yurok teacher at McKinleyville High School, replacing a retiring language-keeper, in addition to his job at EHS.

3. A pseudonym for an anonymous interviewee.

4. Mission kits are craft supply kits sold in California that provide things like popsicle sticks, glue, cotton balls, and a thick cardboard base in a tidy package that families sometimes purchase to facilitate their fourth graders' completion of the "build-your-own-mission" assignment.

5. Alice Birney Elementary School is part of Eureka City Schools and has a reputation for being a tough school because it is in one of Eureka's lowest-income neighborhoods, and one of the most affected by methamphetamine and other drug addictions.

6. Davies-Hughes served in this role during the period of research for this book and was my main point of contact in the district. In 2021, he was named Superintendent of Schools for Humboldt County, filling an elected seat left open in the midst of a term.

7. See https://www.eurekacityschools.org/for_parents/indian_education_program for more information.

8. See Questions 14–23 in Appendix 5.

9. Some districts have found better ways to do this. Boston Public Schools, for example, provide universal free breakfast and lunch to all students regardless of need. Such an approach circumvents barriers to access by avoiding an application process and reduces the stigma for students who access the food.

10. Individual Education Plans (IEPs) are state-mandated instruments used to personalize curricula for students who may be facing a range of challenges, from learning disabilities to behavioral issues, articulating which teachers and support staff will be involved with the students and what the plan is for their academic success.

Conclusion

1. Pseudonym.
2. Pseudonym.

Appendix 1

I reproduce the English text of the research instruments here in the appendices as they were at the time of first implementation in 2017–2019. The informational and permission forms were also made available in Spanish at all schools.

Appendix 6

1. This is survey question 9.

2. In English, Day of the Dead. Dia de los Muertos is derived from an Aztec ritual now celebrated annually on November 1 and 2 to honor ancestors and family members who have died. It also traditionally recognized the harvest time, and the coming of autumn and a darker period in the year's calendar. Skeletons, traditional skull-shaped sweets, and alters with family photographs and marigolds are symbols of contemporary Dia de los Muertos celebrations.

3. In English, Good Samaritan's Day, observed on the fourth Friday of Lent and based on a passage in the bible where a Samaritan woman gave Jesus a drink of water at a well. In Oaxaca, this is celebrated by people setting up tables and giving away free *aguas* (flavored waters or fruit juices) to those who pass by. BIC 29 students participate in this event in Teotitlán del Valle each year.

REFERENCES

Adams, David Wallace. (1995). *Education for Extinction: American Indians and the Boarding School Experience, 1875–1928*. Lawrence: University Press of Kansas.

Adams, Melissa, & Busey, Christopher L. (2017). "They Want to Erase That Past": Examining Race and Afro-Latin@ Identity with Bilingual Third Graders. *Social Studies and the Young Learner, 30*(1), 13–18.

Aguirre Beltrán, Gonzalo. (1957). *El proceso de aculturación y el cambio sociocultural en México*. México: Universidad Nacional Autónoma de México.

Ai Camp, Roderic, & Mattiace, Shannan L. (2020). *Politics in Mexico: The Path of a New Democracy*. Oxford: Oxford University Press.

America Counts Staff. (2021). *California: 2020 Census: California Remained Most Populous State but Growth Slowed Last Decade*. https://www.census.gov/library/stories/state-by -state/california-population-change-between-census-decade.html.

Anaya-Muñoz, Alejandro, & Frey, Barbara. (2019). Introduction. In Alejandro Anaya-Muñoz & Barbara Frey, eds., *Mexico's Human Rights Crisis*, 1–20. Philadelphia: University of Pennsylvania Press.

Anaya-Muñoz, Alejandro, & Saltalamacchia, Natalia. (2019). Factors Blocking the Compliance with International Human Rights Norms in Mexico. In Alejandro Anaya-Muñoz & Barbara Frey, eds., *Mexico's Human Rights Crisis*, 207–226. Philadelphia: University of Pennsylvania Press.

Anderson, Robert. (2018). [Interview with author. #63CA #03HVHS. 1/17/18. HVHS, Hoopa, California].

Anonymous. (2018a). [Intervew with author. #47CA #35EHS. 1/15/18. EHS, Eureka, California].

Anonymous (2018b). [Interview with author. #68Mexico #14CEDARTMC. 4/23/18. CEDAR-TMC, Oaxaca de Juárez, Oaxaca, Mexico.]

Anonymous. (2018c). [Interview with author, #10Mexico #08BIC29. 3/2/18. BIC 29, Teotitlán del Valle, Oaxaca, Mexico].

Anonymous. (2018d). [Interview with author. #08Mexico #06BIC29. 2/26/18. BIC 29, Teotitlán del Valle, Oaxaca, Mexico].

Anonymous. (2018e). [Interview with author. #36CA #24EHS. 1/12/18. EHS, Eureka, California].

Anonymous. (2018f). [Interview with author. #03Mexico #01BIC29. 2/26/18. BIC 29, Teotitlán del Valle, Oaxaca, Mexico].

Anonymous. (2018g). [Interview with author. #04Mexico #02BIC29. 2/26/18. BIC 29, Teotitlán del Valle, Oaxaca, Mexico].

Anonymous. (2018h). [Interview with author. #06Mexico #04BIC29. 2/26/18. BIC 29, Teotitlán del Valle, Oaxaca, Mexico].

Anonymous. (2018i). [Interview with author. #08 Mexico #06BIC29. 2/26/18. BIC 29, Teotitlán del Valle, Oaxaca, Mexico].

Anonymous. (2018j). [Interview with author. #14Mexico #12BIC29. 3/2/18. BIC 29, Teotitlán del Valle, Oaxaca, Mexico].

Anonymous. (2018k). [Interview with author. #16Mexico #02IIAC. 3/2/18. IIAC, A.C., Oaxaca de Juárez, Oaxaca, Mexico].

Anonymous. (2018l). [Interview with author. #17CA #05EHS. 1/10/18. EHS, Eureka, California].

Anonymous. (2018m). [Interview with author. #18Mexico #04IIAC. 3/5/18. IIAC- Centro de Aprendizaje, Oaxaca de Juárez, Oaxaca, Mexico].

Anonymous. (2018n). [Interview with author. #21CA #09EHS. 1/11/18. EHS, Eureka, California].

Anonymous (2018o). [Interview with author. #37CA #25EHS. 1/12/18. EHS, Eureka, California].

Anonymous. (2018p). [Interview with author. #51Mexico #17BIC29. 4/12/2018. BIC 29, Teotitlán del Valle, Oaxaca, Mexico].

Anonymous. (2018q). [Interview with author. #52CA #40EHS. 1/15/18. EHS, Eureka, California].

Anonymous. (2018r). [Interview with author. #58Mexico #07CEDARTMC. 4/16/18. CEDAR-TMC, Oaxaca de Juárez, Oaxaca, Mexico].

Anonymous. (2018s). [Interview with author. #59Mexico #08CEDARTMC. 4/16/18. CEDAR-TMC, Oaxaca de Juárez, Oaxaca, Mexico].

Anonymous. (2018t). [Interview with author. #62Mexico #10CEDARTMC. 4/18/18. CEDAR-TMC, Oaxaca de Juárez, Oaxaca, Mexico].

Anonymous. (2018u). [Interview with author. #65Mexico #11CEDARTMC. 4/20/18. CEDAR-TMC, Oaxaca de Juárez, Oaxaca, Mexico].

Anonymous. (2018v). [Interview with author. #66Mexico #12CEDARTMC. 4/20/18. CEDAR-TMC, Oaxaca de Juárez, Oaxaca, Mexico].

Anonymous. (2018w). [Interview with author. #67Mexico #13CEDARTMC. 4/23/18. CEDAR-TMC, Oaxaca de Juárez, Oaxaca, Mexico].

Anonymous. (2018x). [Interview with author. #68CA #55EHS. 1/18/18. EHS, Eureka, California].

Anonymous. (2018y). [Interview with author. #69Mexico #15CEDARTMC. 4/25/18. CEDAR-TMC, Oaxaca de Juárez, Oaxaca, Mexico].

Anonymous. (2018z). [Interview with author. #74CA #12YT. 7/3/18. Eureka, California].

Anonymous. (2018aa). [Interview with author. #80CA #10HVHS. 11/1/18. HVHS, Hoopa, California].

Anonymous. (2018ab). [Interview with author. EHS student. 1/10/18. Eureka, CA].

Anonymous. (2018ac). [Interview with author. #37CA #25EHS. 1/12/18. EHS, Eureka, California].

Anonymous. (2018ad). [Personal communication with author. 2/21/18. Oaxaca de Juárez, Mexico].

Anonymous. (2018ae). Interview with author. #95CA #25HVHS. 11/6/18. HVHS, Hoopa, California.

Anonymous. (2020). [Informal conversation with author. 3/4/20. BIC 29, Teotitlán del Valle, Oaxaca, Mexico].

APSA QMMR. (2019). *Qualitative Transparency Deliberations: Reports*. https://www.qualtd.net/.

Aruaz, Esmeralda. (2018). [Interview with author. #78CA #08HVHS. 11/1/18. HVHS, Hoopa, California].

Auerbach, Randy P., Mortier, Philippe, Bruffaerts, Ronny, Alonso, Jordi, Benjet, Corina, Cuijpers, Pim, . . . WHO WMH-IES Collaborators. (2018). WHO World Mental Health Surveys International College Student Project: Prevalence and Distribution of Mental Disorders. *Journal of Abnormal Psychology, 127*(7), 623–638.

Bacon, Jules M. (2019). Settler Colonialism as Eco-social Structure and the Production of Colonial Ecological Violence. *Environmental Sociology, 5*(1), 59–69.

Baker, Colin. (2011). *Foundations of Bilingual Education and Bilingualism*. Bristol: Multilingual Matters.

Baldy, Cutcha Risling. (2018). *We Are Dancing for You: Native Feminisms and the Revitalization of Women's Coming-of-Age Ceremonies*. Seattle: University of Washington Press.

Ballotpedia. (2016). California Proposition 58, Non-English Languages Allowed in Public Education. Encyclopedia of American Politics. https://ballotpedia.org/California_Proposition_58,_Non-English_Languages_Allowed_in_Public_Education_(2016).

Banks, James A. (2004). Teaching for Social Justice, Diversity, and Citizenship in a Global World. *Educational Forum, 68*(4), 296–305.

Barabas, Alicia M. (2016). La migración de los indígenas de Oaxaca, México, a Estados Unidos y su movilización social. *Comparative Cultural Studies-European and Latin American Perspectives, 1*(1), 77–86.

Bardzell, Shaowen, & Bardzell, Jeffrey. (2011). Towards a Feminist HCI Methodology: Social Science, Feminism, and HCI. Paper presented at the Proceedings of the SIGCHI Conference on Human Factors in Computing Systems, Vancouver, BC.

Baum, Fran, MacDougall, Colin, & Smith, Danielle. (2006). Participatory Action Research. *Journal of Epidemiology and Community Health, 60*(10), 854–857.

Bautista, Jacob. (2020). [Interview with author. #91Mexico #26BIC29. 3/4/20. BIC 29 Teotitlán del Valle, Oaxaca, Mexico].

Bénéï, Véronique. (2008). *Schooling Passions: Nation, History, and Language in Contemporary Western India*. Stanford, CA: Stanford University Press.

Benvenuto, Jeff. (2015). What Does Genocide Produce? The Semantic Field of Genocide, Cultural Genocide, and Ethnocide in Indigenous Rights Discourse. *Genocide Studies and Prevention, 9*(2), 26–40.

Blancas Moreno, Elsa María, & Vázquez Rodríguez, Saúl. (2017). El derecho a la educación de los niños y las niñas que asisten a escuelas primarias rurales de los cursos comunitarios del CONAFE Oaxaca. In Ana Margarita Alvarado Juárez & Virginia Guadalupe Reyes de la Cruz, eds., *La Educación en México: Escanarios y Desafíos*, 129–156. México: Universidad Autónoma Benito Juárez de Oaxaca y Juan Pablos Editor, S.A.

Blatter, Joachim. (2017). Truth Seeking AND Sense Making: Towards Configurational Designs of Qualitative Methods. *Qualitative and Multi-Method Research, 15*, 2–14.

Bleck, Jaimie, Dendere, Chipo, & Sangaré, Boukary. (2018). Making North-South Research Collaborations Work. *PS: Political Science and Politics, 51*(3), 554–558.

Bonds, Anne, & Inwood, Joshua. (2015). Beyond White Privilege: Geographies of White Supremacy and Settler Colonialism. *Progress in Human Geography, 40*(6), 715–733.

Bradbury, Hilary, ed. (2015). *The SAGE Handbook of Action Research*. London: SAGE Publications.

Brydon-Miller, Mary, Greenwood, Davydd, & Maguire, Patricia. (2003). Why Action Research? *Action Research Journal, 1*, 9–28.

Buckley, Thomas C. T. (2002). *Standing Ground: Yurok Indian Spirituality, 1850–1990*. Berkeley: University of California Press.

Burch, Traci. (2013). *Trading Democracy for Justice: Criminal Convictions and the Decline of Neighborhood Political Participation*. Chicago: University of Chicago Press.

Bush, Jamie. (2018). [Interview with author. #43CA #31EHS. 1/12/18. EHS, Eureka, California].

California Department of Education. (2000). *Proposition 227 Final Report*. https://www.cde.ca.gov/sp/el/er/prop227summary.asp.

California Department of Education. (2017). *English Learner Roadmap*. https://www.cde.ca.gov/sp/el/rm/.

California Freshworks. (2020). Increasing Access to Food in California's Hoopa Valley. *California Freshworks*. http://www.cafreshworks.com/hoopavalley/.

Campbell, Howard. (1994). *Zapotec Renaissance: Ethnic Politics and Cultural Revivalism in Southern Mexico*. Albuquerque: University of New Mexico Press.

Campbell, Rebecca, & Wasco, Sharon M. (2000). Feminist Approaches to Social Science: Epistemological and Methodological Tenets. *American Journal of Community Psychology, 28*(6), 773–791.

Canclini, Néstor García. (1989). *Culturas híbridas: Estrategias para entrar y salir de la modernidad*. Mexico, D.F.: Editorial Grijalbo.

Cárdenas González, Alfonso. (2018). [Interview with author. #44Mexico #01CEDARTMC. 4/9/2018. CEDARTMC, Oaxaca de Juárez, Oaxaca, Mexico].

Cardinal, Linda, & Sonntag, Selma K., eds. (2015). *State Traditions and Language Regimes: A Historical Institutionalism Approach to Language Policy*. Toronto: McGill-Queen's University Press.

Carpenter IV, Chance Edward. (2018). "NINIS'A:N M'IXINE:WHE' YIŁCHWE": Towards a Local Land Based Pedagogy in Northern California's North Coast for Local Indigenous Heritage Languages. Thesis for Master of Arts in Education: Composition Studies and Pedagogy, Humboldt State University. https://digitalcommons.humboldt.edu/cgi/viewcontent.cgi?article=1216&context=etd.

Centellas, Miguel, & Rosenblatt, Cy. (2018). Do Introductory Political Science Courses Contribute to a Racial "Political Efficacy Gap"? Findings from a Panel Survey of a Flagship University. *PS: Political Science and Politics, 51*(3), 641–647.

Ceylan, Deniz Tarba, & Irzik, Gürol. (2004). *Human Rights Issues in Textbooks: The Turkish Case*. Istanbul: History Foundation of Turkey.

Chassagne, Natasha. (2019). Sustaining the "Good Life": Buen Vivir as an Alternative to Sustainable Development. *Community Development Journal, 54*(3), 482–500.

CNEI-UCIEP A.C. (2011). *Hacia la Contrucción de una educación indígena e intercultural desde los pueblos y para los pueblos*. In Congreso Nacional de Educación Indígena e Intercultural (Ed.). México: Comité Promotor del Congreso Nacional de Educación Indígena y la Unidad de Capacitación e Investigación Educativa para la Participación, A.C.

Cohen, Jeffrey H., & Ramirez Rios, Bernardo. (2016). Internal Migration in Oaxaca: Its Role and Value to Rural Movers. *International Journal of Sociology, 46*(3), 223–235.

Cole, Elizabeth A., ed. (2007). *Teaching the Violent Past: History Education and Reconciliation*. Lanham, MD: Rowman and Littlefield.

Cole, Taylor. (2018). [Interview with author. #89CA #19HVHS. 11/5/18. HVHS, Hoopa, California].

Colegrove-Raymond, Adrienne. (2019). A Time of Reflection: The Role of Education in Preservation. In Kishan Lara-Cooper & Walter J. Lara Sr., eds., *Ka'm-t'em: A Journey Toward Healing*, 277–283. Pechanga, CA: Great Oak Press.

Collier, David. (1993). The Comparative Method. In Ada W. Finifter, ed., *Political Science: The State of the Discipline*. Washington, DC: American Political Science Association.

Combs, Mary Carol, González, Norma, & Moll, Luis C. (2014). US Latinos and the Learning of English. In Teresa L McCarty, ed., *Ethnography and Language Policy*, 184–203. New York: Routledge.

Contreras García, Eulogio. (2018). [Interview with author. #15Mexico #13BIC29. 3/2/18. BIC 29, Teotitlán del Valle, Oaxaca, Mexico].

Cook, Maria Lorena. (1996). *Organizing Dissent: Unions, the State, and the Democratic Teachers' Movement in Mexico*. University Park: Pennsylvania State University Press.

Córdova, Abby, & Layton, Matthew L. (2015). When Is "Delivering the Goods" Not Good Enough? How Economic Disparities in Latin American Neighborhoods Shape Citizen Trust in Local Government. *World Politics, 68*(1), 74–110.

Cornelson, Craig. (2018). [Interview with author. #82CA #12HVHS. 11/1/18. HVHS, Hoopa, California].

Corntassel, Jeff. (2012). Re-envisioning Resurgence: Indigenous Pathways to Decolonization and Sustainable Self-determination. *Decolonization: Indigeneity, Education & Society, 1*(1), 86–101.

Cortés Reyes, Saúl Gamaliel. (2018). [Interview with author. #45 Mexico #02CEDARTMC. 4/9/18. CEDARTMC, Oaxaca de Juárez, Oaxaca, Mexico].

Cramer, Katherine. (2015). Transparent Explanations, Yes. Public Transcripts and Fieldnotes, No. Ethnographic Research on Public Opinion. *Newsletter of the American Political Science Association, Organized Section for Qualitative and Multi-Method Research, 13*(1), 17–20.

Crawford, Susan E., & Alaggia, Ramona. (2008). The Best of Both Worlds?: Family Influences on Mixed Race Youth Identity Development. *Qualitative Social Work, 7*(1), 81–98.

Cruz, Ana (Writer). (2012). Las Sufragistas [The Suffragists]. In EPF Media. https://www .epfmedia.com/the-suffragists.

Crystal, David. (2013). *English as a Global Language*. Cambridge: Cambridge University Press.

Crystal, David. (2014). *Language Death*. Cambridge: Cambridge University Press.

Cyr, Jennifer. (2016). The Pitfalls and Promise of Focus Groups as a Data Collection Method. *Sociological Methods & Research, 45*(2), 231–259.

Daniels, Greg. (2018). [Interview with author. #66CA #53EHS. 1/18/18. EHS, Eureka, California].

Danielson, Michael S., & Eisenstadt, Todd A. (2009). Walking Together, but in Which Direction? Gender Discrimination and Multicultural Practices in Oaxaca, Mexico. *Politics and Gender, 5*, 153–184.

DataQuest. (2022). *Eureka Senior High Report: Enrollment Multi-Year Summary by Ethnicity*. https://dq.cde.ca.gov/dataquest/dqcensus/EnrEthYears.aspx?cds=12755151232206 &agglevel=School&year=2017-18&ro=y:.

DataQuest. (2020). *Eureka Senior High Report: Enrollment Multi-Year Summary by Ethnicity*. https://dq.cde.ca.gov/dataquest/dqcensus/EnrEthYears.aspx?cds=12755151232206&agglevel =School&year=2017-18&ro=y:.

Davies, Nancy. (2007). *The People Decide: Oaxaca's Popular Assembly.* New York: Narco News.

Davies-Hughes, Michael. (2017). [Interview with author. #10 CA. 7/24/17. Eureka, California].

Deloria Jr., Vine. ([1969] 1988). *Custer Died for Your Sins: An Indian Manifesto.* Norman: University of Oklahoma Press.

DeLugan, Robin Maria. (2012). *Reimagining National Belonging: Post–Civil War El Salvador in a Global Context.* Tucson: University of Arizona Press.

Desposato, Scott. (2018). Subjects and Scholars' Views on the Ethics of Political Science Field Experiments. *Perspectives on Politics, 16*(3), 739–750.

Dionisio, Maria Pérez (2018). [Interview with author. #39Mexico #14BIC29. 3/22/18. BIC 29, Teotitlán del Valle, Oaxaca, Mexico].

Dor, Danny. (2004). From Englishization to Imposed Multiculturalism: Globalization, the Internet, and the Political Economy of the Linguistic Code. *Public Culture, 16*(1), 97–118.

Duran, Eduardo. (2006). *Healing the Soul Wound: Counseling with American Indians and Other Native Peoples.* New York: Teachers College Press.

Earl, Jennifer, Maher, Thomas V., & Elliott, Thomas. (2017). Youth, Activism, and Social Movements. *Sociology Compass, 11*(4), 1–14.

Eber, Christine, & Kovic, Christine, eds. (2003). *Women in Chiapas: Making History in Times of Struggle and Hope.* London: Routledge.

EdData. (2020). *Eureka High School: Demographics.* http://www.ed-data.org/district/Humboldt /Eureka-City-Schools.

Enrique, Salmón. (2012). *Eating the Landscape: American Indian Stories of Food, Identity, and Resilience.* Tucson: University of Arizona Press.

Enrique López, Luis. (2006). Cultural Diversity, Multilingualism and Indigenous Education in Latin America. In Ofelia García, Tove Skutnabb-Kangas, & Maria E. Torres-Guzmán, eds., *Imagining Multilingual Schools: Languages in Education and Glocalization,* 238–261. Buffalo: Multilingual Matters.

Esteban. (2020). [Interview with author. #92Mexico #27BIC29. 3/4/20. BIC 29, Teotitlán del Valle, Oaxaca, Mexico].

Ewing, Eve. (2020). I'm a Black Scholar Who Studies Race. Here's Why I Capitalize "White." https://zora.medium.com/im-a-black-scholar-who-studies-race-here-s-why-i-capitalize -white-f94883aa2dd3.

Faingold, Eduardo D. (2018). *Language Rights and the Law in the United States and Its Territories.* Boulder, CO: Lexington Books.

Faudree, Paja. (2013). *Singing for the Dead: The Politics of Indigenous Revival in Mexico.* Durham, NC: Duke University Press.

Fenelon, James V. (1998). *Culturicide, Resistance, and Survival of the Lakota (Sioux Nation).* New York: Garland Publishing.

Fenelon, James V. (2002). Dual Sovereignty of Native Nations, the United States, & Traditionalists. *Humboldt Journal of Social Relations, 1,* 106–145.

Field, Margaret C., & Kroskrity, Paul V. (2010). Introduction: Revealing Native American Language Ideologies. In Paul V. Kroskrity & Margaret C. Field, eds., *Native American Language Ideologies: Beliefs, Practices, and Struggles in Indian Country,* 3–28. Tucson: University of Arizona Press.

Firchow, Pamina, & Gellman, Mneesha. (2021). Collaborative Methodologies: Why, How, and for Whom? *PS: Political Science & Politics, 54*(3), 525–529.

Fishman, Joshua A. (2006). Language Loyalty, Language Planning, and Language Revitalization: Recent Writings and Reflections from Joshua A. Fishman. In Nancy H. Hornberger & Martin Pütz, eds., 29–259. Buffalo: Multilingual Matters.

Focus Group. (2018a). [Focus group with author. #01CA #01EHS. Senior Civics students. 1/18/18. EHS, Eureka, California].

Focus Group. (2018b). [Informal focus group with Yurok III students. #03CA #01HVHS. 10/31/18. HVHS, Hoopa, California].

Focus Group 1.1. (2018). [Focus group with author. 8th semester Zapotec students. 3/12/18. UABJO, Oaxaca de Juárez, Oaxaca, Mexico].

Focus Group 9.2. (2018). [Focus group with author. Three second semester English students. 5/5/18. CEDARTMC, Oaxaca de Juárez, Oaxaca, Mexico].

Focus Group 3.1 BIC 29. (2018). [Focus group, BIC 29 students with author. 3/22/18. BIC 29, Teotitlán del Valle, Oaxaca, Mexico].

Focus Group 4.2 BIC 29. (2018). [Focus group, BIC 29 students with author. 3/22/18. BIC 29, Teotitlán del Valle, Oaxaca, Mexico].

Focus Group 5.3 UABJO. (2018). [Focus group, UABJO college students and recent graduates with author. 3/22/18]. UABJO, Oaxaca de Juárez, Oaxaca, Mexico.

Foxworth, Raymond, Liu, Amy H., & Sokhey, Anand Edward. (2015). Incorporating Native American History into the Curriculum: Descriptive Representation or Campaign Contributions? *Social Science Quarterly, 96*(4), 955–969.

Fregoso, Dora. (2018). [Interview with author. #34CA #22EHS. 1/12/18. EHS, Eureka, California].

Galindo, Estalita. (2018). [Interview with author. #79CA #09HVHS. 11/1/18. HVHS, Hoopa, California].

García, Ofelia, Skutnabb-Kangas, Tove, & Torres-Guzmán, Maria E. (2006). *Imagining Multilingual Schools: Languages in Education and Globalization.* Buffalo: Multilingual Matters.

Gay, Geneva. (2010). *Culturally Responsive Teaching: Theory, Research, and Practice.* New York: Teachers College Press.

Gellman, Mneesha. (2015). Teaching Silence in the Schoolroom: Whither National History in Sierra Leone and El Salvador? *Third World Quarterly, 36*(1), 147–161.

Gellman, Mneesha. (2017). *Democratization and Memories of Violence: Ethnic Minority Rights Movements in Mexico, Turkey, and El Salvador.* New York: Routledge.

Gellman, Mneesha. (2019). The Right to Learn Our (M)other tongues: Indigenous Languages and Neoliberal Citizenship in El Salvador and Mexico. *British Journal of Sociology of Education, 40*(4), 523–537.

Gellman, Mneesha. (2020a). Covid-Closures: When School Cancellation Means Return to a War Zone/Cierres por Covid: Cuando la cancelación de la escuela significa el regreso a una zona de guerra. *ReVista: Harvard Review of Latin America.* https://revista.drclas.harvard.edu/book/covid-closures?admin_panel=1.

Gellman, Mneesha. (2020b). "Mother Tongue Won't Help You Eat": Language Politics in Sierra Leone. *African Journal of Political Science and International Relations, 14*(4), 140–149.

Gellman, Mneesha. (2021a). Collaborative Methodology with Indigenous Communities: A Framework for Addressing Power Inequalities. *PS: Political Science and Politics, 54*(3), 535–538.

Gellman, Mneesha. (2021b). "No nos importaba a nadie": Navegando en la búsqueda del éxito académico en Oaxaca, México. *Polis: Revista Latinoamericana, 20,* 59–78.

Gellman, Mneesha, & Bellino, Michelle. (2019). Fighting Invisibility: Indigenous Citizens and History Education in El Salvador and Guatemala. *Latin American and Caribbean Ethnic Studies, 14*(1), 1–23.

Gensaw, James. (2017). [Interview with author. #05CA, 7/14/17. Eureka, California].

Gensaw, James. (2019). [Personal communication with author. Yurok language teacher. 11/18/19. Eureka High School, California].

Gensaw, Melanie. (2017). [Interview with author. #06CA, 7/14/17. Eureka, California].

Gillespie, Evelyn. (2018). [Interview with author. #18CA #06EHS. 1/10/18. EHS, Eureka, California].

Gobierno de Oaxaca. (2020). *Sistema Normativa Indígena*. http://www.ieepco.org.mx/sistemas-normativos.

Goering, Elizabeth M. (2013). Engaging Citizens: A Cross Cultural Comparison of Youth Definitions of Engaged Citizenship. *Universal Journal of Educational Research, 1*(3), 175–184.

Gómez de García, Jule, Axelrod, Melissa, & Lachler, Jordan. (2010). English Is the Dead Language: Native Perspectives on Bilingualism. In Paul V. Kroskrity & Margaret C. Field, eds., *Native American Language Ideologies: Beliefs, Practices, and Struggles in Indian Country*, 99–122. Tucson: University of Arizona Press.

Gone, Joseph. (2014). Colonial Genocide and Historical Trauma in Native North America. In Alexander Hinton, Andrew Woolford Laban, & Jeff Benvenuto, eds., *Colonial Genocide in Indigenous North America*, 273–291. Durham, NC: Duke University Press.

Gopar, Mario E. López. (2016). Introducción. In Mario E. López Gopar, ed., *Historias de vida de estudiantes universitarios de origen indígena*, 11–14. Oaxaca: Universidad Autónoma "Benito Juárez" de Oaxaca.

Gopar, Mario E. López, Bohórquez Martínez, Marlene B., Cruz Ramírez, Marlene, López Aparicio, Luis P., & Peña Garcia, Isabel. (2016). Isabel: Una mujer retadora de costumbres. In Mario E. López Gopar, ed., *Historias de vida de estudiantes universitarios de origen indígena*, 121–136. Oaxaca: Universidad Autónoma "Benito Juárez" de Oaxaca.

Gopar, Mario E. López, López, Susana Marín, Montes, Tanibet Silva, Mendoza Manuel, Gerardo J., & Bautista García, Merie. (2016). Merie: Una migrante en busca de sueños. In Mario E. López Gopar, ed., *Historias de vida de estudiantes universitarios de origen indígena*, 33–44. Oaxaca: Universidad Autónoma "Benito Juárez" de Oaxaca.

Gopar, Mario E. López, Vásquez Miranda, Alba Eugenia, León Jiménez, Edwin Nazaret, & Pacheco Cruz, Elisa M. (2016). Fernando: Un médico veterinario chinanteco. In Mario E. López Gopar, ed., *Historias de vida de estudiantes universitarios de origen indígena*, 80–92. Oaxaca: Universidad Autónoma "Benito Juárez" de Oaxaca.

Government of Mexico. (2011 [1917]). *Constitución Política de los Estados Unidos Mexicanos*. México, D.F. Last reformed 10/13/11.

Government of Mexico. (2003). *Ley General de Derechos Lingüísticos de los Pueblos Indígenas/General Law on Linguistic Rights of Indigenous Peoples*. Publicada en el Distrito Federal el día 13 de marzo de 2003.

Greenson, Thadeus. (2019). Duluwat Island Is Returned to the Wiyot Tribe in Historic Ceremony. *North Coast Journal*, October 21. https://www.northcoastjournal.com/NewsBlog/archives/2019/2010/2021/duluwat-island-is-returned-to-the-wiyot-tribe-in-historic-ceremony.

Greenson, Thadeus. (2021). Dishgamu Humboldt: A Groundbreaking, Wiyot-Led Effort to Heal and Rebuild While Putting Land Back in Native Hands. *Northcoast Journal, 31*(27), 12–16.

Guerrettaz, Anne Marie. (2019). "We Are the Mayas": Indigenous Language Revitalization, Identification, and Postcolonialism in the Yucatan, Mexico. *Linguistics and Education, 58*, 1–15.

Gutmann, Matthew C. (2007). *The Meanings of Macho: Being a Man in Mexico City*. Berkeley: University of California Press.

Hale, Charles R. (2008). *Engaging Contradictions: Theory, Politics and Methods of Activist Scholarship*. Berkeley: University of California Press.

Hamel, Rainer Enrique. (2008). Indigenous Language Policy and Education in Mexico. In *Encyclopedia of Language and Education*, 301–313. Berlin: Springer.

Hamilton, Katherine. (2019). "It's Called a Genocide": The Strength of Language in U.S. Government Apologies to Native Americans. *Cultural Survival*. https://www.culturalsurvival.org/news/its-called-genocide-strength-language-us-government-apologies-native-americans.

Hammond, Zaretta. (2015). *Culturally Responsive Teaching and the Brain: Promoting Authentic Engagement and Rigor Among Culturally and Linguistically Diverse Students*. Thousand Oaks, CA: Corwin: A SAGE Company.

Hassanpour, Amir, Sheyholislami, Jaffer, & Skutnabb-Kangas, Tove. (2012). Introduction. Kurdish: Linguicide, Resistance and Hope. *International Journal of the Sociology of Language, 2012*(217), 1–18.

Haun, Jess. (2018). [Interview with author. #73CA #60EHS. Eureka High School English teacher. 6/19/18. McKinleyville, California].

Herrera, Allison. (2019). Indigenous Educators Fight for an Accurate History of California. *High Country News*, April 19. https://www.hcn.org/issues/2051.2017/tribal-affairs-indigenous-educators-fight-for-an-accurate-history-of-california-missions.

Herrera, Veronica, & Post, Alison E. (2019). The Case for Public Policy Expertise in Political Science. *PS: Political Science and Politics, 52*(3), 476–480.

Heugh, Kathleen, & Stroud, Christopher. (2019). Diversities, Affinities and Diasporas: A Southern Lens and Methodology for Understanding Multilingualisms. *Current Issues in Language Planning, 20*(1), 1–15.

Higginbottom, Andy. (2008). Solidarity Action Research as Methodology: The Crimes of the Powerful in Colombia. *Latin American Perspectives, 35*(5), 158–170.

Hornberger, Nancy H. (2008). *Can Schools Save Indigenous Languages? Policy and Practice on Four Continents*. New York: Palgrave Macmillan.

Hornberger, Nancy H. (2009). Multilingual Education Policy and Practice: Ten Certainties (Grounded in Indigenous Experience). *Language Teaching, 42*(2), 197–211.

Hornberger, Nancy H., & Cassels Johnson, David. (2014). The Ethnography of Language Policy. In Teresa L. McCarty, ed., *Ethnography and Language Policy*, 273–289. New York: Routledge.

Hornberger, Nancy H., & De Korne, Haley. (2018). Is Revitalization Through Education Possible? In Leanne Hinton, Leena Huss, & Gerald Roche, eds., *The Routledge Handbook of Language Revitalization*, 94–103. New York: Routledge.

Huang, Jane. (2018). [Interview with author. #26CA #14 EHS. 1/11/18. EHS, Eureka, California].

Huerta Córdova, Vilma. (2018). [Interview with author. #46 Mexico #21UABJO. Faculty at UABJO and staff at CEDARTMC. 4/9/18. CEDARTMC, Oaxaca de Juárez, Oaxaca, Mexico].

Hussar, Bill, Zhang, Jijun, Hein, Sarah, Wang, Ke, Roberts, Ashley, Cui, Jiashan, . . . Dilig, Rita. (2020). *The Condition of Education 2020-NCES 2020-144*. https://nces.ed.gov/pubs2020 /2020144.pdf.

Imbler, Sabrina. (2019). Is the End Coming for a Problematic California Grade School Tradition? The Mission Model Project Has Long Glossed over the Brutal Treatment of Native Americans. *Atlas Obscura*, September 12.

Indian Land Tenure Foundation. (2020). *Education*. https://iltf.org/grants/education/

Indigenous Peoples of Oaxaca Forum. (2006). Pronunciamiento Conjunto de los Pueblos Indígenas y la Sociedad Civil de Oaxaca. In *La Batalla por Oaxaca*, 271–276. Oaxaca: Ediciones Yope Power.

Indigenous Peoples of Oaxaca. (1992). ¡*Ahora o Nunca! Luchemos por Nuestro Destino: Declaración de Lucha de los Pueblos Mixtecos, Chocholtecos, Triquis, Tacuates y Amuzgos*, 1–15. Tlaxiaco, Oaxaca, June 1992.

INEGI. (2015). *Lengua Indígena: Información General. Instituto Nacional de Estadística y Geografíia (National Institute of Statistics and Geography)*. https://en.www.inegi.org.mx /temas/lengua/#General_Information.

INEGI. (2020a). *Lengua indígena*. https://www.inegi.org.mx/temas/lengua/.

INEGI. (2020b). *Migration*. https://en.www.inegi.org.mx/temas/migracion/.

Inong, Kay. (2017). [Interview with author. #02CA. 6/29/17. HVHS, Hoopa, California].

Jackson, Sarah. (2019). A Huge Shift: How California Is Making Up for 20 Years of English-Only Education. *Pacific Standard*, May 3.

Jacob, Michelle M. (2013). *Yakama Rising: Indigenous Cultural Revitalization, Activism, and Healing*. Tuscon: University of Arizona Press.

Jacob, Michelle M., & RunningHawk Johnson, Stephany, eds. (2020). *On Indian Ground: A Return to Indigenous Knowledge: Generating Hope, Leadership and Sovereignty Through Education*. Charlotte, NC: Information Age Publishing.

Jasper, James M. (1997). *The Art of Moral Protest: Culture, Biography, and Creativity in Social Movements*. Chicago: University of Chicago Press.

Jiménez Naranjo, Yolanda. (2017). Política pública y educación indígena: Entre la asimilación que no cesa y el pluralismo que no llega. In Ana Margarita Alvarado Juárez & Virginia Guadalupe Reyes de la Cruz, eds., *La Educación en México: Escanarios y Desafíos*, 97–127. Oaxaca de Juárez: Universidad Autónoma Benito Juárez de Oaxaca y Juan Pablos Editor, S.A.

Johnson, Melissa A. (2019). *Becoming Creole: Nature and Race in Belize*. New Brunswick, NJ: Rutgers Unversity Press.

Joseph, Kisdyante. (2019). "I Have a Voice" (17 years old). In Kishan Lara-Cooper & Walter J. Lara Sr., eds., *K'am-t'em: A Journey Toward Healing*, 305–309. Pechanga, CA: Great Oak Press.

Kemmis, Stephen, McTaggart, Robin, & Nixon, Rhonda. (2014). *The Action Research Planner: Doing Critical Participatory Action Research*. Singapore: Springer Science & Business Media.

Kendi, Ibram X. (2016). *Stamped from the Beginning: The Definitive History of Racist Ideas in America*. New York: Bold Type Books.

Kessler-Mata, Kouslaa T. (2017). *American Indians and the Trouble with Sovereignty: Structuring Self-Determination Through Federalism*. Cambridge: Cambridge University Press.

Kimmerer, Robin Wall. (2013). *Braiding Sweetgrass: Indigenous Wisdom, Scientific Knowledge, and the Teaching of Plants*. Minneapolis: Milkweed Editions.

Kindon, Sara, Pain, Rachel, & Kesby, Mike, eds. (2007). *Participatory Action Research Approaches and Methods: Connecting People, Participation and Place*. New York: Routledge.

King, Kendell A., & Haboud, Marleen. (2014). International Migration and Quichua Language Shift in the Ecuadorian Andes. In Teresa L McCarty, ed., *Ethnography and Language Policy*, 138–159. New York: Routledge.

King, Thomas. (2018). *The Inconvenient Indian: A Curious Account of Native People in North America*. Minneapolis: University of Minnesota Press.

Kittrie, Orde F. (2016). *Lawfare: Law as a Weapon of War*. Oxford: Oxford University Press.

KTJUSD. (2020). *Program Overview*. Klamath Trinity Joint Unified School District. http://www.ktjusd.k12.ca.us/Departments/Indian-Education-Program/Program-Overview/index.html.

Koomler, Alexis, Gill, Judith, Esson, Katharine, & Yuen, Rosalina. (2017). A Girl's Education: Schooling and the Formation of Gender, Identities, and Future Visions. *Journal of Youth and Adolescence, 46*(9), 2073–2077.

Kovats Sánchez, Gabriela. (2018). Raffirming Indiginous Identity: Understanding Experiences of Stigmatization and Marginalization Among Mexican Indigenous College Students. *Journal of Latinos and Education, 19*(2), 1–14.

Kroeber, Alfred Louis. (1925). *Handbook of the Indians of California*. Vol. 78. Washington, DC: U.S. Government Printing Office.

Lara-Cooper, Kishan. (2017). Protecting the Treasure: A History of Indigenous Education in California. In Joely Proudfit & Nicole Quinderro Myers-Lim, eds., *On Indian Ground: A Return to Indigenous Knowledge: Generating Hope, Leadership and Sovereignty Through Education*, 1–18. Charlotte, NC: IAP-Information Age Publishing.Lara-Cooper, Kishan. (2019). "More than a Boat": Bias, Institutional Frameworks, and Testimonial Injustice. In Kishan Lara-Cooper & Walter J. Lara Sr., eds., *Ka'm-t'em: A Journey Toward Healing*, 15–38. Pechanga, CA: Great Oak Press.

Lara-Cooper, Kishan, & Lara Sr., Walter J., eds. (2019). *Ka'm-t'em: A Journey Toward Healing*. Pechanga, CA: Great Oak Press.

Layna Sarmiento, Desiree Marion. (2018). [Interview with author. #73Mexico #17CEDARTMC. 5/2/18. CEDARTMC, Oaxaca de Juárez, Oaxaca, Mexico].

Lewis, Carole. (2017). [Interview with author. #01CA. 6/29/17. HVHS, Hoopa, California].

Leyva Solano, Xochitl, Alonso, Jorge, Hernández, R. Aída, Escobar, Arturo, Kohler, Axel, Cumes, Aura, & Sandoval, Rafael, eds. (2015). *Prácticas otras de conocimiento(s): Entre crisis, entre guerras. Tomo 1*. Buenos Aires: CLACSO.

Lindsay, Brendan C. (2015). *Murder State: California's Native American Genocide, 1846–1873*. Lincoln: University of Nebraska Press.

Liu, Cindy H., Stevens, Courtney, Wong, Sylvia H. M., Yasui, Miwa, & Chen, Justin A. (2019). The Prevalence and Predictors of Mental Health Diagnoses and Suicide Among US College Students: Implications for Addressing Disparities in Service Use. *Depression and Anxiety, 36*(1), 8–17.

Loader, Brian D., Vromen, Ariadne, & Xenos, Michael A. (2014). The Networked Young Citizen: Social Media, Political Participation and Civic Engagement. *Information, Communication & Society, 17*(2), 143–150.

Loether, Christopher. (2010). Language Revitalization and the Manipulation of Language Ideologies: A Shoshoni Case Study. In Paul V. Kroskrity & Margaret C. Field, eds., *Native American Language Ideologies: Beliefs, Practices, and Struggles in Indian Country*, 238–254. Tuscon: University of Arizona Press.

Lopez, Luis. (2018). [Interview with author. #45CA #33EHS. 1/15/18. EHS, Eureka, California].

Love, Bettina L. (2019). *We Want to Do More than Survive: Abolitionist Teaching and the Pursuit of Educational Freedom*. Boston: Beacon Press.

Lowry, Chag. (2014). *History & Hope*. Film. Self-produced. https://www.youtube.com/watch?v=4FSiiuMAfFo.

Mac Ionnrachtaigh, Feargal. (2013). *Language, Resistance and Revival: Republican Prisoners and the Irish Language in the North of Ireland*. New York: Pluto Press.

MacLean, Lauren M., Posner, Elliot, Thomson, Susan, & Wood, Elisabeth Jean. (2018). *Research Ethics and Human Subjects: A Reflexive Openness Approach*. https://papers.ssrn.com/sol3/papers.cfm?abstract_id=3332887.

Maher, Anne. (2018). *Saga of the G-O Road, 30 Years Later*. https://www.yournec.org/GO-Road-30yr-anniv

Mahoney, James. (2001). *The Legacies of Liberalism: Path Dependence and Political Regimes in Central America*. Baltimore: Johns Hopkins University Press.

Mako, Shamiran. (2012). Cultural Genocide and Key International Instruments: Framing the Indigenous Experience. *International Journal on Minority and Group Rights, 19*(2), 175–194.

Maldonado Alvarado, Benjamín. (2000). *Los Indios en Las Aulas: Dinámica de Dominación y Resistencia en Oaxaca*. Oaxaca: Instituto Nacional de Antropología e Historia.

Maldonado Alverado, Benjamin. (2010). Comunidad, comunalidad y colonialismo en Oaxaca, México: La nueva educación comunitaria y su contexto. PhD thesis, Leiden University.

Marcos, Subcommandante Insurgente, & Ponce de Leon, Juana. (2001). *Our Word Is Our Weapon: Selected Writings*. New York: Seven Stories Press.

Marshall, Joe. (2018). [Interview with author. #76CA #06HVHS. 10/31/18. HVHS, Hoopa, California].

Martinez Covarubbias, Francisco Vicente. (2018). [Interview with author. #71Mexico #20BIC29. 4/27/18. BIC 29, Teotitlán del Valle, Oaxaca, Mexico].

Martinez Covarubbias, Francisco Vicente. (2020). Informal conversation with author. Director of BIC 29. 1/29/20. BIC 29, Teotitlán del Valle, Oaxaca, Mexico.

Martínez de Bringas, Asier. (2013). Los Sistemas Normativos Indígenas en el marco del pluaralismo Jurídico: Un Análisis Desde los Derechos Indígenas. *Revista de Derecho Político, 86*(enero–abril), 411–444.

Martínez Martínez, Esteban de Jesús (2018). [Interview with author. #54Mexico #03CEDARTMC. 4/13/18. CEDARTMC, Oaxaca de Juárez, Oaxaca, Mexico].

Mata Moreles, Monserrat. (2018). [Interview with author. #05Mexico #03BIC29. 2/26/18. BIC 29, Teotitlán del Valle, Oaxaca, Mexico].

May, Stephen. (2012). *Language and Minority Rights: Ethnicity, Nationalism and the Politics of Language*. New York: Routledge.

McAdam, Doug. (1988). *Freedom Summer*. New York: Oxford University Press.

McAdam, Doug, Tarrow, Sidney G., & Tilly, Charles. (2001). *Dynamics of Contention*. Cambridge: Cambridge University Press.

McCarty, Teresa L., ed. (2014). *Ethnography and Language Policy*. New York: Routledge.

McCarty, Teresa L., Romero-Little, Mary Eunice, Warhol, Larisa, & Zepeda, Ofelia. (2014). Critical Ethnography and Indigenous Language Survival. In Teresa L. McCarty, ed., *Ethnography and Language Policy*, 30–51. New York: Routledge.

McCovey, Shaunna Oteka. (2006). Resilience and Responsibility: Surviving the New Genocide. In Marijo Moore, ed., *Eating Fire, Tasting Blood: Breaking the Great Silence of the American Indian Holocaust*, 287–295. Philadelphia: Running Press.

McQuillen, Barbara. (2017). [Interview with author. #12CA. Barbara McQuillen, Del Norte High School language teacher and staff member of Yurok Tribe's Education Department. 7/24/17. Klamath, CA].

McQuillen, Jim. (2017). [Interview with author. #11CA. Jim McQuillen, Education Director of the Yurok Tribe. 7/24/17. Klamath, CA].

McQuillen, Jim. (2019). Next Steps: The Education System; Inclusiveness, School Dropouts, and Cultural Pride. In Kishan Lara-Cooper & Walter J. Lara Sr., eds., *Ka'm-t'em: A Journey Toward Healing*, 285–289. Pechanga, CA: Great Oak Press.

Meek, Barbra A. (2010). *We Are Our Language: An Ethnography of Language Revitalization in a Northern Athabascan Community*. Tuscon: University of Arizona Press.

Méndez Vera, Mónica Haniel. (2018). [Interview with author. #55Mexico #04CEDARTMC. 4/13/18. CEDARTMC, Oaxaca de Juárez, Oaxaca, Mexico].

Mendoza Jiménez, Carlos. (2020). [Interview with author. #86Mexico #24BIC29. 2/12/20. BIC 29, Teotitlán del Valle, Oaxaca, Mexico].

Mendoza Zuany, Rosa Guadalupe. (2017). Inclusión educativa por interculturalidad: Implicaciones para la educación de la niñez indígena. *Perfiles Educativos, 39*(158), 52–69.

Métais, Julie. (2018). The Tortuous Politics of Recognition: Local Festivities, Protest, and Violence in Oaxaca, Mexico. In Nicole Gombay & Marcela Palomino-Schalscha, eds., *Indigenous Places and Colonial Spaces*, 155–175. London: Routledge.

Meyer v. State of Nebraska. 262 US 390. (1923). Taft Court. *Oyez*. https://www.oyez.org/cases/1900-1940/262us390.

MICS. (2015). *Encuesta Nacional de Niños, Niñas y Mujeres 2015*. https://mics-surveys-prod.s3.amazonaws.com/MICS5/Latin%20America%20and%20Caribbean/Mexico/2015/Key%20findings/Mexico%202015%20MICS%20KFR_Spanish.PDF.

Middleton Manning, Beth Rose, & Reed, Kaitlin. (2019). Returning the Yurok Forest to the Yurok Tribe: California's First Tribal Carbon Credit Project. *Stanford Environmental Law Journal, 39*, 71–124.

Middleton-Manning, Beth Rose, Gali, Morning Star, & Houck, Darcie. (2018). Holding the Headwaters: Northern California Indian Resistance to State and Corporate Water Development. *Decolonization: Indigeneity, Education & Society, 7*(1), 174–198.

Modiano, Nancy. (1984). Bilingual-Bicultural Education in Mexico: Recent Research. *Contemporary Educational Psychology, 9*(3), 254–259.

Moksnes, Heidi. (2012). *Maya Exodus: Indigenous Struggle for Citizenship in Chiapas*. Norman: University of Oklahoma Press.

Montero, Ashley. (2018). [Interview with author. #41CA #29EHS. 1/12/18. EHS, Eureka, California].

Moorehead Jr., Virgil. (2019). American Indian Mental Health in Northwest California: A Call for Structural Interventions. In Kishan Lara-Cooper & Walter J. Lara Sr., eds., *Ka'm-t'em: A Journey Toward Healing*, 63–83. Pechanga, CA: Great Oak Press.

Mora, Mariana. (2015). The Politics of Justice: Zapatista Autonomy at the Margins of the Neoliberal Mexican State. *Latin American and Caribbean Ethnic Studies, 10*(1), 87–106.

Morton, Rebecca B., & Williams, Kenneth C. (2010). *Experimental Political Science and the Study of Causality: From Nature to the Lab.* New York: Cambridge University Press.

Mukherjee, Shomik. (2019). New Superintendent Backs Out of Offer to Lead Klamath-Trinity School District. *Times-Standard*, July 10.

Nash, June C. (2001). *Mayan Visions: The Quest for Autonomy in an Age of Globalization.* New York: Routledge.

Nash, June C. (2010). Autonomy Begins at Home: A Gendered Perspective on Indigenous Autonomy Movements. *Caribbean Studies, 38*(2), 117–142.

National Center for Education Statistics. (2019). *Status and Trends in the Education of Racial and Ethnic Groups 2018.* https://nces.ed.gov/pubs2019/2019038.pdf.

National Congress of American Indians. (2019). *Becoming Visible: A Landscape Analysis of State Efforts to Provide Native American Education for All.* https://nnigovernance.arizona.edu/becoming-visible-landscape-analysis-state-efforts-provide-native-american-education-all.

Navarro Tomás, Alejandra. (2018). [Interview with author. #56Mexico #05CEDARTMC. 4/13/18. CEDARTMC, Oaxaca de Juárez, Oaxaca, Mexico].

Norgaard, Kari Marie. (2019). *Salmon and Acorns Feed Our People: Colonialism, Nature, and Social Action.* New Brunswick, NJ: Rutgers University Press.

Norton, Jack. (1979). *Genocide of Northwestern California: When Our Worlds Cried.* San Francisco: Indian Historian Press.

Norton, Jack. (2019). The Past Is Our Future: Thoughts on Identity, Tradition and Change. In Kishan Lara-Cooper & Walter J. Lara Sr., eds., *Ka'm-t'em: A Journey Toward Healing*, 115–133. Pechanga, CA: Great Oak Press.

OECD. (2013). *Education Policy Outlook: Mexico.* http://www.oecd.org/mexico/EDUCATION%20POLICY%20OUTLOOK%20MEXICO_EN.pdf.

Ogulnick, Karen. (2006). Popular Education and Language Rights in Indigenous Mayan Communities: Emergence of New Social Actors and Gendered Voices. In Ofelia García, Tove Skutnabb-Kangas, & Maria E. Torres-Guzmán, eds., *Imagining Multilingual Schools: Languages in Education and Globalization*, 150–168. Buffalo: Multilingual Matters.

Olthuis, Marja-Liisa, Kivelä, Suvi, & Skutnabb-Kangas, Tove. (2013). *Revitalising Indigenous Languages: How to Recreate a Lost Generation.* Bristol: Multilingual Matters.

Orcutt, Michael. (2019). Tribal Water Rights: Klamath-Trinity River. In Kishan Lara-Cooper & Walter J. Lara Sr., eds., *Ka'm-t'em: A Journey Toward Healing*, 201–212. Pechanga, CA: Great Oak Press.

Ornelas, Carlos. (2008). El SNTE, Elba Esther Gordillo y el Gobierno de Calderón. *Revista mexicana de investigación educativa, 13*(37), 445–469.

Ortiz Mendoza, Gabriela. (2020). [Interview with author. #87Mexico #25BIC29. 2/12/20. BIC 29, Teotitlán del Valle, Oaxaca, Mexico].

Osorio Méndez, Juan Carlos. (2018). [Interview with author. #57Mexico #06CEDARTMC. 4/16/18. CEDARTMC, Oaxaca de Juárez, Oaxaca, Mexico].

Pachirat, Timothy. (2015). The Tyranny of Light. *Newsletter of the American Political Science Association, Organized Section for Qualitative and Multi-Method Research, 13*(1), 27–31.

Pachirat, Timothy. (2018). *Among Wolves: Ethnography and the Immersive Study of Power.* New York: Routledge.

Payton, Nathan. (2018). [Interview with author. #22CA #10EHS. 1/11/18. EHS, Eureka, California].

Pérez-Torres, R. (2006). *Mestizaje: Critical Uses of Race in Chicano Culture.* Minneapolis: University of Minnesota Press.

Phanhsavang, Lannah. (2018). [Interview with author. #13CA #01EHS. 1/10/18. EHS, Eureka, California].

Pole, Lelencia. (2018). [Interview with author. #93CA #23HVHS. 11/6/18. HVHS, Hoopa, California].

Proudfit, Joely, & Myers-Lim, Nicole Quinderro, eds. (2017). *On Indian Ground: A Return to Indigenous Knowledge: Generating Hope, Leadership and Sovereignty Through Education.* Charlotte, NC: Information Age Publishing.

Pruim, Sandra. (2014). Ethnocide and Indigenous Peoples: Article 8 of the Declaration on the Rights of Indigenous Peoples. *Adelaide Law Review, 35,* 269–308.

Pye, Geralyn, & Jolley, David. (2011). Indigenous Mobilization in Oaxaca, Mexico: Towards Indianismo? *Journal of Iberian and Latin American Research, 17*(2), 179–195.

Qin, Amy. (2019). As It Detains Parents, China Weans Children from Islam. *New York Times,* December 29, pp. 1, 10–11.

Qu, Yang, Pomerantz, Eva M., Wang, Meifang, Cheung, Cecilia, & Cimpian, Andrei. (2016). Conceptions of Adolescence: Implications for Differences in Engagement in School over Early Adolescence in the United States and China. *Journal of Youth and Adolescence, 45*(7), 1512–1526.

Ragin, Charles C. ([1987] 2014). *The Comparative Method: Moving Beyond Qualitative and Quantitative Strategies.* Oakland: University of California Press.

Ramírez Castañeda, Elisa. (2014). *La educación indígena en México.* Ciudad de México: Universidad Nacional Autónoma de México.

Ray, John. (2018). [Interview with author. #81CA #11HVHS. Superintendent, Klamath Trinity Joint Unified School District. 11/1/18. KTJUSD office, Hoopa, California].

Reed, Jacob. (2018). [Interview with author. #88CA #18HVHS. 11/5/18. HVHS, Hoopa, California].

Reed, Kaitlin. (2019). The Environmental & Cultural Impacts of Cannabis Cultivation on Yurok Tribal Lands. PhD diss., University of California, Davis.

Reed, Kaitlin. (2020). We Are a Part of the Land and the Land Is Us. *Humboldt Journal of Social Relations, 42,* 27–49.

Reyes de la Cruz, Virginia Guadalupe. (2015). Migrantes retornados: Comunidad y políticas públicas. In Virginia Guadalupe Reyes de la Cruz & Ana Margarita Alvarado Juárez, eds., *Efectos de la Migración en el Medio Rural.* Oaxaca de Juárez: Instituto de Investigaciones Sociológicas-Universidad Autonoma "Benito Juárez" de Oaxaca, y MAPorrúa.

Risling Baldy, Cutcha. (2017). *The San Diego Mission and Kumeyaay Revolt: A (Decolonized) Mission Report Written by my Nine Year Old Daughter or Don't Try to Tell Me That Fourth Graders Can't Understand a More Complex View of History.* http://www.cutcharislingbaldy .com/blog/the-san-diego-mission-and-kumeyaay-revolt-a-decolonized-mission-report

-written-by-my-nine-year-old-daughter-or-dont-try-to-tell-me-that-fourth-graders
-cant-understand-a-more-complex-view-of-history. 6/13/17.

Risling Baldy, Cutcha, & Begay, Kayla. (2019). Xo'ch Na:nahsde'tl-te: Survivance, Resilience and Unbroken Traditions in Northwest California. In Kishan Lara-Cooper & Walter J. Lara Sr., eds., *Ka'm-t'em: A Journey Toward Healing*, 39–61. Pechanga, CA: Great Oak Press.

Robles Lomeli, Jafte Dilean, & Rappaport, Joanne. (2018). Imagining Latin American Social Science from the Global South: Orlando Fals Borda and Participatory Action Research. *Latin American Research Review, 53*(3), 597–612.

Robson, James, Klooster, Daniel, Worthen, Holly, & Hernández-Díaz, Jorge. (2018). Migration and Agrarian Transformation in Indigenous Mexico. *Journal of Agrarian Change, 18*(2), 299–323.

Rojas Crotte, Ignacio Roberto. (2017). Mundo de la vida, sistema y colonización en el aula de educación superior: Una propuesta de investigación. In Ana Margarita Alvarado Juárez & Virginia Guadalupe Reyes de la Cruz, eds., *La Educación en México: Escanarios y Desafíos*, 261–291. Oaxaca de Juárez: Universidad Autónoma Benito Juárez de Oaxaca y Juan Pablos Editor, S.A.

Ruiz López, Arturo. (2017). Migración, trabajo infantil y educación: El caso de los niños de San Martín Peras, Oaxaca. In Ana Margarita Alvarado Juárez & Virginia Guadalupe Reyes de la Cruz, eds., *La Educación en México: Escanarios y Desafíos*, 47–71. México: Universidad Autónoma Benito Juárez de Oaxaca y Juan Pablos Editor, S.A.

Rus, Jan, Hernández Castillo, Rosalva Aída, & Mattiace, Shannan L. (2003). *Mayan Lives, Mayan Utopias: The Indigenous Peoples of Chiapas and the Zapatista Rebellion*. Lanham, MD: Rowman and Littlefield.

Sadowski, Michael. (2008). *Adolescents at School: Perspectives on Youth, Identity, and Education*. Cambridge, MA: Harvard Education Press.

Saldaña-Portillo, María Josefina. (2016). *Indian Given: Racial Geographies Across Mexico and the United States*. Durham, NC: Duke University Press.

Sánchez Martínez, Liliana. (2017). *Reporte Cuestionario de Ingreso 1er Semestre: Ciclo escolar 2017–2018: Liliana Sánchez Martínez, Orientación Educativa*. Internal document, CEDARTMC.

Sánchez Martínez, Liliana. (2018). [Interview with author. #60Mexico #09CEDARTMC. 4/16/18. CEDARTMC, Oaxaca de Juárez, Oaxaca, Mexico].

Santiago Reyes, Estefany. (2018). [Interview with author. #16Mexico #02IIAC. 3/2/18. Centro de Aprendizaje, IIAC, Oaxaca de Juárez, Oaxaca, Mexico].

Schabas, William A. (2008). Genocide Law in a Time of Transition: Recent Developments in the Law of Genocide. *Rutgers Law Review, 61*(1), 161–192.

Schreiber, Hanna. (2017). Cultural Genocide—Culturecide: An Unfinished or Rejected Project of International Law? In Grażyna Michałowska & Hanna Schreiber, eds., *Culture(s) in International Relations*, 319–346. Bern: Peter Lang.

Schultze-Kraft, Markus. (2018). *Crimilegal Orders, Governance and Armed Conflict*. Berlin: Springer.

Schwartz-Shea, Peregrine. (2014). Judging Quality: Evaluative Criteria and Epistemic Communities. In Dvora Yanow & Peregrine Schwartz-Shea, eds., *Interpretation and Method: Empirical Research Methods and the Interpretive Turn*, 120–146. New York: M. E. Sharpe.

Scott, James C. (1985). *Weapons of the Weak: Everyday Forms of Peasant Resistance*. New Haven, CT: Yale University Press.

Scott, James C. (1990). *Domination and the Arts of Resistance: Hidden Transcripts*. New Haven, CT: Yale University Press.

Secretaría de Educación Media Superior. (2014). *Plan de Estudios 2014: Modelo Educativo Integral Indígena (MEII)*. https://www.academia.edu/34542328_Funciones_de_las_lenguas_en_el_Modelo_Integral_Ind%C3%ADgena_2015_CSEIIO.

Selbin, Eric. (2010). *Revolution, Rebellion, Resistance: The Power of Story*. London: Zed.

Shlossberg, Pavel. (2018). Heritage Practices, Indigenismo, and Coloniality: Studying-Up into Racism in Contemporary Mexico. *Cultural Studies, 32*(3), 414–437.

Short, Damien. (2010). Cultural Genocide and Indigenous Peoples: A Sociological Approach. *International Journal of Human Rights, 14*(6), 833–848.

Simon, Theodora, Nelson, Linea, & Chambers, Taylor. (2020). *Failing Grade: The Status of Native American Education in Humboldt County*. https://www.aclunc.org/sites/default/files/ACLU%20Humboldt%20report%2010%2026%2020%20final%20web.pdf.

Simpson, Leanne. (2008). Our Elder Brothers: The Lifeblood of Resurgence. In Leanne Simpson, ed., *Lighting the Eighth Fire: The Liberation, Resurgence, and Protection of Indigenous Nations*, 73–88. Winnipeg: Arbeiter Ring Publishing.

Skocpol, Theda. (1979). *States and Social Revolutions: A Comparative Analysis of France, Russia, and China*. Cambridge: Cambridge University Press.

Skutnabb-Kangas, Tove, Phillipson, Robert, Panda, Minati, & Mohanty, Ajit K. (2009). Mulilingual Education Concepts, Goals, Needs, and Expense: English for All or Achieving Justice? In Tove Skutnabb-Kangas, Robert Phillipson, Ajit K. Mohanty, & Minati Panda, eds., *Social Justice Through Multilingual Education*, 320–344. Bristol: Multilingual Matters.

Smith, Andrea. (2009). *Indigenous Peoples and Boarding Schools: A Comparative Study*. https://www.un.org/esa/socdev/unpfii/documents/E_C_19_2009_crp1.pdf.

Smith, Peter H. (2013). *Talons of the Eagle: Latin America, the United States, and the World*. New York: Oxford University Press.

Snelgrove, Corey, Dhamoon, Rita, & Corntassel, Jeff. (2014). Unsettling Settler Colonialism: The Discourse and Politics of Settlers, and Solidarity with Indigenous Nations. *Decolonization: Indigeneity, Education & Society, 3*(2), 1–32.

Sonntag, Selma K., & Cardinal, Linda. (2015). State Traditions and Language Regimes: Conceptualizing Language Policy Choices. In Linda Cardinal & Selma K. Sonntag, eds., *State Traditions and Language Regimes*, 3–26. Toronto: McGill-Queen's University Press.

Sowerwine, Jennifer, Mucioki, Megan, Sarna-Wojcicki, Daniel, & Hillman, Lisa. (2019). Reframing Food Security by and for Native American Communities: A Case Study Among Tribes in the Klamath River Basin of Oregon and California. *Food Security, 11*(3), 579–607.

Speed, Shannon. (2006). At the Crossroads of Human Rights and Anthropology: Toward a Critically Engaged Activist Research. *American Anthropologist, 108*(1), 66–76.

Speed, Shannon, & Collier, Jane F. (2000). Limiting Indigenous Autonomy in Chiapas, Mexico: The State Government's Use of Human Rights. *Human Rights Quarterly, 22*(4), 877–905.

Speed, Shannon, Hernández Castillo, Rosalva Aída, & Stephen, Lynn. (2006). *Dissident Women: Gender and Cultural Politics in Chiapas*. Austin: University of Texas Press.

Stephen, Lynn. (2007). *Transborder Lives: Indigenous Oaxacans in Mexico, California, and Oregon*. Durham, NC: Duke University Press.

Stephen, Lynn. (2013). *We Are the Face of Oaxaca: Testimony and Social Movements*. Durham, NC: Duke University Press.

Stephen, Lynn, & Speed, Shannon, eds. (2021). *Indigenous Women and Violence: Feminist Activist Research in Heightened States of Injustice*. Tuscon: University of Arizona Press.

Tacelosky, Kathleen. (2018). Transnational Education, Language and Identity: A Case from Mexico. *Society Register, 2*(2), 63–84.

Tamés, Regina. (2019). The Invisible Violence Against Women in Mexico. In Alejandro Anaya-Muñoz & Barbara Frey, eds., *Mexico's Human Rights Crisis*, 86–103. Philadelphia: University of Pennsylvania Press.

Tarrow, Sidney. (2005). *The New Transnational Activism*. New York: Cambridge University Press.

Tavanti, Marco. (2003). *Las Abejas: Pacifist Resistance and Syncretic Identities in a Globalizing Chiapas*. New York: Routledge.

TEDNA. (2010). *Tribal Education Departments Reports*. https://www.narf.org/nill/resources/education/reports/tednareport2011.pdf.

Telles, Edward, & Sue, Christina A. (2019). *Durable Ethnicity. Mexican Americans and the Ethnic Core*. Oxford: Oxford University Press.

Thachil, Tariq, & Vaishnav, Milan. (2018). The Strategic and Moral Imperatives of Local Engagement: Reflections on India. *PS: Political Science and Politics, 51*(3), 546–549.

Thiong'o, Ngũgĩ wa. (1986). *Decolonising the Mind: The Politics of Language in African Literature*. London: J. Currey.

Thomson, Susan. (2021). Reflexive Openness as Ethical Research Practice. *PS: Political Science & Politics, 54*(3), 530–534.

Tilly, Charles. (2002). *Stories, Identities, and Political Change*. Lanham, MD: Rowman and Littlefield.

Tripp, Aili Mari. (2018). Transparency and Integrity in Conducting Field Research on Politics in Challenging Contexts. *Perspectives on Politics, 16*(3), 728–738.

Tuck, Eve, & Yang, Wayne K. (2012). Decolonization Is Not a Metaphor. *Decolonization: Indigeneity, Education & Society, 1*(1), 1–40.

Tuhiwai Smith, Linda. (2012). *Decolonizing Methodologies: Research and Indigenous Peoples*. New York: Zed Books.

Tutsch, Sonja F., Fowler, Patrick, Kumar, Gaurav, Weaver, Adam, Minter, Christian I. J., & Baccaglini, Lorena. (2019). Universal Anxiety Interventions in United States Schools: A Systematic Review. *Health Behavior and Policy Review, 6*(5), 438–454.

UN. (1948). Universal Declaration of Human Rights. http://www.un.org/en/universal-declaration-human-rights/.

UNESCO. (1953). *The Use of Vernacular Languages in Education*. http://www.inarels.com/resources/unesco1953.pdf.

UNESCO. (1983). *Study of the Problem of Discrimination Against Indigenous Nations*. Commission of Human Rights. https://www.un.org/esa/socdev/unpfii/documents/MCS_xv_en.pdf.

U.S. English. (2021). Making English the Official Languge. https://www.usenglish.org/.

Valadez, Kimberly. (2018). [Interview with author. #57CA #45EHS. 1/15/18. EHS, Eureka, California].

Valdés, Guadalupe, Fishman, Joshua A., Chávez, Rebecca, & Pérez, William. (2006). *Developing Minority Language Resources: The Case of Spanish in California*. Clevedon Hill: Multilingual Matters.

Velásquez, Luis Ignacio. (2020). Concentra Oaxaca pobreza del país. *Noticias: Voz e Imágan de Oaxaca*. https://www.nvinoticias.com/politica/oaxaca/concentra-oaxaca-pobreza-del-pais/57815.

Vizenor, Gerald. (1994). *Manifest Manners: Postindian Warriors of Survivance*. Hanover, NH: Wesleyan University Press.

Vizenor, Gerald. (2010). *Native Liberty: Natural Reason and Cultural Survivance*. Lincoln: University of Nebraska Press.

Vizenor, Gerald, ed. (2009). *Survivance: Narratives of Native Presence*. Lincoln: University of Nebraska Press.

War Soldier, Rosa Soza. (2019). "Tilted History Is Too Often Taught": Activism, Advocacy, and Restoring Humanity. In Kishan Lara-Cooper & Walter J. Lara Sr., eds., *Ka'm-t'em: A Journey Toward Healing*, 99–113. Pechanga, CA: Great Oak Press.

Wear, Kimberly. (2021). Historic Klamath Dam Removal Project Takes Another Step Forward. *Northcoast Journal* (June 17). https://www.northcoastjournal.com/NewsBlog/archives/2021/2006/2017/historic-klamath-dam-removal-project-takes-another-step-forward.

Whittier, Nancy. (2001). Emotional Strategies: The Collective Reconstruction and Display of Oppositional Emotions in the Movement Against Child Sexual Abuse. In Jeff Goodwin, James M. Jasper, & Francesca Polletta, eds., *Passionate Politics: Emotions and Social Movements*, 233–250. Chicago: University of Chicago Press.

Wilshire, Bruce. (2006). *Get 'Em All! Kill 'Em!: Genocide, Terrorism, Righteous Communities*. Lanham, MD: Lexington Books.

Wilson, Shawn. (2008). *Research Is Ceremony: Indigenous Research Methods*. Halifax: Fernwood Publishing.

Wonnacott, Brittany. (2018). [Interview with author. #14CA #02EHS. 1/10/18. EHS, Eureka, California].

World Population Review. (2020). Hoopa, CA: Population 2020.

Wright, Melissa W. (2011). Necropolitics, Narcopolitics, and Femicide: Gendered Violence on the Mexico-US Border. *Signs: Journal of Women in Culture Society, 36*(3), 707–731.

Yanow, Dvora. (2014). Neither Rigorous nor Objective? Interrogating Criteria for Knowledge Claims in Interpretive Science. In Dvora Yanow & Peregrine Schwartz-Shea, eds., *Interpretation and Method: Empirical Research Methods and the Interpretive Turn*, 97–119. New York: M. E. Sharpe.

Yanow, Dvora, & Schwartz-Shea, Peregrine. (2014a). Wherefore "Interpretive": An Introduction. In Dvora Yanow & Peregrine Schwartz-Shea, eds., *Interpretation and Method: Empirical Research Methods and the Interpretive Turn*, xiii–xxxi. New York: M. E. Sharpe.

Yanow, Dvora, & Schwartz-Shea, Peregrine, eds. (2014b). *Interpretation and Method: Empirical Research Methods and the Interpretive Turn*, 2nd ed. New York: M. E. Sharpe.

Yashar, Deborah J. (2005). *Contesting Citizenship in Latin America: The Rise of Indigenous Movements and the Postliberal Challenge*. Cambridge: Cambridge University Press.

Young, Sativa. (2018). [Interview with author. #71CA #58EHS. 1/18/18. EHS, Eureka, California].

INDEX

Printed in the USA
CPSIA information can be obtained
at www.ICGtesting.com
JSHW022309220324
59760JS00002B/108